COMHAIRLE CHON

SOUTH DUBLIN

COUNTY LIBRARY, TOWN CENTRE, TALLAGHT
TO RENEW ANY ITEM TEL: 462 0073
OR ONLINE AT www.southdublinlibraries.ie

Items should be returned on or before the last date below. Fines,
as displayed in the Library, will be charged on overdue items.

21-4-15		

C000213011

QUIET REVOLUTIONARIES

*Irish Women in Education,
Medicine and Sport, 1861–1964*

Dr Margaret Ó hÓgartaigh

The
History
Press
Ireland

*For Lindsey Earner-Byrne, Michael Laffan, Matthew Macfadyen and in
memory of Catherine Hacket*

Index compiled by Helen Litton

First published 2011

The History Press Ireland
119 Lower Baggot Street
Dublin 2
Ireland
www.thehistorypress.ie

British Library Cataloguing in Publication Data.
A catalogue record for this book is available from the British Library.

ISBN 978 1 84588 696 7

Typesetting and origination by The History Press
Printed in Malta

Contents

Acknowledgements

'Why don't you look at professional women,' suggested Tom Bartlett. From this acorn of an idea grew this book. Many editors have helped me; Lisa Hyde, Joost Augusteijn, Seamus MacGabhann, Maeve Convery, Ciara Breathnach, Ronan Colgan, Bernadette Whelan, Jim Rogers, Donal O Driscoill, Anne Macdona and Rena Lohan. I am very grateful to Irish Academic Press, Four Courts Press, New Island books, *Irish Educational Studies Journal*, *New Hibernia Review*, *Irish Archives*, *Saothar, Journal of the Irish Labour History Society*, *Clogher Record*, Rathmines, Rathgar and Ranelagh Historical Association, University of Texas Medical Branch, *Australian Journal of Irish Studies, Journal of the Irish Dental Association*, *The Irish Pharmacy Journal*, *Irish Veterinary Journal*, *High Ball* and *Ríocht na Midhe*, *Records of the Meath Archaeological and Historical Society*, who originally published these articles.

Margaret Mac Curtain contributed a perceptive foreword. My All Hallows College colleague, Bernadette Flanagan, was very support- ive. My superb copy editor Micheal Heffernan deserves high praise. Thanks also to his sister Carol for all the yummies. I am grateful to all at Crusader's Athletics Club. Mel Watman's publications were inspira- tional. Anne McLelland, Declan Downey and Finola Kennedy were very encouraging and I am grateful to them. Ciarán, my husband, make all this possible and I am indebted to him for so much.

The award of a Fulbright Fellowship facilitated research in the United States and I am grateful to the Irish Studies programme at Boston College, especially Kevin O'Neill, Peg Preston, Rob Savage, Cathy McLaughlin and the librarians at the O'Neill library. The History Press both in Ireland and the UK has been a joy to work with, my thanks to them all, especially the ever-calm Ronan Colgan and the ever-efficient Beth Amphlett.

Finally, I am delighted to acknowledge the help of Lindsey Earner-Byrne who has stimulated so much Irish women's history. The all-round decency and good sense of Michael Laffan, as well as the kindness of Catherine Hacket will never be forgotten. Matthew Macfadyen has made the past accessible, engaging and exciting and I am grateful for his gifts. This book is dedicated to that talented quartet.

Foreword

Just when it seemed that the impulses which had energised women's history had ebbed in the early years of the twenty-first century, along comes Margaret Ó hÓgartaigh's zesty collection of essays examining Irish women's performance in the fields of education, medicine, pharmacy, dentistry and sport over the last century. Intrepid adventurers all, women had even entered the field of veterinary surgery by the 1930s.

The essays, drawn from contributions to specialist journals and local history publications, are in the nature of investigations and as such there is an equivalence between the studies that appeared in journals dealing with medicine and dentistry and the experience of qualified women as they applied their professional skills in a community setting. Female teachers, their formation and cultural background prepared them for the acceptance of trade union negotiation in the recognition of levels of qualification and tenure. Moving chronologically from the teaching profession, the author examines the choices women doctors and nurses made in the beginning decades of the twentieth century. Possibly Dr Kathleen Lynn and Dr Dorothy Stopford-Price had a formative influence by their focus on children's illnesses on women in medicine, dentistry, and nursing including midwifery. There was opposition and Dr Ó hÓgartaigh illuminates pockets of resistance to appointments in rural areas and the spectre of women being paid for work, Councillor Tully of County Meath is a witty case–study in male rural attitudes. It is to be hoped that the writer of these richly variegated essays will be encouraged to develop her explorations of women's entry into the field of sport, certainly her two offerings in this collection, on camogie and its impact on women's sport, and her nuanced investigation of hockey and mixed athletics in the 1930s and mid-twentieth century whet the curiosity of the reader for more.

Dr Ó hÓgartaigh, a scholar of repute, who has published full-scale biographies of Dr Kathleen Lynn and of the 1798 historian Edward Hay has once again shed light on important and neglected areas of Irish life.

Margaret Mac Curtain, 2011

Introduction

> If you please, no reference to examples in books. Men have
> had every advantage of us in telling their own story. Education
> has been theirs in so much higher a degree; the pen has been
> in their hands. I will not allow books to prove anything.
>
> *Anne Elliot to Captain Harville in Jane Austen's,* Persuasion,
> *published in 1816.*

It is a truism that without sources, history is very difficult to write.
Records must come first. Hence, this book begins with an article on
sources for the history of professional women in Ireland. The role of
education in stimulating the growth of professional women is the
focus of chapter two. Ironically, the cloistered atmosphere of many
educational institutions provided the intellectual means for many
women to pursue professional careers. In chapter three, the impact
of the Intermediate Education Act of 1878 is analysed. The gradual
standardisation of the educational curriculum at second-level paved
the way for university entry for a small minority of women in the late
nineteenth century. The experiences of these women are discussed in
chapter four. One of the most popular professions for women was
primary education. Chapter five concentrates on the cultural formation of teachers at the training colleges and helps to explain their
role as servants of the state. Despite a culture of compliance, teachers'
unions were important in the profession as chapter six emphasises.
The personal experiences of Susan Stephens, a teacher in County
Monaghan at the beginning of the twentieth century, are the focus
of chapter seven. The individual professional experiences of teachers
and nurses in the west of Ireland are discussed in chapter eight.

One of the outstanding doctors of her generation, Kathleen Lynn,
as well as her style of maternal medicine, is explained in chapter
nine. Several of the professional careers of her St Ultan's Hospital
for Infants colleagues are also described. The most original of these
doctors was Dorothy Stopford-Price whose work in eliminating
childhood tuberculosis has been forgotten or ignored. Her career is
the centre point of chapter ten which also suggests that the innova-
tions of the 1930s tend to be lost in the concentration on politics.
The essential services provided by nurses and midwives are examined

in chapter eleven. While their work was recognised by contemporaries, historians have been slow to analyse this gendered aspect of the history of medicine.

Many of the developments in Irish medicine in the early twentieth century drew their inspiration from international examples. The Babies' Clubs in Ireland are compared with the Children's Bureau in the United States in chapter twelve. The following chapter compares children's hospitals in Australia and Ireland. Moving to the local in chapter fourteen, a row in County Meath over the appointment of a medical officer discusses the timeless theme of professionalism in conflict with local aspirations. The following three chapters discuss briefly the role of women in pharmacy, dentistry and veterinary science. Finally, women's participation in sport aroused comical levels of derision with all kinds of fictional medical reasons used to prevent women enjoying sporting opportunities as chapters eighteen and nineteen suggest. The last chapter assesses the extent to which working women posed a threat to more paranoid members of Ireland's political class. The voice may be that of Mr Tully, but the facts suggest that women had made their mark in education, medicine and sport. 'History is a conversation and sometimes a shouting match between present and past, though often the voices we most want to hear are barely audible', suggests Pulitzer prize-winning historian, Laurel Thatcher Ulrich.[1] This book makes quiet revolutionaries audible.

Chapter 1

Archival sources for the history of professional women in late-nineteenth-century Ireland

Publications relating to the history of Irish women have multiplied in the last two decades. Correspondingly, new sources, and the innovative use of old sources, have provided historians with the necessary material to write about women's lives. However, much recent work has focussed on women in poorly-paid employment. Professional women have been neglected. Use of the sources relating to these women described below may help to expand our knowledge of women working in the professions. Not surprisingly, women dominated in certain occupations. This is reflected in the range of sources that relate to female teachers and nurses. Predictably, there are few sources that document women's careers in law and accountancy. It is possible that gaining access to the archival sources described might require specific permission. An initial enquiry should be made to the organisation or institution in which the material is held.

Education Archives

Ireland has a wide variety of archival sources which refer to women in education. The Association of Secondary Teachers (ASTI) Archives in Winetavern Street, Dublin has carefully catalogued its extensive archives. Official programmes of annual conventions, the minutes of these conventions as well as the register of intermediate (that is, second-level) teachers all contain material relating to women. Furthermore, women featured regularly in Dublin branch

minutes of the ASTI. Regrettably, the Irish National Teachers'
Organisation (INTO), Parnell Square, Dublin has yet to catalogue
its holdings. Nonetheless, they have considerable archives. Central
Executive Committee minutes and Congress minutes refer to female
teachers, though women rarely featured in the management of the
INTO. The programme for students in training contains fascinating details on the different approaches adopted in the preparation
of male and female teachers. More particular details of difficulties in
specific areas are available in the County Louth National Teachers'
Association minutesm, which date from 1917. The papers for Baggot
Street, later Carysfort, College are currently being catalogued in the
Mercy Central Archives, Herbert Place, Dublin. They have a wide
range of varied material from student memoirs to letters which
recount the efforts of the Mercy Order to establish their college
in the face of economic difficulties. Not surprisingly, the National
Archives, Bishop Street, Dublin has extensive education holdings. The Commissioners for National Education kept meticulous
records. In particular, ED8 (the reports of inspectors) and ED11 (letters to commissioners) have much of interest. The National Library
of Ireland, Manuscript Department, Kildare Street, Dublin, has more
specific material relating to professional women. The minutes of
the Commission on Vocational Education (Ms. 922-941) include
evidence from various educational organisations. Additionally, the
papers of Mary Hayden (the first professor of modern Irish history
at UCD), as well as the large collection of papers of teacher and suffragette, Hanna Sheehy-Skeffington, give us specific information on
the careers of two professional women. The matriculation certificates
held at National University of Ireland, in Merrion Square, Dublin
provide an unexpected rich source of information. These certificates
often contain vital genealogical and educational information on the
matriculation students, such as dates of birth, parents' occupation/s
and schools attended. Possibly some of the best archival sources
of information for women in education are in the Public Record
Office of Northern Ireland (PRONI), Balmoral Avenue, Belfast.
This repository holds the records of such varied groups as the Irish
Protestant National Teachers' Union (D/517), Ulster Headmistresses'
Association (D/3820), Ulster Teachers' Union (D/3944), as well as
the Ministry of Education Reports (ED25). These general sources are
supplemented by material relating specifically to various educational
institutions where women worked. For example, the archives of

Bangor School (D/1341), the Lodge School (D3114/10 and D/3712 and the Ladies Collegiate School (T/1389/3) provide us with a picture of the experiences of both pupils and teachers. University archives are also worth visiting. Trinity College Dublin's Manuscript Department contains the papers of the Central Association of Irish Schoolmistresses (Ms. 9722). This group was very influential in the early years of the twentieth century. They were established in 1889 in order to 'promote [the] higher education of girls and promote co-operation among schoolmistresses'.[1] Meanwhile, University College Dublin's Archives Department holds the National University Women Graduates' Association papers. They cover a range of issues which affected professional women. Additionally, the Mary MacSwiney papers provide a window on the career of this controversial republican, as well as her establishment of Scoil Íde. The registers of the Royal College of Science, which became the UCD Science faculty, provide details of the academic careers of female scientists. We are fortunate that the extensive records of the Church of Ireland Training College have been deployed by Susan Parkes in her history of that institution.[2] Unfortunately, few second-level schools themselves have kept records of their activities. An exception is Alexandra College which has records dating from its foundation in 1866. Material ranges from memoirs of past pupils to reports of the principal. Also included are fascinating files on the position of women in the universities, the federation of university women, plus a broad-ranging survey of universities within the former British Empire.

Health Archives

After teaching, one of the most popular professions for women was nursing. An Board Altranis (the nursing board) has detailed archives relating to the profession, including the minutes of the Central Midwives Board and the General Nursing Council which provide us with a picture of this emerging profession in the 1920s. Some hospitals have also kept records. Belfast Maternity Hospital (D/1326) and Queen Charlotte's Lying-In Hospital (D/1326) papers are available in PRONI. The Rotunda Hospital, Dublin also has impressive records.[3] From them it is possible to ascertain the nationality, age profile, marital status, type of pre-training and length of training of Rotunda midwives based on their records. On a more personal level, the National Maternity Hospital, Holles Street, Dublin is fortunate in possessing the matron's register of midwives in training.

These registers contain the matron's comments (positive and otherwise) on the qualities of her staff. Health professionals frequently worked abroad and missionary activity was the focus of the career of Lady Hermione Blackwood, whose papers are deposited in PRONI (D/1071). Possibly one of the best institutional archives is located at Peamount Hospital, Newcastle, Dublin.[4] The hospital was established by the Women's National Health Association. They were prominent in the fight against tuberculosis. The annual reports of the hospital, as well as the association's journal, *Sláinte*, provide us with information on the careers of both nurses and doctors.[5] Archival material on female physicians is more elusive. Were it not for the energetic efforts of the Registrar of the Royal College of Physicians, Dr T.P.C. Kirkpatrick, it would be difficult to trace the careers of the first and second generation of Irish female doctors. Kirkpatrick assembled files on over 10,000 Irish doctors and this includes over 300 females. Hence, these records, which are available in the Royal College of Physicians, Dublin, can be used to illuminate the careers of female physicians.[6] Furthermore, the college's archives also contain the papers of St Ultan's Hospital, which was established and managed by female doctors. Dr Kathleen Lynn's copious diaries are also available in the college. Additionally, the reports of the Queen's University Belfast Women Graduates' Association in the QUB Special Collections Department detail the range of careers adopted by a variety of female physicians. Information on specific doctors is also available in the file of the Alexandra College Guild which was established with the encouragement of Dr Katherine Maguire. A memorial to Dr Maguire also exists in the Alexandra College Archives. The National Library of Ireland's Manuscripts Department and the TCD Manuscipts Department also hold the Dr Dorothy Stopford-Price papers. She introduced the BCG vaccination in 1937 which helped to eliminate tuberculosis.[7] There are other Price papers in the Crowley family correspondence. The varied career of Dr Bridget Lyons-Thornton can be tracked in the Military Archives, Cathal Brugha Barracks, Dublin (PC519). The papers of less well-known doctors, such as Nan Watson (D/3270) and Florence Stewart (D/3612), have been deposited in PRONI.

Higher Professions' Archives

As one would expect, there were very few female accountants or barristers in the early years of this century. However, some archives

elucidate the lives of women in the higher professions. The Dental
Council in Merrion Square, Dublin has registers which include
women's names and addresses, as well as year of qualification.
Likewise, the Institute of Engineers, Clyde Road, Dublin has scattered information on female engineers, for example, in the *Irish
Engineers Handbook*. More revealingly, King's Inn's in Dublin has
memorials of female barristers and these include genealogical
information. The minutes of the benchers also refer to women's
attempts to gain access to the profession and their subsequent successes.[8] Only three female accountants qualified in Ireland prior to
1930, however, one of them was Emma Bodkin, whose family was
prominent in Irish life. The Bodkin papers in the National Archives
(1155) contain letters written by Emma Bodkin. It is extremely fortunate that the Pharmaceutical Society of Ireland has a full-time
librarian.[9] The annual *Calendar of the Pharmaceutical Society of Ireland*
includes female pharmacists, as well as their date of registration and
address. Additionally, the Society has a range of periodicals, such as
The Chemist and Druggist which help to provide a fuller picture of
the profession. Unfortunately, for researching veterinary surgeons,
it is necessary to visit the Royal College of Veterinary Surgeons,
Wellcome Library in London. However, the visit is worthwhile as
the archives include biographical information on Irish female veterinary surgeons as well as the registers of the profession. Finally, the
register of the Royal Institute of Architects in Ireland includes lists of
female architects.

Conclusion

Though the history of the professions in general have been
neglected, it is clear that there are various sources which can illuminate the lives of those women who enjoyed professional careers. In
addition to well-known archives in health and education, it is necessary to examine the archives of the larger archival institutions, such as
PRONI and the National Archives, and these can be supplemented
by rarely-used material in the archives of the various institutions that
shaped the careers of professional women.

Chapter 2

Emerging from the educational cloisters:[1] educational influences on the development of professional women

Introduction

This paper discusses the educational factors which influenced the emergence of professional women in late-nineteenth and early twentieth-century Ireland. Three developments are explored: first, the Intermediate Education Act of 1878; secondly, the establishment of the Royal University of Ireland in 1879; and finally, the statutory registration introduced by many professions in the 1910s.

One historian has argued that, 'Daughters were largely redundant in nineteenth-century Ireland.'[2] Second-level education was an option for a small minority of the population. However, increasing participation rates at primary level as well as socio-economic factors ensured that by 1911 97.8 per cent of females could read and write compared to 26.8 per cent in 1841.[3] The growth of secondary education can be traced back to the mid-nineteenth century with the establishment of secondary schools for girls by religious orders.[4] Despite the increasing number of second-level schools for females, many commentators feared that women's health would suffer if they sought academic success. It was suggested that:

> Darwinistic theories of evolution, declared that the health of the nation would suffer and the reproductive functions of women would be hampered by over-stressing the brain with intellectual work.[5]

In an era when women benefited from increasing educational opportunities it was almost inevitable that many would then seek employment commensurate with their qualifications. Between 1881 and 1911 many women sought jobs in the professional sector. By the latter date more than 37,000 women (or 10 per cent of the working female population) were classified as 'professional'.[6] A profession has been described as a job which is based on, 'Trained expertise and selection by merit.'[7]

The qualifications required for a professional career encouraged the pursuit of education. Many professions (law, medicine and education) required higher education. Between 1880 and 1930 women became members of prestigious professions such as law, medicine and accountancy.[8] Fortuitously, just as these professions both in Ireland and elsewhere were establishing regulations regarding entry, women were availing of the necessary educational requirements for professional life. The first step in acquiring professional status was to follow a uniform examination syllabus. This was provided by the Intermediate Education Act of 1878.

Intermediate Education Act of 1878

One of the most significant developments in relation to secondary education in the late-nineteenth century was the 1878 Intermediate Act. In many ways it was a catalyst that encouraged a far more focused approach to education. Traditionally, second-level schools for females (for the most part convents) concentrated on 'accomplishments', or, according to one pupil of the French order of the Faith Companions of Jesus in Bruff, Co. Limerick, *bonne tenue* (good appearance) French-style.[9] In a work on the history of women in Western Europe between 1500 and 1800 Hufton points out that female, 'Education was directed toward the acquisition of social skills, singing, dancing, an attractive appearance, the right manners, delicate needlework, as well as to basic literacy.'[10]

This tradition persisted right up until the late-nineteenth century in Ireland. However, the establishment of a recognised national examination for all students who received a second-level education ensured that, in time, schools provided a more rigorous academic curriculum. This in itself encouraged teachers to concentrate on the rigidly defined curriculum of the Intermediate Certificate at junior, middle and senior grades. However, the process was a gradual one.

At the Dominican Convent in Galway Sr Hyacinth, the mistress of schools, wrote to the Roman Catholic bishop Revd McEvilly for advice on the examination. He replied:

> For my part I thought keeping aloof would do no harm to your excellent school. I would at once say unhesitantly: have nothing to do with them: pursue the course you have hitherto so successfully pursued with such advantage to religion and society.

The school did not enter for the examinations until 1897.[11] On the other hand the progressive Roman Catholic Archbishop of Dublin, William Walsh, encouraged the Dominican nuns in Eccles Street and Sion Hill and the Loretos in Stephen's green to enter their students for the examination.[12]

Many students concentrated on modern languages to the neglect of the classics and, to a lesser extent, mathematics. The Report of the Intermediate Education Board for 1918 states that 2,741 girls and 3,957 boys passed the examinations in that year, comprising 56.5 per cent of girls and 55.1 per cent of boys taking the examination. However, only 2 girls took Greek as opposed to 1,174 boys. The figures for Latin were not as extreme with 751 girls and 4,879 boys taking the subject. It is clear, though, that the classical nature of boys' schooling gave them an advantage when they entered the jobs market. The neglect of the classics was to have profound implications for the career options of convent-educated students. Once choices were made at second-level then it was difficult to begin a new subject at a later stage.[13]

These biases related in part to the widely held view that females were unsuited to the logical or analytical requirements of the classics or mathematics, though it is clear that females were catching up in mathematics with 4,825 girls and 7,150 boys taking arithmetic in 1918.[14] This was due, in part, to the increasing number of females studying for a BSc at third-level. For example, Kathleen Phelan MSc was a professor of science and mathematics at St Mary's College, Belfast (a training college for female primary teachers) and she had been a science teacher at St Dominic's High School in Belfast.[15] The records of the Royal College of Science also detail the subjects taken by women who wanted classes in preparation for university science degrees. The first woman to enter for a science degree was Annie Frances Farrell who studied mathematics in 1901.

The advantage of this institution was that students could enter for whatever subjects they wished without being confined to a rigid course. Another student, Elizabeth White, did a diploma in applied chemistry and received eight certificates for various courses. It was also possible to attend as an occasional student. As early as 1879 Helen Webb from Foxrock studied Heat, Light and Sound.[16] The Royal College of Science was similar in some respects to the Royal Institution in London since both were used by women to further their scientific knowledge. Elizabeth Garrett, the first woman doctor in Britain, studied at the Royal Institution.[17] However, despite the fact that more females were taking science subjects, Hanna Sheehy-Skeffington, a well-known suffragette, was described as 'masculine' because she could reason.[18]

For the first decade and a half after the Intermediate Act, it was primarily schools under Protestant management who sat for the examinations. The prizes allocated to successful students enabled schools to promote themselves. Margaret Byers, who established the Ladies Collegiate in 1859 (later known as Victoria College, Belfast), took great pride in the success of the school in the Intermediate examinations.[19] Additionally, the tradition of mixed education in Ulster was a factor in encouraging students to take what were traditionally seen as 'male subjects'. There were also religious differences: Protestant students were more likely to study the classics and maths. In 1911 more Presbyterian females (1,308) were studying maths than their male co-religionists (1,119).[20] This can be compared with Roman Catholics where 4,036 females as compared to 10,672 males studied maths.[21]

In Dublin, Alexandra College was also excelling in these examinations under the dynamic direction of Isabella Mulvany.[22] However, many catholics attended or taught at Alexandra School and College. Dr Mulvany chaired a committee which presented a memorial to the Board of Intermediate Education in 1906 as it was the Board which established the regulations for prizes. After all, the Board allocated the prizes and exhibitions. The Committee was worried that schools were motivated only by the prizes offered and certain subjects were being neglected as a result. They pointed out that forty-four exhibitions worth £775 were awarded to students in modern literature while only two were awarded in classics and one in mathematics worth £30 and £310 repectively.[23] Parents and teachers, it was argued, selected subjects because they were 'profitable'. Many schools were dependent on the prizes won by their students in these exams. Dr Mulvany believed it was:

> Undoubtedly easier to win marks in the modern literary and sci-
> ence [domestic science and hygiene] courses than in the classical
> and mathematical ones.[24]

Students, she felt, needed to be encouraged to take the latter subjects as they were the 'foundation' of University teaching. She also felt that these subjects were also

> The passports to the professions and the higher ranks of the civil
> service.[25]

The pursuit of examination prizes and all the publicity attendant on success also favoured students who concentrated on subjects that were considered 'safer' and more likely to yield high marks. The Group System meant that students concentrated on a group of sub-jects which were linked. The groups were modern literature, classics, mathematics and science. This system also encouraged early speciali-sation. The Central Association of Irish Schoolmistresses (CAISM) was established in 1889 to promote the higher education of females and co-operation between school mistresses.[26] This association was critical of the 'group system' whereby students specialised at an early age on a particular group of subjects, for example, literature, classics, mathematic or science.[27] It felt that this system was not desirable as it encouraged, 'Students more and more to confine themselves to the lighter subjects of the programme and to neglect those which give the most solid and valuable training.'

Before the introduction of the group system in 1900 students in the, 'Senior and Middle Grades took Latin, Greek or Mathematics, almost all taking both Latin and Mathematics, and in the junior Grade all except one candidate did the same.'[28]

However, by 1905 those taking literature (the most popular option for females) did not study Greek or mathematics.[29] This was partly because most teachers had themselves studied for a BA thereby lim-iting their students to these subjects.

While Alexandra and Victoria College, Belfast (VCB) were enjoy-ing the publicity that their exam successes brought, many schools, which had previously shunned the exams as being too demanding for the 'weaker sex', decided that the students would benefit from the curriculum. Religious rivalry between schools was evident. The amount of prizes won by students was frequently cited in the prospectus of the schools. The *Dublin Evening Mail* in a reference to VCB asked its readers had they heard of, 'Anything more scandalous than the avarice of this female Orange and Freemason nursery in Belfast?[30]

The *Lyceum*, a Catholic 'magazine and review', made the rivalry quite clear:

> It is possible to provide for Catholic girls, under Catholic influences, similar educational advantages to those non-Catholic girls enjoy … We see no reason, if our efforts be directed wisely, why we should not compete on equal terms with non-Catholic institutions.[31]

Once the concept of regular examinations was accepted the push for women's entry to university became stronger. As at second-level, it was Alexandra and VCB which pioneered the preparation of women for university examinations. Additionally, Magee College and Methodist College, Belfast also prepared students for third-level examinations. Religious as well as academic rivalry increased the numbers of females studying at second and third-level.

Royal University of Ireland 1879-1908

Students enthusiastically entered for the examinations of the Royal University of Ireland after it was established in 1879, even though it was only an examination body. By 1904, when Trinity finally opened its doors to women, over a third of the Royal's graduates were female.[32] This gave women the opportunity to study in the preparatory colleges established by secondary schools. Very few women attended the Queen's Colleges in Galway, Cork and Belfast prior to the establishment of the National University of Ireland in 1908. Additionally, by the early 1900s many of the students of the Royal University had come from convent schools which twenty years earlier had focused on 'showy accomplishments'.[33] Many convent schools had gradually shed their genteel traditions in response to the example set by Protestant schools. By 1893 the Catholic schools which prepared students for matriculation were primarily the Irish-based French orders, Ursuline, Dominican, Loreto and St Louis as well as Mercy and Presentation, which were Irish foundations. However, some commentators were convinced that some students still focused on:

> ... goody-goody-ness, and superficiality, and helplessness, trumpery accomplishments, and total unfitness for home and wifehood.[34]

A 'Catholic barrister' maintained that the girls were:

> ... fit for nothing under heaven except casting flowers before the Banner of the Sodality.

The schools were described as, 'conventual factories of incapacity.'[35] More revealingly, we are told that if the students, 'Were even brought to be skilled teachers, zenana doctors, etc, they might be able to be of some use proportionate to their silent and pitiable self-sacrifice.'[36]

These comments were written just as students were beginning to excel at examinations. Indeed, some of the RUI graduates went on to be teachers and the Royal College of Physicians accepted female examinees from 1876. Even when schools did well in State examinations they did not cease to remind their students of the importance of accomplishments. Kate O'Brien's semi-autobiographical novel, *The Land of Spices*, which is set in FCJ convent at Laurel Hill, Limerick during the early twentieth century, details the ever-present focus on gentility. Few females received their third-level education from the Queen's Colleges at Belfast, Cork and Galway. Between 1891 and 1900, 216 females received RUI degrees while studying at Victoria College, Belfast, Alexandra College, Dublin, Loreto Convent, Dublin and St Mary's College, Dublin. For the same period only thirty-nine women graduated from the Queen's Colleges in Belfast, Cork and Galway and Magee College, Derry.[37] Even though it was theoretically possible to study anywhere for the RUI examinations it was very difficult to obtain tuition outside of Dublin, Cork or Belfast. The *Lyceum* commented in 1893 that:

> Intermediate Education suffers by distance from centres of intellectual activity; and that distance would render Higher Education, in any true sense, under present circumstances, and for a long time to come, quiet impossible.[38]

However, by 1918, the results of the matriculation examinations, which were used for university entrance to the University College in Dublin, Cork and Galway, indicate that students throughout the country were sitting the exam, 306 males and 123 females passed. Given that Queen's College, Belfast did not require matriculation it is not surprising that only one female from what was to become Northern Ireland passed the exam. Dublin (thirty-two), Cork (fifteen), Limerick (seven) and Galway (seven) provided 61 of the successful candidates. The rest of successful females had studied in 'rural' schools, though this would have included areas like Monaghan and Waterford.[39]

Once women reached third-level their choice of subjects was greatly influenced by what they had studied at second-level. By 1931 66 per cent of females who studied at National University of Ireland (NUI) took Arts degrees. Commerce was also a popular option as 73 per cent of all NUI graduates in this faculty in 1931 were female.[40] Latin was not required to study commerce, therefore it was attractive to many women who did not get the opportunity to study Latin at second-level. However, many did not work in business, becoming teachers instead.

The move to open Trinity to females was another educational influence on professional women. The preparatory colleges for women such as VCB, Alexandra and the Dominican run St Mary's were soon to return to being secondary schools though Alex continued to run successful courses for teachers in its secondary department.[41] The vast majority of women were in favour of mixed third-level education, despite, or perhaps because, most had been educated in single-sex schools. Francis Sheehy-Skeffington, a noted supporter of women's rights, perceptively noted that a separate women's college:

> Would tend to encourage the unfounded and already too common division of the intellectual sphere into two distinct and usually unequal portions-the masterful man appropriating all that is of any permanent or intrinsic value while permitting women to cultivate the curios fringes of the field of learning.[42]

The vast majority of female graduates gained work as teachers. By 1924 more than half of the secondary teachers working in the Irish Free State were female.[43]

The Possibilities of Suitable Employment

What, then, was the effect of the increased educational opportunities for women between 1880 and 1930? In a submission to the Robertson Commission on University Education (1903) Mary Hayden, a graduate of the Royal University and later Professor of Irish History at UCD, noted that if women were educated separately at third-level it required:

> ... no special gift of prophecy to foretell on which sex the burden of the injustice would, in actual fact, fall.[44]

However, even with mixed third-level education and increased opportunities women still followed traditional career routes as they dominated the semi-professions of teaching and nursing. One contemporary saw teaching as:

> ... a cul-de-sac a the end of [women's] collegiate career.[45]

Such was the desire of women graduates to extend their employment opportunities that they proposed the establishment of a library school in 1926. The resolution was supported by Professor Mary Macken of the UCD German Department who sought to 'extend the possibilities of suitable employment' for female graduates. The graduates also established an employment bureau with Anna Whelan BA, as its secretary in 1926.[46] This bureau eventually developed into the UCD careers office. The National University Women's Graduates' Association asked that the Civil Service equalise the marks allocated for maths and classics with those for modern languages and commerce. They felt that those taking classics and maths (usually male) had an 'unfair advantage'.[47] Hence the type of education females received was to limit their career choices and ensure that they dominated in certain professions.

All these developments indicate the difficulties faced by women who aspired to professional status. Women were still concentrated in the lower-paid professions, they were discriminated against in their choice of subjects as higher-paid positions remained the preserve of those who had that elusive stamp of class, a 'classical education'. Taught in the main by women who themselves had focused on 'female subjects', it was almost inevitable that the next generation would follow a similar career path. William Starkie, a Resident

Commissioner of Education and a classical scholar whose daughter Enid graduated with first class honours from Oxford University, declared in 1911:

> A woman, though unskilled, has a natural sympathy for babies, she understands their ways, and even if she can teach them little, she knows how to make them happy.[48]

Starkie's voice was not a lone one. With the establishment of the Irish Free State in 1922 the apparent gains of the previous half century seem to have come to nought. However, the move from being part of the British Empire with its vast resources for soaking up under-employed professionals (many doctors, for instance, worked in colonies) to a very under-funded Irish Free State government meant that State employment was considerably reduced. Female professionals, moreover, were more likely to be found in public professions such as health and education as opposed to private professions like law and accountancy. Therefore, they were all the more affected by the cutbacks in public expenditure in the 1920s. Additionally, a woman's entrance into the workforce, especially if it was a reasonably well-paid job, was viewed with suspicion since she was perceived as preventing a man from gaining employment. Marriage bans were introduced in 1919. Edward Cahill, S.J., declared that in a:

> Christian State women should be excluded even by law from occupations unbecoming or dangerous to female modesty.[49]

This viewpoint was not unique in Ireland as it was felt in England after the First World War that many women needed to learn domestic science since they were forgetting their roles as mothers.[50]

Economic independence in these circumstances was difficult to obtain. Modern societies have been described as ones which place 'merit before hereditary status.'[52] Educational attainments are one measure of merit and ones which are particularly valued in a profession. However, the professions in which women dominated were neither self governing nor rigid in their insistence on particular qualifications. Registration councils were established for secondary teachers in 1918 and for nurses in 1919 but many within these professions remained unregistered and continued to work.

Conclusion

The paradox of this era was that increasing educational opportunities and professionalisation did not ensure the emergence of the fully professional female. Flexible entry requirements and a refusal to insist that all entrants to the profession undergo a uniform system of education was to prevent many from enjoying the full fruits of a professional career. The growth of professions led to a demand for an educated class. The increasing participation of women in education went some way toward meeting that demand. Ironically, the constraints of that participation, particularly in terms of subject choice, meant that women's involvement in the professions, while relatively numerous, was in a limited number of areas.

Chapter 3

A Quiet Revolution: Irish women and second-level education, 1878-1930

In 1902, the maverick politician Frank Hugh O'Donnell wrote the *The Ruin of Education in Ireland*, in which he declared that female students were 'fit for nothing under heaven except casting flowers before the Banner of the Sodality.'[1] For many in Ireland, education was the avenue to economic independence. However, in both pre- and post-Independence Ireland, education beyond first level was constrained both by gender and by class. Nonetheless, by the late-nineteenth century, changes in the educational system began to facilitate the entry of professional women into the labour market. The census of 1881 noted that a 'very decided advance in the superior [second-and third-level] education of females' had taken place in the last decade. The number of females studying Latin had increased from 2,292 to 770; in the case of Greek, from 35 to 122; and in mathematic from 510 to 1,082.[2] These subjects were critical for university entry.[3] This quiet revolution in female education was most strongly felt in the area of employment. Educated females now sought access to jobs commensurate with their educational attainments.

Several authors have noted the emphasis on 'refinement' in female education in the nineteenth century.[4] Yet, criticism of this focus by educational reformers, combined with the need to provide for unemployed females who had enjoyed – or perhaps, endured – a 'polite' education, gradually led to changes in the curriculum. As in the eighteenth century, Irish education in the closing decades of the nineteenth century still emphasised the alleged differences between male and female students. Such influential texts as Rousseau's *Emile* had argued that women were dependent on men.[5] The writer Frances Power Cobbe felt that 'everything was taught in inverse ratio of its true importance.'[6] Segregated gender education, particularly at second-level, was the norm well into the nineteenth century. At national schools for first-level students, usually aged five to fourteen, the curriculum reflected the economic and cultural needs of the day, and domestic science was prominent in the curriculum for girls.[7]

The development of convent schools in the late-nineteenth century meant that, as Caitriona Clear has noted, 'a proportionately greater number of women were in a position to access the education and training which led to white collar work.'[8] However, Martha Vicinus's study of independent women in Britain noted that the educated women had 'virtually no other option' other than teaching, which she describes as 'a narrow staircase leading to more education as an ill-paid but respected-teacher.'[9] Other professions, such as accountancy, law and medicine, remained male-dominated. It was the teacher who exerted the most profound educational influence on professional women.

Mary Colum, writing of her school days at the St Louis Convent in Monaghan town in the late-nineteenth century, commented that 'education turned out a considerable number of trained and scholarly minds, but the country was too small to use as many of them as were turned out.'[10] This may in part be due to the focus on modern languages in women's education, at the expense of science and business. Because many women did not study Latin or science, they were effectively excluded from many facilities at university. But Latin was not required for the commerce faculty at the National University of Ireland, where, in the early twentieth century, women accounted for the majority of those studying commerce. A tracking of their careers reveals that many opted for the Higher Diploma in Education, the professional preparation for a teaching career.[11]

Criticism of female education in Ireland persisted. Henrieta White, the principal of Alexandra College in Dublin, declared that the 'cult of ignorance in woman did not lack adherents even in the latter half of the nineteenth-century.'[12] A Dr Kirkpatrick, in a speech to the Queen's Institute of Female Professional Schools – established in 1861 to prepare women for such careers as teaching – discerned a 'want of thoroughness in the education of girls; a want of acquaintance with rudiments; a want of accuracy and continuity of plan.'[13] Such criticisms were not unique to Ireland. In a work discussing the educational preparation of French schoolgirls, Linda Clark points out that their education was not designed to 'prepare pupils for pro- fessional careers.' For example, the exclusion of Latin, a difficulty also faced by Irish students, meant that they 'lacked an essential subject for baccalaureat and university entrance.'[14] Mixed education was also discouraged. There were no female school inspectors, as women were considered to lack the 'impartiality' require for inspection.[15] Likewise, in Britain there were separate curricula for males and females; girls were allowed to drop science and substitute domes- tic science.[16] However, it was noted that 'no hindrance should be placed in the way of their [females] following the boys' curriculum if they wished.'[17] in Ulster, which had a tradition of mixed educa- tion, females were more likely to undertake what were seen as male subjects. By 1911, the numbers of Presbyterian females – who would have been more likely to have mixed education – studying math- ematics surpassed their male contemporaries.[18]

The schools' investment in 'cultural capital' is notable.[19] Such extracurricular activities as music and deportment helped to impart a particular view of female behaviour. This preparation was con- sidered to be particularly important for those women whose work would expose them to the public – for instance, nurses and teach- ers, both professions in which women predominated. This is not to say that these were the only professions open to women. The Irish Association for Promoting the Training and Employment of Women, which replaced the Queen's Institute in 1883, focused on technical training for women who sought employment.[20] However, this small institution impinged little on the career choices of the vast majority of Irish women. It was the local national school that influenced Irish women who were not educated properly.

By 1881, just three years after the introduction of the Intermediate Education (Ireland) Act, there were 675,036 students receiv- ing instruction at the primary level. By 1911, this had decreased to 669,293, chiefly due to an overall drop in population, though the percentage of those being educated at second-level increased slightly from 12.85 per cent to 13.8 per cent.[21] More significantly, in 1881 only 3,654 teachers of out of a total of 10,621, or just a third, were actually trained.[22] It is therefore difficult to ascertain the quality of education, given the low proportion of trained teachers, though many of the teachers had informal training as monitors or trainee teachers. The number of trained teachers was to increase with the establishment of training colleges. By 1899, 47.8 per cent of primary teachers were trained.[23]

The development of first-level education provided jobs for professional women as primary teachers. Tom Garvin has argued that 'school was the way out of the Parish. Education was the route to position for men [*sic*] of intelligence and no capital, and it was scarcely a reliable one.'[24] The potential for entry into professional life for these teachers should not be underestimated. It was still possible to sit a university entrance examination, such as the matriculation for the National University of Ireland or the entrance exam for Trinity College, Dublin, after receiving only primary education, topped up by attendance at 'grinds-that is extra classes'. For instance, after passing the 1918 matriculation, Kathleen Doyle of St Aidan's National School, Kiltimagh, County Mayo, qualified to study at the NUI. Two years later Nora Stack of Dublin passed the Trinity entrance exam without the benefit of second-level education. She went on to gain a first-class honours medical degree.[25] These were rare occurrences, however. The majority of women who received a second-level education came from at least modestly comfortable backgrounds.

Because so many rural primary schools were two-teacher institutions, many females were educated in coeducational environments, in contrast to secondary schools. Traditionally, the female teacher taught the younger classes and the male teacher taught the older students. In urban areas, single-sex primary schools were more common. William Starkie, a Resident Commissioner for Education, felt that infants should not be entrusted to men who were 'naturally unacquainted with the ways of infants, and interested solely in the instruction of the older children [whereas] a woman though unskilled, has a natural sympathy for babies, she understands their ways, and even if she can teach them little, she knows how to make them happy.'[26] Given this attitude, it is clear that not much knowledge was expected to be imparted to younger students. Older students could benefit from the monitress system, whereby candidates from the senior classes would be selected to prepare for a teaching career. They would learn by doing, and they could then sit the entrance examinations for the training colleges having had the experience of teaching classes. In this sense, primary teachers could exert a powerful influence on women. Patronage – that is, selection for a monitorship by one's teacher – could work in favour of females.

Certain schools, usually second-level institutions, gained reputations for preparing students for teaching careers. The primary school at Carysfort was used by prospective teachers in their teaching practise; students there observed future teachers operating, and the experience may have induced some to pursue a teaching career. King's and Queen's scholarships were available to capable primary students who passed the entrance exam for the primary teaching training colleges. The primary school could be a significant educational influence by preparing candidates for secondary school scholarships. Like third-level scholarships, they were few and far between; begun in the early 1900s by county councils, only 188 were awarded in the Irish Free State in 1924.[27] In the 1920s there were still primary schools operating as semi-second-level schools. A total of 136 females attending seventeen primary schools were prepared for the Intermediate Certificate, while eighteen females sat their Leaving Certificate from primary school. In contrast, only one boy sat each exam from primary school.[28] As it was possible to remain at primary level until age sixteen, and from there, to begin training for a career as a primary school teacher, the profession was accessible to the less well-off. Few other professions could facilitate those who had not received second-level education.

However, it was the kind of second-level education received by females, and not their primary education, that had the greater bearing on their subsequent careers. Second-level education was a rarity for the majority of the population between 1878 and 1930.[29] By the latter date, 93 per cent of the population of the Irish Free State had received only primary education. But in the same period substantial gains were made by females in the education system. Many of these gains derived from the 1878 Intermediate Education Act, which gave women access to all the examinations of the Intermediate Board. Isabella Mulvanny, the principal of Alexandra School, pointed out that prior to the act, 'instruction in Classics and Mathematics was available in certainly not more than half a dozen schools located in … Dublin or Belfast.' In 1879, 736 females sat the Intermediate exam. By 1906 that number had increased to 3,656.[30] It remained, however, the preserve of the middle class. In time the curriculum of girls' schools reflected the academic nature of these examinations.

The establishment of Queen's Institute in 1861 was part of a move to make female education more relevant to the job market.

The professional schools of the Queen's Institute sought to prepare middle-class women for work rather than marriage. But the change was gradual. Some schools, particularly convents, persisted in emphasising accomplishments – that is, extracurricular classes in such subjects as elocution, music, and art appreciation that were expected to enhance girls' social graces – over academic achievements. The growing tendency toward examinations was noted by the Endowed Schools (Ireland) Commission in 1880, which reported that females were staying longer at school in order to train as teachers.[31] There was little cooperation between primary and secondary education. The system was managed in an entirely different manner. The second-level system depended on voluntary fee payments, while most primary schools were part of the State system. Females (and males from working-class backgrounds) had little chance of receiving a second-level education.

Victoria College Belfast, originally Ladies' Collegiate, was unusual in having its own kindergarten; Margaret Byers, the founder of the school, felt it was important that the students had a good foundation before they moved on to the higher classes. By the time the students were twelve years old they had thirty-nine hours of classes per week for twelve subjects with mathematics (ten hours) taking up the most time.[32] Byers often argued that academic subjects were frequently neglected in girls' schools. She also felt that Protestant girls had lost out educationally, as there were few schools available to them, unlike the many convent schools open to Catholic girls. However, at least initially it was the Protestant schools that excelled at the intermediate examinations. Indeed, the impetus to improve female education was initiated by Protestant schools.[33] The Quaker Anne Jellicoe, who helped to found Alexandra College in 1866, was part of this movement. Alexandra College provided a solid academic education – students studied Latin, mathematics, science and modern languages – which in time produced numerous professional women among its graduates.[34] Under the dynamic direction of Isabella Mulvany, who was appointed headmistress in 1880, Alexandra School provided many middle-class women with the opportunity to prepare for professional careers. Many of the early doctors, Isabella Ovenden, Kathleen Lynn, Katherine Maguire as well as the first female chartered accountant, Eileen Woodworth, were past pupils.

Jellicoe was also involved in the Queen's Technical Training Institute for Women, which trained pupils for teaching careers and prepared students for third-level examinations. The 'High School movement' that sought to establish academic second-level schools in the early twentieth century provided an important example of academic training for Irish educationalists. St Leonard's School in Scotland, an academically rigorous institution that became the model for Enid Blyton's Malory Towers series of girls' books in the 1940s, educated Constantia and Euphran Maxwell, an historian and oph-thalmologist respectively in Dublin. Alexandra College and School; Victoria College, Belfast; and the High School, Cork, were modelled on English high schools. The Ladies Institute – the Belfast version of the Queen's institute – also provoked change by emphasising the employment of women.[35]

Advances in women's education did not always run smoothly and were not universally applied. As late as 1905, two English school inspectors in Ireland reported that less than 10 per cent of women teachers, and less than 30 per cent of male teachers in second-level schools were graduates, and that 'no distinction is made between the experienced teacher and the student in his first year at col-lege.'[36] Ironically, teachers at primary level were more likely to be trained, because members of religious orders had their own training establishments. Convents in particular were slow to reform female education; the majority of teachers in convent schools had no aca-demic qualifications. In 1894, the Catholic bishop of Limerick, at the annual prize-giving for the Faithful Companions of Jesus Laurel Hill Convent, declared that the intermediate examination system was 'discordant with feminine idiosyncrasies,' and praised the nuns for not entering their students for the examinations.[37] In 1883, the Catholic bishop of Meath deplored 'the advent of the new woman who demanded equal rights with her brother in admission to a study of the exact sciences and to the Pagan literature of Greece and Rome [apparently it was acceptable for males, especially those studying for the priesthood, to imbibe this paganism] as well as to the realms of Law and Medicine and all the liberal professions'.[38] Yet by 1926 women constituted more than 10 per cent of the medical profession.[39]

A clear measure of the gradual improvement of opportunities for Catholic students is the fact that only twenty women's schools were found in the results of the Intermediate Board in 1892; only six years later, the number had more than doubled to forty-five. In part, this stems from the desire of Catholic schools not to be outclassed in examinations by Protestant schools. The *Lyceum*, a Catholic intellectual periodical, announced in 1893 that, 'We see no reason, if our efforts be directed wisely, why we should not compete on equal terms with non-Catholic institutions. We go further, even, and believe we may out-distance rivals, if we are only true to ourselves, and utilise all the conditions of success which are at our disposal.'[40] Some schools adapted quickly to the changes. At the Dominican school in Galway, Sr Hyacinth, the mistress of schools, had been advised by Dr McEvilly, the Roman Catholic Bishop of Galway, to have 'nothing to do with the examinations'; the school did not even enter the examination until 1897. Yet by 1903 they had equipped a science laboratory for their students.[41] This step was all the more innovative given that the Intermediate Education Board exempted schools from compulsory experimental science if they lacked the 'necessary equipment or teaching staff.'[42] Meanwhile, at the St Louis secondary school in Monaghan town, which had previously concentrated on 'the courtesies', German, Italian, Latin, and mathematics were added to the curriculum. In 1889 the school took first place among girls' schools in the Intermediate examination, much to the joy of the *Freeman's Journal*.[43] The school's success was not surprising; a professor from the diocesan seminary taught the students extra mathematics and the president of the seminary taught Latin to the students once a week.[44] The school was also noted for its pioneering work in promoting the Irish language in the 1890s.[45] Not all Catholic clergy opposed education for women, and many Protestant women benefited from Sunday Schools established by clergymen.

The success of candidates in these intermediate examinations was also hugely influenced by subject choice. There were clear biases in the allocation of marks (the weighted academic points awarded to each subject). Greek, Latin, and English were allocated 1,200 marks. French and German – which were more favoured by female candidates – were worth only 700 marks. Science subjects fared better, with chemistry allocated 500 marks and botany ('for girls only') given 300 marks.[46] Clearly, the classical bias in Irish education was bolstered by the examination system. Traditionally girls' schools had placed emphasis on languages. As Judith Harford has noted, 'even before public examinations for girls had been introduced, Loreto pupils were periodically examined English, French, Italian and German.'[47] Many women did not have access to Greek or Latin, and were thus limited in their university choices as virtually all faculties required Latin. This denied young women access to the higher professions, and in turn, also explains why women congregated in such professions as nursing and teaching.

When the Central Association of Irish School Mistresses (CAISM) was established in 1889 to 'promote [the] higher education of girls and promote cooperation among schoolmistresses,' the matter of subject choices made by females was one of the key issues the association hoped to address.[48] CAISM did much to raise the status of Irish teachers, and it continually encouraged female students to sit examinations in Latin, Greek and mathematics. The association criticised the 'group system' in which second-level students concentrated on a group of subjects such as literature, mathematics, or science; as late as 1905 those taking literature (the most popular option for females) did not study Greek or mathematics.[49] Because this inevitably restricted their choices at third-level, females predominantly studied for arts degrees and then pursued teaching careers. This specialisation was partly financial, as students felt they had a better chance of excelling in modern languages and winning prize money.[50] By 1930, the situation had changed. In 1929, almost equal numbers of females took mathematics (223) and French (239) in the Leaving Certificate, the State examination for those completing their second-level education.[51]

CAISM was also quick to defend students from changes in the curriculum that might affect their future careers. In 1922 domestic science became compulsory for first- and second-year female secondary students taking the science option. This left less time for other, crucial science subjects like physics and chemistry. The association warned that the 'disadvantage would be more marked in the case of medical students, as the Medical Council had already decreed that after 1923 entrants to the medical school would have to pass before entrance, an examination in the sciences which now forms part of the first year medical course.' Owing to their intervention with the educational authorities, the domestic science requirement was postponed indefinitely.[52] Many Protestant schools at second-level were unenthusiastic, with some notable exceptions, about the emphasis placed on Irish. However, they were less than successful in their attempts to challenge the stress placed on the national language.[53] In 1924, CAISM – at that point dominated by schools under Protestant management, such as Rutland School in Dublin and

Rochelle in Cork – protested against the proposed introduction of compulsory Irish in 1928. They argued that for their 'students who enter the profession there is not sufficient scope in Ireland when qualified.' Again in 1926 they maintained that Irish crowded out Latin and French and this was a 'serious handicap to students intending to proceed to a university or enter upon a professional career.'[54] The CAISM did not dwell on the negative, however. Its meetings often featured speakers who outlined careers for women. For example, in 1929 Miss Honor Brown gave a paper on 'the training and qualifications necessary for girls desiring to take up teaching of physical culture as a profession.'[55]

An analysis of the summer matriculation examination of 1918 indicates the extent to which convent schools had adapted to changes in the curriculum and were preparing students for third-level education. Dublin accounted for thirty-two of the successful female candidates, followed by Cork (fifteen) Limerick and Galway (seven). More than half of the females, sixty-two in total, had studied outside the bigger cities, in such small towns as Swinford, County Mayo; Skibbereen, County Cork; and Ballymahon, County Longford.[56] Furthermore there was a tendency to send females from rural areas to urban boarding schools. Clearly, it was not just the urban areas that benefited from the educational changes of the late-nineteenth century.

Mixed-gender education was not entirely absent. Methodist College Belfast, established in 1868, had taken in female students from the beginning. It opened with fifty females, many of whom went on to professional careers in medicine, science and education.[57] The school catered primarily to Presbyterians, Episcopalians and Methodists; by 1901 one-third of the students were female, about 110 girls.[58] This tradition of mixed-gender education in Ulster may also explain the greater likelihood of Ulster females to study what were seen as 'male' subjects; in 1879, the first year of the Intermediate examinations, seventy-two female (or 68 per cent of the total number of females who passed mathematics) were from Ulster.[59] The report of the inspectors Dale and Stephens noted that, of the mixed schools that had entered students for the 1903 Intermediate examinations, there were twenty-three in Ulster, five in Leinster, three in Munster – including remarkably, two in Kilmihil, County Clare, a village with a population of 185 – and one in Connaught.[60] Single-sex education was by no means unique to Ireland; in Portugal, it was not until 1920 that girls were allowed to attend boys' secondary schools the same year as the first mixed convent school opened on Ireland in Louisburg, County Mayo.[61]

As so many future female professionals received their education at convent secondary schools, it is worth examining the regimen that existed in a typical school, St Louis Secondary School, Carrickmacross, County Monaghan. There, students rose at 6.45 a.m., with Mass at 7.30. After a breakfast described as 'frugal, not delicate but wholesome and abundant – plenty of tea, bread and butter,' classes began at 9 a.m. with dinner and recreation at 1 p.m. Classes continued between 2 p.m. and 4 p.m. Subjects studied included Irish, English, German, French, mathematics, bookkeeping, experimental and practical science, music, religious instruction and painting. After formal classes there was another meal and then a walk. Study began at 5 p.m., with a break for prayers at 6 p.m, followed by supper. Between 7 and 9 p.m. there was recreation (usually dancing), and then the girls went to bed.[62]

By 1931, Mercy nuns taught in fifty-one secondary schools, with the Loreto sisters teaching in eighteen schools. The Dominican and Presentation orders taught in ten and eleven schools, respectively. Because scholarships were rare, most of their student came from middle-class backgrounds; in the mid-1920s only 3.5 per cent of all secondary students received scholarships.[63] Scarce as they were, scholarship for intellectually able students at second-level often made a professional career possible. An example is Dr Dorothy Stopford-Price. She was a foundation scholar at St Paul's in London, her mother having moved to England after the death of her father. She won junior and senior scholarships at St Paul's before studying medicine at Trinity College.[64]

Not all schools established by enterprising women were antagonistic toward examinations. Mary MacSwiney – more noted for her political activities in the Independence era – established Scoil Íte (St Ita's) after her release from prison in 1916. It was to exert a powerful influence on Mary O'Sullivan, a professor of education in UCC in the 1930s once said that when meeting a new class of students, she could always 'pick out the St Ita's pupils after a few weeks – there was something distinctly different about them.' The education received by students at St Ita's included training 'in Ecumenism'.[65] MacSwiney's republicanism informed the teaching of history in St Ita's; although she did not teach history, the course was taught from an 'Irish point of view'. When the students were required to answer a question in a history examination on the counties that bordered Northern Ireland, she refused to let the students answer it, as she wanted no one taught history 'according to a British Act of Parliament'.[66]

Profiles of a variety of schools published in 1915, demonstrate the range of activities enjoyed by students. St Louis, Rathmines, pursued 'Swedish hygienic exercise'. The faithful Companions of Jesus school in Bunclody, County Wexford, had an art room as well as a science laboratory where students were prepared for the 'Technical Board (science) exams'. These progressive schools still emphasised the importance of accomplishments.[67] One of Dorothy Price's teachers noted her 'steady enthusiasm for social work', and the philanthropic activities of many secondary schools may partly explain female involvement in such philanthropic professions in the early twentieth century as factory inspection.[68] This kind of work was also seen as suitable for females. Alexandra College had its very active 'Guild' which established model tenement houses. Victoria College Belfast supported Shamrock Lodge, a home for impoverished females.[69] Dr Nan Watson, a physician, left an impressive amount of material relating to her schooldays in Victoria College Belfast, and her papers reflect a striking emphasis on prize-giving. Watson won a prize for 'first general place senior class' in 1917.[70] The following year she won a prize for Latin, mathematics, and domestic science. Her exercise book for the latter subject contains the oft-repeated refrain that 'less attention is now given to spelling than formerly'.[71]

The extension of second-level education to females is one of the quiet revolutions of late-nineteenth- and early twentieth-century Ireland. Despite anomalies in the subjects studied – a stunning example of which occurred in 1918, when one girl and 219 boys passed Greek in the senior grade – by 1911 one-third of all students attending 'superior schools' were female. In Western Europe, only England, Wales and Norway had a higher percentage of females at second-level. More significant, Ireland was second only to Finland in the percentage of women at university.[72]

Frank Hugh O'Donnell's lamentable assessment in 1902 that schools were manufacturing 'young feminine failures and non-values for the decline, the depression, and the destruction of the Irish nation' could not be further from the truth.[73] It was through education that many of the values of the new nation were communicated. New schools

like Louise Gavan-Duffy's all-Irish Scoil Bhríde and the more established institutions educated women who were prominent in many of
the causes in early twentieth-century Ireland and who additionally
had a profession to pursue.[74]

The numbers of women availing of second-level education indicates the increasing availability of educational opportunities. The
quarter-century after the 1878 Intermediate Education Act saw a
five-fold increase in female participants, from 736 to 3,656. Moreover,
the development of a more academic education for women opened
up careers for these women, although the emphasis on modern languages and other curricular restraints restricted the scope of their
educations. Additionally, because most second-level schools were
fee-paying, the 'revolution' in female education was confined to the
middle classes. The publications produced by female educational
institutions in Ireland impart a sense of their atmosphere. The focus
was on such female-dominated professions as teaching and public
health; nonetheless, these schools created an environment in which
female ambitions were encouraged and networks were established,
and students were alerted to employment opportunities.

Between 1878, when the Intermediate Education Act took effect,
and 1930, which saw the introduction of the Vocational Educational
Act, Ireland witnessed a dramatic development of professions for
women in health and education. Many of these women had benefited from the education that commentators like O'Donnell were
so quick to deride. An indication of the success of Intermediate
education is that by 1921, 43 per cent of the students who sat its
examinations were female.[75] For the second-level schools, there were
8,706 females and 22,807 males attending second-level schools, but
there were 877 (10 per cent) females compared to 1,560 (7 per cent)
males at A schools, where all instruction was in Irish, and B schools,
which offered some classes in English. Females were thus over-repre-
sented in this category.[76] In 1929, of all females in fourteen-to-sixteen
age group, 27 per cent were in primary school and only 10.7 per cent
were at second-level.[77] However, very few young women continued
in formal education after the age of fourteen.

Without the educational developments of the late-nineteenth
century – in particular, the 1878 Intermediate Act and the opening up of the universities – women would not have been able to
capitalise on increasing educational opportunities. Regrettably, it
was primarily those who had already had some financial resources

who derived most from these opportunities, and, having entered the professions and other leadership roles in Ireland, they did little to change the structure of society. Their inaction ensured that a professional career was possible only if one had the necessary contacts for a professional apprenticeship, or the finances for advanced education.

The most forceful arguments for the developments of female education arose from the desire to eliminate superficiality from the curriculum. In 1919, Hanna Donovan, an MA graduate from Cork would declare, 'a new aristocracy has arisen among women – the aristocracy of intellect – the sole passport of admission to which is the value of work done.'[78] This was an optimistic view, but Donovan's claim was a product of the quiet revolutionary changes in female education during the previous four decades. This was an era during which intellectual strait-jackets were gradually transformed into academic gowns.

Chapter 4

Women in university education in Ireland: the historical background

University education for women in Ireland began with the establishment of the Royal University of Ireland (RUI) in 1879. The Queen's Colleges in Galway, Cork and Belfast quickly followed suit, with all facilities in those colleges available to women by 1895. Dublin University – or Trinity, as it was popularly known – was closed to females until 1904.

The experiences of females in third-level education can be gleaned from college magazines. *St Stephen's* (of the Catholic University, later UCD) gives a hint of such experiences in a regular piece in entitled 'Girl Graduates' Chat'. (The title was later changed to 'From the Ladies' Colleges', following charges that the original title was frivolous and suggested 'childish babble'.[1]) The contributors were primarily students from St Mary's Dominican College, Alexandra College, and Loreto College, Stephen's Green, all of whom were studying for RUI degrees. They exchanged gossip and described efforts to obtain employment for university graduates. Lively debates in Irish were reported from St Mary's, with Agnes O'Farrelly, a future Professor of Irish at UCD, to the fore.[2] Students who excelled at examinations were singled out for praise. Miss Ada English was congratulated on her success in medical examinations, as was Agnes Perry on becoming the first woman to gain honours in the MA in mathematics.[3] *St Stephen's* noted with delight that female medical students were 'well known' and excited 'little or no extraordinary attention in moving through Dublin social circles'. However, it was felt that in certain homes, where daughters were 'trained to no method of earning their bread', university students were 'received with ill-concealed envy and jealousy'.[4]

Alexandra College Magazine likewise gives an insight into the activities of that college. Like *St Stephen's*, it regularly praised its illustrious graduates. Regular reports from societies (such as the Literary Society), as well as games activities (particularly hockey) featured. The magazine also devoted space to possible openings for women, and talks were given on topics such as 'Journalism as a Profession for Women' and 'Women as Poor Law Guardians'.[5] Opportunities for women in the colonies were also alluded to, and the Debating Society debated the topic, 'Should Women Enter the Professions?' Nineteen supported the motion and six were against. An indication of the manner in which the debate over women's work had progressed, partly in response to the First World War, is evident from a motion discussed in 1917. The topic by then was 'That every Woman should receive Professional Training'.[6] Readers of *Alexandra College Magazine* should keep in touch with events in the educational field through reports on the International Federation of University Women. Past pupils also recounted their experiences of other educational institutions, such as Danish high schools. Student publications alerted graduates to opportunities in the jobs market, as well as providing news of social activities.

It is worth bearing in mind that, for most females, third-level education until the early 1910s was by way of Ladies' Colleges. Graduates numbers between 1891 and 1900 were as follows; Victoria College Belfast, ninety-five; Alexandra College Dublin, eighty-four; Loreto College Dublin, twenty; Queen's College, Belfast, nineteen; St Mary's Dominican College Dublin, seventeen; Magee College, Derry, seventeen; Queen's College Cork, two; Queen's College Galway, one.

Many of the aforementioned institutions were single-sex environments. Mary Hayden, while presenting evidence in 1902 to the Robertson Commission on University Education, proposed that co-education would alleviate many of the disparities suffered by women at third-level. This was achieved with establishment of the National University of Ireland in 1908.[8] A contemporary of Hayden's, Mary Macken, remembered her time at Loreto College, Stephen's Green, where tuition in Latin and Science was difficult to obtain. P.A.E. Dowling helped the first arts students with the compulsory mathematics and science. Macken also noted the excellent teaching in Latin and logic of Sr Mary Eucharia, who gave her a letter of introduction to Monsignor Macken, one of the trustees of the Catholic University.

Mary Macken here alerts us to the need for students to have a 'sponsor' who would see that they were catered for. Catholic connections were fully utilised by religious orders in placing their students at universities abroad for language study. When Sr Eucharia went to Cambridge as Superior, Mary Macken went with her and studied at Newnham, one of the women's colleges at Cambridge University.[9] These links were vital to the development of professional and social networks for women, and should not be underestimated. Male students were at an academic advantage in that the Royal University appointed fellows to teach on their courses, whereas women were more likely to be taught by non-graduates. Hence, the pursuit of qualifications abroad was essential.

Trinity officially opened its doors to women in 1904. Alexandra College undoubtedly viewed the opening of Trinity in an ambivalent manner. Many, particularly Isabella Mulvany, the headmistress at Alexandra School, thought it would benefit females in the pursuit of suitable employment; Henrieta White, the principal of Alexandra College, thought it would adversely affect student numbers at her institution. In the long run, hers was as accurate assessment. Nonetheless, for a quarter of a century before Trinity was available, Alexandra provided the essential qualifications for a professional career.

By 1934, there were 242 females and 1,484 males in Trinity. The presence of Oxbridge female students who came to Trinity to graduate since they could not graduate from their home universities, may also have opened intellectual doors for Irish women. The writer Mary Colum describes the visitors as, 'intellectual dragons, they knew all sorts of things like biology and modern science such as our more literary training discounted'.[10] As regards college activities, the 'Ex-Science Association' (an association for students who had graduated with a science degree) was the first college society to accept women as ordinary members, and their exclusion from the Classical Society was all the more puzzling given they were taking Classical courses, and winning prizes.[11]

In a work focusing on American women, Barbara Miller Solomon suggests that female collegians 'came from a range of families within the broad and expanding middle class'.[12] From the evidence available

on Irish university women, there is nothing to contradict the view
that Ireland was any different. Education was expensive, and scholarships scarce. True, some students resourcefully worked their way
through college, but these appear to have been exceptions. Family
support was often crucial. Just as interested staff sought opportunities for their students, extended family members were also vital in
providing support systems for female students. It was not unusual for
women to be aged twenty before commencing a university degree.
Some worked before preparing for a second profession. Several medical graduates took a BA degree, a Higher Diploma in Education, or
a music degree before they opted for a medical career.

As noted above, the ladies' colleges were at a disadvantage in the
RUI as they did not have the benefits of university Fellows on the
staff. However, university graduates taught in some of the ladies' colleges. When the first RUI degrees were awarded in 1884, five of the
nine female graduates were teaching at Alexandra.[13] Not surprisingly,
there was a strong link between these educated women and their
efforts as activists in the Central Association of Irish Schoolmistresses,
to improve female access to higher educated women. In March 1891,
for example, the CAISM discussed the possibility of establishing a
course in the RUI to train teachers. This group of educated women
was heavily involved in the opening Trinity to women, and making
the Junior Fellowships of the RUI available to them also.

Northern women, particularly those in Belfast, could attend
Victoria College Belfast, Methodist College Belfast, or St Dominic's.
Alternatively, they could sit the RUI exams through private study.
This was preferable for Catholics in particular, since Queen's College
Belfast (after 1908, Queen's University Belfast) was perceived as a
Presbyterian institution. There were only 208 male and female
Catholics in QUB in 1920. In 1947, Catholics constituted only 20
per cent (400) of the student population.[14] Magee College in Derry
admitted women students in 1883. Eight matriculated female stu-
dents entered, including Mary Kennedy, who subsequently went to
Girton in Cambridge and was placed first in the Natural Science
Tripos. Unlike Queen's in Belfast, where women were eligible for
all prizes from 1895, the Magee females were immediately eligible
for all prizes. With the establishment of the NUI, Magee was linked
with Trinity. Some Magee students excelled in the Trinity examinations, and the females were particularly prominent in languages.[15]
The Royal College of Science also provided aspiring professional

women with qualifications. Their register of students indicates that women who were taking science for practicals and specific courses. Some students were registered as 'teachership in training' and most had their fees paid, possibly by the Department of Agriculture and Technical Instruction. The register for 1905 to 1926 (when the college was transferred to UCD, and became the university's Science Faculty) indicates that over forty female students were awarded Royal College of Science diplomas. Many of these described themselves as teachers in training or National School teachers.[16]

There was also scope for occasional students to study at the Royal College of Science. In 1881, Isabella Mulvany registered for Practical Physics, as did ten students from Alexandra, probably at her prompting. However, they did not complete the course. Amelia Grogan, who later became a medical doctor, completed several courses in 1887. Emily Dickson, the first female Fellow of the Royal College of Surgeons, was awarded the second prize in Botany in 1890.[17] Kathleen Maguire, who graduated from the RUI with a First class honours medical degree in 1891, passed examinations in Botany and Zoology in 1887.[18]

It is interesting to note that women were admitted to the Cecilia Street Medical School (subsequently the UCD Medical School) before they were admitted to lectures at the Catholic University. The RUI recognised Royal College of Science courses as part of one's medical training.[19] These opportunities were vital for women who were starved of science courses at second-level. The possibilities for women in science contrast favourably with continental development. It was not until 1920 that women in Germany were granted official permission to obtain a doctorate, while Rosalind Clarke, for example, who pursued an academic career in chemistry at UCG, was awarded a DSc in 1914 by that university.[20] At second-level, the numbers of women taking Science had improved, no doubt because they were benefiting from trained science teachers. By 1921, 31 per cent of those taking science at second-level were female.[21]

By 1930, women were well established in Irish universities. In one of the smallest of Irish universities, University College Galway, which had 263 students in 1926, there was an equal number of male and female students by 1930.[22] In University College Cork, for the 1917–18 academic year, there were 111 (20 per cent) female students of a total of 566.[23] How do these figures compare internationally? In 1925, 11 per cent of German university students were female;

in Italy, women constituted 17 per cent of university students. Meanwhile in France, the figure was 20 per cent, whereas in Finland, one third of university were female. Ireland was on a par with Finland, as by 1925, 30 per cent of all Irish university students were female.[24] The Irish figures therefore compare well with other Western European countries.

Higher education, it was believed, would allow women to lead 'a richer, freer life and made fuller personal development possible freeing women from mere eccentricity, political faddism, philanthropic hysteria and busy-body shallow restlessness.'[25] This was an inaccurate assessment. Ironically, it was the experience of college life that propelled many women into political activity and philanthropic professions. University education provided women with opportunities. They had the chance to excel at examinations, therein finding the motivation to seek professional occupations. University careers also aided the development of female networks that furthered professional careers. Moreover, the presence of female role models stimulated aspiring professional women. Records indicate that, having received a university education, female graduates were indeed more likely to pursue professional careers.

What had changed for UCD women by the end of the twentieth century? An essay of this brevity could not even attempt to chart the changes and, more importantly, the absence of change. Perhaps the following statistic will provide food for thought: in 1998 there were sixty-four sports scholarships students in UCD. Four of them were women.[26]

Ad Astra and *Comhthrom na Féinne* – and *Fair Play* – are the Latin and Irish phrases on the crest of University College Dublin. Their university years, for some women, provided an opportunity to reach for the stars, but for many others there was very little fair play.

Chapter 5

Books and baths and run all the way: the cultural and education formation of female primary teachers in the early twentieth century

This paper discusses the role of female primary teachers in the development of a national system of education. Their preparation at the various training colleges as well as the academic and cultural environment of these institutions is examined. More specifically, the role of extra-curricular activities, particularly sporting endeavours, in the formation of female primary teachers is assessed. The paper suggests that the traditional picture of restrictions on females in the sporting arena may have to be modified. Finally, the importance of teachers in passing on cultural and sporting traditions is discussed.

Despite influencing generations of Irish school children, very little is known about the cultural and educational formation of primary school teachers. Garvin has noted that primary teachers were the 'radical intellectuals of the parish.' While he describes teachers as 'Men in the Middle', Garvin points out that female teachers were important in passing on Gaelic traditions.[1] He also notes the ambivalent position of primary teachers: 'they possessed education and quite considerable cultural influence in village society while having little real security or political independence'.[2]

These 'village intellectuals' were to exert considerable hidden influence on generations of school children. However, they were not operating as independent professionals. In 1921, J.J. O'Kelly, Minister for Education, declared that teachers were 'servants of the nation' and the 'nation who employs them must have a right to specify the nature of the work they do'.[3] Coolahan in his examination of the Royal Commission of Inquiry into Primary Education (Powis), 1870 noted that forty-three per cent of teachers were female.[4] This article will focus on the professional preparation of those female primary teachers in the early twentieth century.

Mary Immaculate Training College in Limerick was established in 1898, while Baggot Street (later Carysfort College) was established in 1877. Both institutions were involved in the formation of female teachers and were managed by the Sisters of Mercy. It is difficult to ascertain the precise background of female students at the training colleges. A careful study of the intake to the training colleges in the 1920s and 1930s noted that the development of the preparatory schools, which were established in 1926 in order to ensure that students were proficient in Irish before entering the training colleges, favoured students from Irish-speaking regions of Ireland. This 'differential recruitment of teachers from economic periphery of Ireland'[5] ensured that, in time, cultural aspirations, in particular the restoration of the Irish language, were given a powerful impetus through careful selection of future teachers. By 1928, forty-six per cent of all entrants to the preparatory colleges were from the Gaeltacht.[6] Given the minimal fees at the training colleges, the teaching profession was attractive for those who could not afford a university education.

Many teachers wished to bring the training colleges closer to the universities with all the intellectual variety and status this would have entailed. Similar ideas were evident in French education circles. Catherine Mahon, who went on to become the first female president of the Irish National Teachers' Organisation, noted that, during the passage of the 1908 University Act, teachers' groups tried to have the training colleges linked to the universities.[7] This was to become a prominent issue in the late 1910s and early 1920s as political changes heralded new developments for the training colleges. The short training period (two years for monitors and one year for experienced teachers) also militated against increased status and pay for primary teachers.

The training of teachers was a topic of debate in Ireland. According to the novelist Canon Sheehan, there was 'a marked difference between the old untrained schoolmaster and the young teachers' who graduated from the training colleges:[8]

With the old generation, teaching was something like what
Carlyle was always dreaming of and talking about – a kind of
lofty vocation, a priestly function, which would not rank lower
than that of a Kirk-minister, or voluntary preacher under the free
Church.

Now that the National Board was more or less in control, it had
'converted the teachers into State officials and destroyed all personal
interest in their pupils.'

This argument does not stand up to analysis, however. Local teachers still wielded considerable authority, particularly in rural Ireland.
While they may have been paid by the State, they were not seen
as anonymous civil servants. Sheehan wanted teaching to be recognised as an 'exalted and honourable vocation'. He believed that its
'influence on humanity' placed it as the 'premier secular profession'.[9]
These grandiose ideas faltered because the poor pay and prospects
rendered it unattractive for the ambitious.

Up until the 1930s, the majority of teachers trained under the
monitorship system, prior to attending training college. In 1920, there
were 1,400 monitors.[10] This suggests that the profession was open to
the less well off. Once these trainee teachers went on to third-level
education, their preparation focussed on cultural capital, as well as
academic preparation. Academically, their course work emphasised a
large range of subjects with none being studied in detail. Attendance
at training college also enhanced one's employment prospects with
the college authorities seeking jobs for their graduates. In 1900, fifty-
five per cent of teachers were trained.[11] There was more competition
for female college places, with 482 males and 1,216 females seeking
admission in 1902 to the training colleges.[12]

The focus of teachers' training reflected the aspirations of the
curriculum. What was the content of the educational curriculum?
Coolahan was critical of the limited 'scope for speculation or intelligent' responses in the curriculum and assessment of teachers.[13] The
subject of 'Education' was an important part of the training of future
teachers. Yet it was not taught in an analytical manner. Unfortunately,
as Coolahan makes clear, the 'examinations tended to favour cramming and memory work based on factual data and practical hints
of the trade rather than encouraging reflection and the intelligent
application of general principle to problem questions.'[14] By 1903
reform of the curriculum ensured that education counted for 250

out of a total of 1,300 marks the allocated to compulsory subjects for male and female students. But there were regular complaints concerning the poor quality of training. Females, in particular, were considered to be overworked. One anonymous contemporary commentator claimed that the course was 'too extended (especially for women), hence the students are overburdened for mere examination purposes, leading to some extent to neglect of real training'.[15] Some attempts were made to introduce students to the 'science' of education, but these efforts were never entirely successful given the range of compulsory subjects.

Despite the heavy workload, there were State officials who were pleased with the training colleges. In 1894, Viscount Morley, one of the Commissioners for Education, was very enthusiastic about the cultural benefits of attending Baggot Street Training College. He wrote:

> [I] can well understand the eagerness for admission. Young women come up from all parts of Ireland, rough and unkempt; are put into the civilising mill; books, baths, infinite tidiness and order, and the friendly guidance and sympathy of the Rev. Mother and Sisters. I must say these women please me vastly. Their atmosphere is human, they are keen about their work; it is all moving and alive with sympathy; not mechanical, all chalk and blackboard.[16]

This emphasis on 'books and baths' indicates the kind of education which was deemed to be appropriate for future teachers. The comments of Morley are remarkably similar to those of a local journalist who visited the Brigidine sisters in Beechworth, Victoria, Australia:

> I have, as a Protestant always associated nuns and nunneries with bondage and confinement with dark cells and cruelty, with terrible penances and dark doings. But in my pleasant run through the Brigidine Convent at Beechworth nothing but intellectual associations, perfect liberty and most commendable cleanliness met my eye everywhere.[17]

In Ireland just as in Australia, teachers were to set an example by their scholarliness and standards of hygiene. In the classrooms, inspectors did not only note academic faults. They also commented on the cleanliness and moral tone of the classroom. As in medicine, women were perceived, and in many cases, perceived themselves, as having characteristics which were particularly appropriate for nurturing of the young. Hence, we see female physicians opting for paediatrics.[18] Because of the discovery of the germ, great emphasis was placed on sanitation and the elimination of dirt, which placed particular stress on maternal vigilance both at home and in school.[19] The duties of the lady inspector included the education of younger children, and the special education of girls, particularly cookery and household management. The social function of female teachers in passing on the ideas of motherhood clearly received encouragement from the curriculum. Women were expected to teach domestic skills to girls.

One of the best-known students of Baggot Street was Jennie Flanagan, later Sineád, Bean de Valera. She was a student in the college between 1898 and 1900. Her future husband was appointed professor of mathematics at Carysfort in 1906 at £120 per annum. Éamon de Valera taught mathematics in an unorthodox manner in the college during the 1910s. Christine Coady (she was later to become Sr M. Pascal) remembered her mathematics classes with de Valera: 'Looking back one can see that many of the problems he set up were based on his study of arms and ammunition ... the principle of the torpedo took up one session'. De Valera left in 1916. Coady also commented on the 'modest entrance fee' to the college, though she was not afraid to be critical of the training she received there:

> Though we were preparing to teach and develop the minds and characters of future generations, our years of training were scarcely geared to that profession. Academically, our minds were enlarged, but our character training was very deficient.

The daily routine, from 6.30 a.m. to 10 p.m., was carefully 'supervised'. One member of staff did not impress her at all: 'He spent a great deal of his time laughing at his own jokes which did not appeal to our sense of humour'. In contrast, she thought highly of a 'lady who had been professor in Belfast' who later trained as a barrister.[20]

As noted earlier, by the 1920s, the Irish language movement was making an impact on the curriculum. Irish examinations were introduced for the first time for students who wished to teach in a bilingual school. Meanwhile, other aspects of college activity were receiving attention. In 1912, the Commission praised 'the con-

tinuous development of a larger spirit of College life. Literary and
debating societies, dramatic and musical performances, [Dr Vincent
O'Brien was appointed lecturer in "Chorus Singing" in 1908] and
other social entertainments now play an important part in the general training of the students'.[21]

What was the daily routine of training college like? For Miss
Elizabeth Calwell, who began training at Kildare Place (the Church
of Ireland training College) in 1906, it was a 'miserable existence'
with every day bringing 'fresh troubles and anxieties'. She rose
at 6.30a.m. and had to make her bed in 'the most peculiar fashion imaginable and woe betide the girl who does not make hers
according to the prescribed method.' The college had dormitory
inspectors who checked the beds. For physical exercise, students
walked between one o'clock and six o'clock on Wednesdays and
Saturdays, with the seniors (second-year students) taking the juniors
for their walk. Calwell spent the afternoon 'parading' up and down
Grafton Street. She declared, 'I am perfectly sick of it, however I
must endure patiently till after Xmas when I can choose companions
more congenial to my tastes'. Students were allowed lady visitors.
However, gentlemen were not admitted unless they sent a 'special
application' to the principal.[22]

Despite this strict routine, some students managed to indulge in
highly unorthodox behaviour by the standards of the time. One student from Tipperary smoked in the bathroom at night, and kept a
'black bottle' in her locker. After lights out, at 10.30, some of the
students were 'all up and alive'. Dancing was also a 'favourite amuse-
ment'. Seniors had permission, on occasion, to clear the halls in
preparation for dancing, but Elizabeth Calwell was a Presbyterian,
and 'did not indulge in that'. Students were not always attentive.
In singing, the male students threw 'chalk and other substances' at
the females. Even the non-dancing 'Lillie, as she called herself, broke
the rules by writing a letter in her study class. Letter writing was only
permitted on Friday nights'.[23]

Did the students have time for any extra-curricular activities?
Valiulis has made much of the Mary Immaculate Modest Dress
and Deportment Crusade. This sought to eliminate immodest dress
amongst prospective primary teachers. She links with the restrictions on mixed athletics, and its ban by John Charles McQuaid, then
President of Blackrock College.[24] O'Connor, the historian of Mary
Immaculate Training College, points out that the crusade 'attracted

thousands of members from all walks of life.' Their fashion guidelines were as follows: 'dresses to be worn not less than four inches below the knee' and 'sleeves to the wrist for Church wear.' Furthermore, members of the deportment crusade were to abstain from 'loud talking and boisterous laughter in public'.[25]

The traditional picture of female restrictions in the sporting arena may have to be modified, when one looks at the training colleges. Many students in Limerick played basketball (hardly a sport noted for its sedate pace), baseball and tennis. This may, in part, be due to the enthusiasm of Sr Veronica Cullinan, who became principal in 1923. She was a great believer in outdoor activities, and loved fresh air. It is surprising that camogie was not popular at that time in training colleges. There may have been a class dimension to these activities, given that tennis was seen as a middle-class and highly respectable sport. Such was the interest in games that the students were allowed to forego their Sunday walk, normally a ritual in all-female boarding establishments, and play basketball matches instead. These games were not associated with the gaelicisation programme but may be seen as part of the European gymnastics movement which contributed, in part, to the revival of the Olympic Games in 1896 and organised games in the early twentieth century. However, this was usually associated with Swedish Drill. Hence, it comes as a surprise to see demure Mary Immaculate students racing around a court. One student, who signed herself as B.L., (1927) wrote the following about her games experiences at Mary Immaculate Training College during the 1920s:[26]

'Run all the Way'

The lockers are opened, 'elastics' [stockings] pulled forth,
As each student makes ready for play,
Then laughing and talking, we merrily race,
For our slogan is – Run all the way!
And when, on the playground, a 'White' or a 'Blue'
Hits a ball that bids starward to stray
There rings in her ears as she speeds on her course,
A chorus of 'Run all the way!'
Alas! Like the ball, we to heaven can't soar,
But thither must climb day by day;
To loiter would show a poor spirit of sport,
So we struggle to run all the way.

The much-maligned 'elastics' were the subject of an article by M.B., a senior student in Limerick during the late 1920s. She pondered:[27]

> Surely the elastics remind you of the Games. Don't you remember the Base-Ball and the Basket-Ball, and don't you remember how awkward you felt the first few days and how hard you found it to be frisky, when encased in a brand new pair of elastics?

A similar development in terms of intellectual vitality can be seen in the training of Protestant primary teachers, when Professor Robert Fynne was appointed, in 1922, to the chair of education in TCD. He believed that 'the students should escape from the elementary atmosphere, and enjoy greater freedom for the cultivation and expression of individuality'.[28]

Female teachers struggled with poor pay and conditions, as well as an autocratic education system. The importance of teachers in providing opportunities through careful nurturing of their students, while difficult to calculate, should not be overlooked. Though they may have been at the bottom of the professional ladder, alongside nurses, in terms of pay and status, female teachers were crucial in the preparation of other women and men for professional lives. Given the class background of teachers, their tendency to seek respectability and security through teaching should not surprise us. However, despite complaints about their poor pay and lack of autonomy, they were unwilling to challenge State or Church authority. Anecdotal evidence would suggest that teachers were often crucial in providing educational and sporting opportunities for their students. Service was teachers' defining characteristic. It is a crucial part of the semi-professional ideal, and female teachers were, for better or worse, as a result of their training and the society of which they were a part, loyal servants of the State.

Acknowledgements

I would like to thank Dr James Kelly and Dr Pauric Travers of St Patrick's College, Drumcondra, for their advance and encouragement, two anonymous referees for their astute comments on an earlier draft and Sr Loreto O'Connor for her help with the extensive Mary Immaculate College of Education archives. I am grateful to Sr Frances Lowe, National Library of Ireland, for facilitating my access to the extensive mercy Archives, and to Sr Magdelena Frisby, archivist at Booterstown Mercy Convent, for all her help and hospitality. My thanks to Sr Rita Minehan of the Brigidine Community, Finglas. The transportation of Brian Whelan and the efficiency of Siobhan Nolan were much appreciated.

Chapter 6

Female teachers and professional trade unions in the early twentieth century

One of the first professions that women entered was teaching. It was to become a profession where the presence of single (and occasionally married) females was acceptable and even encouraged. In this context, it is interesting that it had all the classic features of a semi-profession: an ill-defined entry system, poor pay, bureaucratic control and indifferent status. All of these factors affected the primary teachers' union, the Irish National Teachers' Organisation (INTO), founded in 1868. The absence of women in management positions permeated in the INTO in the early part of the twentieth century. Despite being a majority in the professions, women were not prominent in the union. There were few female delegates for the 1904 congress in Belfast,[1] and in 1905 only one woman was nominated for the Central Executive Committee (CEC) of the INTO. However, she was 'insufficiently nominated', ensuring no female presence on the executive[2] In 1907, Catherine Mahon became the first woman elected to the CEC.

The voice of the profession, *Irish School Weekly* (*ISW*), founded in 1904, frequently discussed professional issues such as poor pay, but without highlighting the gender dimension. While the journal had a regular 'Women's World' column, its focus was on domestic issues, such as needlework;[3] given that female primary teachers had to teach needlework and cooking, it is not surprising that these items were discussed, yet issues such as pay differentials and the absence of women in management positions were never raised. It was not until the early 1910s, during the INTO presidency of Catherine Mahon, that such matters received any prominence. Many of the issues discussed by the Viceregal Committee of Enquiry into Primary Education in Ireland (the Killanin Committee) were the focus of activity by the INTO.[4] The union general secretary (1916-48) was T.J. O'Connell, who, as a Labour Party TD, 1922-32, and party leader, 1927-32, pushed educational issues to the fore. O'Connell told the committee that the profession 'does not attract the proper type. In fact, in the case of men, it does not attract enough of any type'. Women teachers were of the 'proper type', but, he acknowl- edged, this was due to the existence of 'few openings for women'. However, he noted that there would 'be more openings in the future for women than there have been in the past' and that while it was possible to 'keep up the supply of women for two or three years ... there are more opportunities offering for ladies in offices and other spheres, and the difficulties will become greater and greater in the case of the supply of women.' The solution of the difficulties which beset the profession, he believed, was also to 'spend a good deal of time in selecting the right candidates.'[5]

O'Connell also dealt with INTO policy regarding female teach- ers. The union believed 'there would be no distinction on account of sex in the salary paid to teachers. In any school where there are boys over a certain age – eight or nine years – it would be an educational advantage that the principal should be a man. There are schools where there are grown girls, and women are more capable than men.' Clearly, O'Connell believed that males should teach males, and females teach females. He also dealt with the issue of resigna- tion on marriage (it is worth noting that O'Connell's wife (Kathleen O'Connor) was also a teacher): 'The English rule by which a mar- ried woman teacher ceases to be a member of the profession has advantages and disadvantages. For a married woman, teaching is dif- ferent from any other class of work' O'Connell believed:

> A married woman is a better teacher because she is better able to deal
> with children than a single woman, but there is a disadvantage in the
> fact that a woman after marriage has to be employed away from her
> home. That is a consideration for the teachers themselves. If not for
> the sake of the teachers themselves I would say they should not be
> employed – that is providing the men teachers were well-paid.

This reflected the dominant belief that the male should be the breadwinner. Yet O'Connell qualified his argument: 'Educationally, it is better that a married women should be employed. I think the records of the Board will show that the married teachers are the best teachers, both men and women'.[6] He also addressed the question of lay assistants in convent schools. O'Connell compared teaching to medicine, arguing that the unqualified should not be permitted to practice. He wanted the elimination of Junior Assistant Mistresses (JAM) – unqualified personnel who provided 'cheap labour', though he believed the monitorial system should be maintained as it formed the 'best apprenticeship to the teaching profession.' Finally, he sought a 'register of trained teachers who leave the colleges in any given year.' This would secure the professional status of teachers and eliminate the unqualified.[7]

Female involvement in the INTO was probably at its peak in the 1910s. O'Connell's own published history of the union pointed out that despite women's eligibility for positions on the executive, female members continually voted for men. In 1919, a Miss Tierney was elected for the southern province but she died the following year. As regards married teachers, Rule 92(j), introduced in 1911, agitated the INTO in the 1910s. Women had to be absent from the school for three months during pregnancy and childbirth, and they had to pay a substitute teacher. The Central Council of the Catholic Clerical Managers' Association approved of the rule, though they suggested that the female teachers should not have to pay a substitute. O'Connell's position was interesting in that his own wife was affected by the rule. Because she returned to her position after the death of her infant child, her salary was withheld for three months. O'Connell saw the rule as an 'insult to motherhood.' It implied that a pregnant woman was not appropriate in a classroom. However, such protective legislation was common in Europe, and was seen as pro-child as well as pro-mother. Catherine Mahon wanted the board to pay for the substitute teacher before imposing the rule. This rule was finally adjusted, and those teachers who had lost out financially were compensated.[8]

The presidency of Catherine Mahon (1912–1916), the first female to head the union, has been discussed in impressive detail by Chuinneagáin.[9] She notes that Mahon's mother was involved in the Irish Women's Franchise League, as well as being an active nationalist. Mahon was also a nationalist, and a member of the Irish

Women's Suffrage Association and the Irish Women's Franchise
League. Women teachers had come under pressure in the 1900s,
with the introduction of rule 127(b), which led to the amalgama-
tion of small schools. As a result, female principals became assistants.
Mahon's 'primary interest was the welfare of women teachers'.
She was particularly critical of the introduction of domestic subjects for females, as women teachers were 'threatened with loss of
increments and promotion if they did not introduce Cookery and
Laundry.' Chuinneagáin argues persuasively that, under Mahon's
presidency, the INTO became stronger and more independent.
During the war bonus controversy,[10] Mahon spearheaded the campaign for equal bonuses for men and women. However, bonuses
were based on civil service rates. They used gender-differentiated pay
structures. Despite Mahon's energetic activity, the 'power structures
of the INTO' remained unaltered.[11] Mahon did not confine her
activities to the INTO. She spoke to the Women's National Health
Association regarding the height of benches in schools, suggesting
that the WNHA call attention 'to the damage done to the children
by these schools.' Other teachers were involved in the WNHA. Mrs
Greer, of Lurgan, said that the school teachers were a 'great help'.
They gave 'educated opinion' which was 'useful'.[12] Lady Aberdeen,
founder of the WNHA, spoke at the INTO congress of 1912 when
Mahon became president. Lady Aberdeen wanted a grant to be made
for the heating and cleaning of schools.[13] Hence, we see women in
medicine and education combining resources in order to extract
the maximum from the State, in pursuit of improved conditions for
themselves and those they served.

The committee of the Irish Protestant National Teachers' Union
(IPNTU) did not have a strong female presence. In 1914, it consisted
of twenty-eight males and two females: Miss Duncan of Derry and
Miss Johnston of Lurgan.[14] In the same year, it urged that 'no official
who has in the past established a reputation for harrying teachers
should be considered eligible for the position' of manager. Financial
constraints restricted both managers and teachers. The manager of a
school in Ballinasloe, where there was not a large Protestant population, tried to obtain a 'teacher who will have somebody to live with
him or her who could act as a JAM'. This policy deprived the current
female teacher of a job. Political issues impacted on teachers, particularly in the heightened political temperature of the mid-1910s.
In 1914, an assistant in Lurgan was 'displaced' because of 'politi-

cal bias'; the inspector was 'unsympathetic'.[15] Political differences created difficulties between the INTO (which had a nationalist bias) and the IPNTU. In 1917 the latter became part of the Ulster National Teachers' Union (UNTU).[16] Miss Evelyn Kennedy, from Lurgan Model School, became vice-president of UNTU in 1922, and president the following year.[17] Despite the election of another female president, Miss S. Allen in 1926, there was no emphasis on specifically female issues in the UNTU. In June 1924, the union discussed the issue of married female teachers. It sought guidance from Mr H. Pollock, at the Ministry of Education: 'The substance of his reply was that the Ministry would not interfere with the discretion of managers or local authorities if they wished to dispense with the services of married women. This communication was regarded as unsatisfactory, and a reply thereto drafted by the secretary was approved of.'[18] Yet, the issue was not discussed in detail.

As in the Irish Free State, the moral tone of schools was considered important. Miss Marshall, Inspector of Schools, instructed 'teachers to give two-and-half hours per week to the teaching of temperance and hygiene.'[19] Religious instruction, rather than hygiene, was a bigger issue for teachers. UNTU members were willing to teach religion, but they did not want it to be compulsory. Teachers were more worried about issues that affected both males and females, such as salaries and security of tenure. However, these issues were perhaps more pressing for women as they received lower salaries and, due to the informal marriage ban, they had less security of tenure. The primary concerns of the UNTU were, therefore, not significantly different from those of the INTO. Both focused on salaries and conditions.

The introduction of registration for secondary teachers, in 1918, was seen as a vital step in professionalisation. Female secondary teachers constituted a small section of the female professional workforce in the 1918-1930 period. They were seen as temporary professionals (or pilgrims passing through educational systems), especially if they intended to get married. Until 1918, and indeed for many years afterwards, anybody could, and did, teach at second-level. The secondary system was primarily private, with Church-controlled schools dominating. As at primary level, but to a far greater degree, female teachers were in competition with members of religious orders for the few jobs that were available. Protestant females were fortunate in that they did not have the same competition. In general, teachers tended to be past pupils of the school. This ensured the development of an enclosed and monopolistic system. Employment opportunities for teachers rested with the managers of schools. These schools remained essentially private institutions. This was not unique to Ireland as, for example, Canadian Roman Catholic school boards employed members of religious orders as teachers, and a similar situation prevailed in France.[20]

The 1878 Intermediate Education Act opened up second-level education for females. It was one of the most significant developments in the history of Irish secondary education. In many ways, the Act encouraged a more focused approach to education. The establishment of a recognised national examination for all students who received a second-level education ensured that in time, schools provided a more rigorous academic curriculum. However, the process was a gradual one. In 1898, 2,368 females and 6,705 completed the intermediate examinations. By 1918, this had increased to 4,848 females and 7,177 males. A decade later, there were 10,090 females in second-level schools in the Irish Free State, as compared to 15,471 males.[21] The Act encouraged female education and this, in turn, led to a demand for secondary teachers. Furthermore, the possibilities for free publicity if a school's students excelled in the intermediate examinations also encouraged schools to enter for the examinations. By 1918, females had been part of the intermediate system for forty years.

The year 1918 also saw the Molony Commission on Intermediate [Secondary] Education.[22] The position of female teachers was discussed by the Commission. Under the Birrell grant scheme of 1914, there was to be, at least, one duly qualified lay teacher per 40 students.[23] This increased professional opportunities for qualified teachers. The grant also aimed to provide 'minimum salaries of £140 a year for men, and £90 for women.'[24] There were three women on the Molony Committee: Henrietta White (principal of Alexandra College), Mary Ryan and Elizabeth Steele. All were teachers. Given that schools primarily survived on the results obtained by their pupils, the emphasis on prizes was discussed: 'it had led to the great evil of over-pressure, particularly in girls' schools, and has given occasion for the very objectionable feature called 'touting' for clever students.'[25] Females were seen as particularly affected by examination stress. This assumption made the task of female teachers, who prepared these students for examinations, more difficult. However, touting for students

was a feature of both male and female schools, and was not a new
development. One recommendation of the Molony Committee was
that there should be no difference in male and female salaries.[26] (This
was eventually achieved in 1973.) There was no unanimity regarding
the positions of teachers. Revd Corcoran, professor of Education at
UCD, in typically forthright style declared his revulsion at State control over Catholic schools:

> The most essential issue in the Catholic nature of Catholic
> schools is full Catholic control of the choice of teachers, reten-
> tion of teachers, and removal of teachers ... when a vacancy on
> a school staff normally and properly occurs, the school should be
> absolutely free to make choice of any teacher, educationally quali-
> fied, that is judged fit to fill the vacancy.

Furthermore, the 'existence of a registration system, with exacting conditions, makes any infringement, direct or indirect, of this
inherent right and duty, an additional and serious grievance.' This
dogmatism was an impediment to the careers of female teachers.
They sought employment in institutions that were not answerable
to the State. Annie McHugh was the only female who signed the
minority report, which totally disagreed with Corcoran's views.[27]

It would be inaccurate to argue that the State played no part in the
running of second-level schools. Inspections were part of the second-level system from 1900. Grants were allocated to schools on the
basis of the inspection. These were known as the 'Inspection Grants'.
However, as at primary level, the 'degree of efficiency shown in the
education of pupils' was only one of the criteria. The number and
attendance of students were also taken into consideration.[28] Teachers
had very little control over the latter two factors.

The Intermediate Education (Ireland) Act of 1914, initiated by
the Chief Secretary Birrell, provided the legislative structure for
the registration of teachers. In 1918, there were '232 schools with
14,710 pupils ... under Roman Catholic management, and 122 with
6,560 [pupils] ... under non-Roman Catholic management.'[29] This
included male and female schools. Hence, Catholics, as a percentage of the population, were underrepresented at second-level. This
had employment implications for Catholic teachers. The salaries
of female teachers averaged £110 per annum. There was no great
difference in the payments received by teachers in Catholic and

Protestant schools. The biggest gap existed on a gender level, with male teachers receiving an average of £180. This gap is most evident if we contrast male and female teachers working in the same institution. In Wesley College, Dublin (a co-educational school since 1912) the five 'duly qualified' male teachers received an average of £174, while the four 'duly qualified' female teachers received an average of £112. As with all other institutions, there was a number of teachers 'not duly qualified' who were paid between £44 and £90. Here, the salary differences between male and female teachers were less startling.[30] Birrell's education initiatives were to have a lasting effect on the professional development of secondary teachers, particularly as the registration system was established as part of the 1914 legislation. However, the 1914 Act was not implemented until 1918.

The Association of Secondary Teachers in Ireland (ASTI) was established in 1909. Was the role of female teachers considered in the ASTI? It has been suggested that there is no evidence that women's pay and promotion was a concern in mixed unions.[31] The ASTI was a small union with 179 members in 1925. Nuns were not permitted to join. This immediately excluded at least half the female teaching force. It was thought, however, that lay female teachers were powerless in the system and needed a union that would fight for their rights. Coolahan comments that it was 'significant' that Elizabeth Steele, the third ASTI member of the Molony Commission, did not sign the minority report, but 'in her note of reservation, supported by the ASTI concern about the appeal procedure' in relation to insecurity of tenure.[32] The ASTI strike of 1920 in Cork, and parts of Limerick, over poor salaries was the first time that secondary teachers asserted their labour power in the face of intolerable conditions. As an indication of the problem in the early 1920s, some secondary teachers received £160 per annum while Dublin Corporation street workers received £195.[33]

In the mid-1920s, when salaries were increased, those who had honours degrees received £40 extra if male, and £20 if female. 'The ASTI got the amount equalised for women in 1926 although basic salaries were still differentiated.'[34] However, the female voice was rarely heard in the ASTI between 1918 and 1930. There had been a ladies' branch of the union between 1911 and 1920, and female members were encouraged to play a part in order to, in the words of E. Hughes Dowling, 'hasten our united victory.'[35] That branch was absorbed in the general restructuring of the association in 1920.

Coolahan suggests that, in the early years, women played a prominent role but this 'tended to decrease some years after their absorption as ordinary members.' Few women made their mark in the Central Executive Committee (CEC), though the first female president was A.J. Mulligan in 1926.[36]

Problems persisted with convent schools. When the union sought incremental salaries for more secular, as opposed to religious, teachers the president of the Conference of Convent Secondary Schools (which represented principals of convent schools) felt it was a bad principal 'to sacrifice justice to charity'. This attitude was less evident in Catholic schools run by males, and the problems seemed to be particularly acute in female schools. Lay teachers were often tolerated rather than respected as professionals. Such was the resentment regarding the insecurity of their position that a wide-ranging pamphlet on the issue was published by the ASTI in 1934. This alluded to the Molony report, and its focus on the insecurity of teachers' positions. There are few specific references to female teachers. Reference was made to CEC negotiations with the Catholic Headmasters' Association (CHMA), but not to the female equivalent, the Conference of Convent Secondary Schools. There is a brief reference to convent schools and the CHMA was to investigate a settlement.[37] The authors noted that, at the annual convention in 1927, the Roscrea branch asked that 'the ASTI adopt a vigorous policy in the matter of conditions of employment in the case of lady teachers.' The result was revealing. 'A circular was sent to every woman member of the Association asking for particulars, even in confidence, of dismissals. Practically no replies were received, and the matter was abandoned.' Following the Maynooth Resolution of 1927, secondary teachers could appeal a dismissal. Teachers in convent schools had 'the right of appeal to the Ordinary [diocesan representative], as in the case of primary teachers.'[38] Female teachers were possibly fearful of repercussions if they complained about conditions, and may have been worried about their own futures. At the ASTI annual convention, in 1926, Miss Doyle of Dublin, enquired about two female teachers who were dismissed from a Dublin convent. The president of the ASTI said 'the ladies concerned had discussed the position with CEC but were not willing to have any action taken.'[39] The following year the motion from Roscrea branch was adopted and 'passed on a division'.[40] Therefore, while the difficulties faced by female teachers were known, and occasionally discussed, there was a reluctance on the part of male and female teachers to pursue the matter.[41]

The ASTI pamphlet of 1934 noted that all 'but a few girls' schools were ... under the control of the Bishop.' The biggest difficulty for the ASTI was its small membership of 179. However, it had the advantage of being 'tightly-knit' and 'well organised', and between 1909 and 1937 the union experienced a 'time of intense and sustained activity'.[42] Unregistered teachers were not allowed to join the ASTI. This also kept the unions' numbers down. Additionally, perhaps many female teachers were wary of joining a union if their position was not permanent. In 1926, Miss Doyle, who was chairing a Dublin branch meeting of the ASTI, pointed out that lay teachers were 'not considered in the grading of classes.' In other words, they did not play a part in the internal organisation of the school. Two years later, she proposed that 'the differentiation between the increments of women teachers and those of men teachers is indefensible, the work done being identical and that the association should press for equal pay for equal work.' The resolution was passed unanimously. The 1929 convention of the ASTI passed a resolution that there were 'absolutely no grounds for discrimination in remuneration.'[43] However it came to nothing.

An ASTI deputation to the Minister of Education (Thomas Derrig) in 1932 pointed out that:

> Security of employment was an essential condition of efficiency; large numbers of lady graduates were produced by the universities and were crowding in to a dwindling market. Some actual cases of harsh treatment were quoted, and the Minister asked to be supplied with the correspondence connected with one case handled by the ASTI in 1931 in which the Episcopal Authority had declined to intervene. The Minister suggested that the fault lay with the universities in sending out large numbers of lady graduates without making some effort to find them employment.[44]

Hence, the educational institutions, which had produced professional women, were blamed for female unemployment. No effort was made to open up schools and ensure that employment was based on merit, rather than on one's membership of a religious community. For those nuns working as secondary teachers there may have been internal pressures, such as the need to teach subjects one was

not qualified to teach. This situation also existed in boys' schools for
priests and brothers.

The position for many teachers in Northern Ireland was quite different. The Minister of Education emphasised that teachers should
hold qualifications in specific subjects. The Ulster Headmistresses
Association (UHMA), which represented Protestant schools, such
as Ashleigh House School and Victoria College Belfast (VCB),
complained of underfunding because of a lack of endowments in
girls' schools. It also noted that competition from England, where
higher salaries were available, deprived schools in Northern Ireland
of the 'most efficient teachers'.[45] The financial situation in schools
run by religious communities was better than in the Irish Free
State. School governing bodies were paid a grant 'equal to the average amount paid in increments to lay teachers of the same sex and
class throughout Northern Ireland.' Most importantly, lay teachers
in these schools were 'paid the appropriate rate of salary in the
same manner as teachers in other schools'.[46] Hence, there seems
to have been fewer difficulties for female teachers in this sector.
However, the lack of evidence on conditions makes it difficult to
be certain.

The UHMA held its first meeting in October 1922. It was represented on the Joint Committee of Secondary Associations which
lobbied the Minister of Education regarding salaries. A frequent issue
in their meetings was remuneration. The president in 1923 was Miss
Anna Matier, headmistress at VCB. The medievalist Helen Waddell,

> described her quite simply as a great teacher; she not only taught
> history she was history. As Waddell said, her pupils had nothing
> to learn about absolute monarchy! 'Historians still marvel at the
> secret of Elizabeth [Queen Elizabeth I], that one so arbitrary, so
> whimsical, so feminine, so despotic could command such absolute
> adoration; we never marvelled. We had known Elizabeth

Anna Matier was unmarried. According to Jordan, schoolmistresses
in the school usually resigned on marriage, even though the school
had been established by a Mrs Byers.[48]

Mirroring T.J. O'Connell's sentiments outlined above, the UHMA
argued that teachers' salaries in Northern Ireland did not 'attract the
best types of men and women.' Pension schemes were sought in 1924,
and payment of part-time teachers was also discussed. Headmistresses

believed that the government rate of five shillings an hour was too high. The UHMA feared that they would not benefit from British educational initiatives. According to a report to the *Belfast Newsletter*, the UHMA thought that Northern Ireland was becoming 'a self-contained area' where no intercourse across the water was possible.[49] On the other hand, the UHMA suggested it could not 'stem the rush of young teachers from Northern Ireland'. The headmistresses were also concerned about specific educational matters. In 1925, the association passed a resolution that 'the publication of a printed list of the names of candidates who have failed at the certificate examinations of the Ministry … [was] undesirable, and not a custom of other examining bodies.' Later, in 1927, there were discussions on the formation of the 'Federated Council of Organisations of Teachers in Northern Ireland,' which, according to a Miss Scott was 'to co-ordinate educational effort and create a bond of professional union among teachers.'

While unity between male and female teachers was discussed, separate subjects were advocated for female pupils. In a talk to the UHMA, W.A. Armour emphasised traditional views regarding the educational needs of male and female students. He 'especially stressed the fact that many countries recognised the necessity of adapting the curriculum to the differing needs of girls and boys.' Preparing students for teacher-training colleges was also a concern. The UHMA felt that the candidates were suffering from 'the strain of an over-burdened curriculum.' A sub-committee was appointed to confer with Mr Henderson of Methodist College Belfast and draw up proposals which were to be sent to the Ministry. There were frequent discussions of examination papers and, on one occasion, the UHMA asked that 'in the setting and marking of the examination papers examiners should be asked to remember the immaturity of mind of the child under 16.' However, the primary focus of the meetings was on finance. In October 1930, Miss Matier resigned as president and was succeeded by Mrs Duncan of Princess Gardens School in Belfast.[50] The minutes of the UHMA, detailing its concerns about attracting committed professional through attractive salaries, make clear that the biggest issue facing female students was remuneration. While the curriculum and daily working conditions were occasionally discussed, concern with financial survival predominated, especially if one was trying to maintain an institution.

It is evident from the activities of the ASTI and the UHMA that the profile of secondary teachers needed to be raised. These organisations sought to influence government policy and increase teacher salaries. Secondary teachers, like nurses and many primary school teachers, worked in a profession which was constrained by religious control. This was not unique in Ireland, and many professional females in France operated under similar conditions. The predominance of religious-run institutions was to impact on the pay and status of these professional women.

The 1878 Intermediate Education Act meant that girls could sit the Intermediate (second-level) examinations. The number of females taking the examination more than doubled (from 2,368 to 4,848) between 1898 and 1918. While secondary teachers had more opportunities than most women, they had very little autonomy. As with their primary school counterparts, there were pay differentials between male and female teachers. In the economic and political atmosphere of the 1920s, teachers were not high on the list of government priorities. Irish female teachers' salaries averaged at about £100 per annum; this contrasted poorly with French teachers who were paid £340 and Norwegian teachers who received £245 per annum. Teachers in Northern Ireland were also better paid than their Irish Free State colleagues. Secondary education in Ireland was generally under-funded. The State spent £14 per student, which contrasts with £27 per student in England and Wales. More worryingly, secondary teachers had very little security of tenure. The presence of unqualified and unregistered teachers, as well as the unwillingness of the government to insist on registration for all, reduced the professional status of teachers. Furthermore, there was an unofficial marriage ban. Few female secondary teachers were married.

Union activity suggests that general issues, such as pay and promotion as well as security of tenure, were seen as important. Specifically female issues were rarely discussed. The UHMA did have the opportunity to improve conditions for their members. They were most concerned about poor salaries, and noted the emigration of teachers to Britain where salaries were superior. Despite these difficulties, secondary teachers were frequently involved in social action movements. Some of these activities such as the Catholic Women's Federation of Secondary School Unions, were based in the schools where they worked.

The professional experience of teachers is one of conflict and acquiescence. The secondary literature tends to focus on conflicts and there were many: between management and staff, between State and individual, as well as between teachers themselves. The overall picture, nonetheless, is one of relative harmony, in the 1920s, once the political changes of the 1918 to 1923 period has been absorbed. This may reflect, in part, lower expectations and the fact that, compared to most women, teachers were comfortably off with a certain degree of independence. Given their relative prosperity and social activism, these teachers were able to exert a significant, if hidden, influence on the community.

Chapter 7

'Susan Stephens: a Monaghan woman's memoir'

The experiences of Susan Stephens (*née* Daly) confirm the presence of a variety of pressures in the daily life of female secondary teachers in the early twentieth century. She was awarded a BA and B.Comm from UCD. It was possible to do both degrees in four years. This was attractive for teachers since they could teach a greater range of subjects. She graduated with first-class honours, and first place in the B. Comm class of 1920. A past pupil of St Louis Convent, Carrickmacross (coming from Clonturk in County Monaghan, between Carrickmacross and Ardee), she had obtained a county council scholarship to study at UCD. Stephens completed her teaching practice hours in Louise Gavan Duffy's, Scoil Bhríde, and thought that 'Revd Dr Corcoran [Timothy Corcoran SJ, Professor of Education at University College, Dublin] was a wonderful professor.' Having completed her Higher Diploma in Education, she went to teach in the St Louis Convent in Carrickmacross, in 1919, prior to obtaining her B.Comm. She remembered that none of the nuns was a graduate when she was a student there. Stephens' background was modest, as she remembered living in a 'three-roomed thatched house, with a hearth fire and a settle bed in the kitchen, a few stools and little of any intrinsic value.' But, compared to other tenants on the Shirely estate, her family were 'landed gentry.' They did not have to go barefoot in the summer. They had a servant boy and girl who were selected at a hiring fair, and were the offered £6 per half-year, plus keep.

Stephens' comments on secondary education in the 1910s indicate the kind of environment in which many teachers worked.

It was more or less a trasitional period at school. The nuns were completely Victorian but the lay teachers were budding rebels, as were the pupils. So the pupils were always wrong; we were not ladylike, we were rough etc. It was class and study all the time and an occasional walk, crocodile-fashion, with nuns fore and aft. We dressed in black and we were not allowed to speak in dormitory or corridors and it was most unseemly to run! On feast days we had hockey or rounders and not much of either ... we were often hungry and there was no freedom or fun but it was no different from other schools ... but I must say this, these nuns did a tremendous job of work and got great results. There were only sixty boarders and some day pupils and yet they put Carrick on the map and built up from nothing to being a first-class school. They accomplished this by downright drudgery on the part of pupils and teachers.

Intriguingly, Stephens was offered a job on Carrickmacross but she did not 'want to go back to teach there'. Elsewhere, she met the usual barriers.

I had enough qualifications but I fear my applications were not very well put together and anyway I had no 'pull'. Nobody wanted me – most of them never even replied. So back to Carrick I went instead of being asked to teach the subjects I had done for the BA, I was put to teach maths and commerce, in which I was not qualified. So off I started, the blind leading the blind.

However, her students were very successful. Stephens was not very happy, nonetheless, as she was 'torn between my love for mother and home, and all the fun I'd have in the digs.' Additionally, there were other pressures. 'We teachers had some difficulties over salaries and had to get Dean Keown [the parish priest] to intervene. The Mistress of Schools [Sr Stanislaus] consulted my pupils behind my back about my teaching.' She then decided to work in a technical school. However, during the summer she told Sr Stanislaus she would not be returning to Carrickmacross. 'She didn't believe me and told me that she had information that I was going to get married. I told her that was not so, that I was going to do the BComm. Later when my BComm results were published, the greatest pressure was brought to bear on me to come back to Carrick, but I refused and stayed in Dublin.' Her determination must have surprised many given the shortage of jobs for secondary teachers.

Stephens found it difficult to get work. Eventually, with some canvassing of the members of Kildare County Council, she began working in Naas. She met a variety of students in the technical school in Naas.

> My classes were hopeless. Except for a very few, they could not add or subtract, but they knew the pedigree of every horse that ever ran at the Curragh or Punchestown, and in order to keep my job I'd go around the houses and ask the children to come to my class and like the Pied Piper, I led the way till they'd be swallowed up in the water tower! [The School was located under the water tower.] If my classes fizzled out, I'd be fizzled out too.

As well as being responsible for the size of her class, she had to contend with the principal. 'He was a tyrant and worst of all, had a notion for me and I had to choke him off and he was real jealous. The inspector and I got on great but Smith [the principal] said that Barrett, the inspector, found fault with my teaching of shorthand.' This proved to be untrue. Once the inspector spoke to the principal, Stephens was left in peace. She also taught in Castledermot, where many of her students were local farmers 'with big farms and [they] were anxious to know what each animal on their farms was really costing and if there was profit and loss.' After her marriage in 1922, she went to work in the family business, a hardware and fancy goods shop in Ballyshannon, where her talents as an accountant were very useful. Stephens was very prominent in the town as she helped set up the *Donegal Democrat* and wrote articles in the newspaper. She also established an Argosy library in the family shop, which supplied school books in south Donegal. Stephens' short teaching career, with continual movement from one post to another, and her eventual marriage and part-time (though vital) work in the family business could be seen as typical of educated females at the time. Her involvement in the community, where her advice on commercial educational matters was valued, can be seen as one of the many roles of professional women in the society of early twentieth-century Ireland.[1]

Chapter 8

Nurses and teachers in the west of Ireland in the late-nineteenth and early twentieth centuries[1]

Any discussion of women working in professional occupations in the late-nineteenth and early twentieth centuries must begin with the admission that we know so little and much remains to be revealed.[2] However, the photographs from the Congested Districts Board (CDB) albums from the West of Ireland discussed in this article reveal hidden aspects of the lives of teachers and nurses and, more importantly, their students and patients.

Nursing

Nursing, it has been argued, 'demonstrated the limitations of a separate female world that lacked an effective power base within its own domain.'[3] A distinct hierarchy was most obvious in the medical world, with nurses (female) invariably subordinate to doctors (usually male): in the hospital setting, nurses were directly controlled by a female matron. However, district nursing managed to surmount these limitations by providing women with much professional autonomy while simultaneously bestowing on them great responsibility for the health and welfare of their patients.

The attraction of a respectable profession, and its association with the traditional female virtues, encouraged many of those who could afford it to opt for a career in nursing. Nurse training was expensive, sometimes as high as 100 guineas per annum, so nurses tended to be drawn from those who had disposable income. Social connections could also play a role in selecting candidates for training. District nurses were always midwives, and were vital public health workers. Jubilee nurses (that is, district nurses) were established in 1887, on the silver jubilee of Queen Victoria. The Dudley nursing scheme was established in 1903, by Lady Dudley (the Viceroy's wife) to provide district nurses in the congested districts of Ireland. These Dudley nurses were prominent in Clare, Donegal, Sligo, Galway, Kerry, Cork and Mayo. The aim of the Jubilee Institute, which trained district nurses, was to create an interest in home nursing, supply home nurses and organise a 'central or country nursing association in every county in Ireland'.[4]

Dudley nurses' work was similar to that of the Women's National Health Association (WNHA): the latter employed district nurses to work towards eliminating tuberculosis.[5] In order to qualify as a Jubilee nurse, one had to be State registered, hold the certificate of the Central Midwives' Board and have three years' general experience.[6] The Dudley nurses' badge featured the motto 'By Love Serve One Another' and they were known affectionately, as late as the 1970s (when the scheme was disbanded) as 'Dudleys'. It was believed that Dudleys were particularly valuable, because it was difficult to entice nurses of Jubilee calibre to the West, where social conditions were appalling. As a rule, nurses were not well paid: such was the voluntarism expected of the profession that salaries were supposed to sustain nurses but not necessarily compensate them for long hours. For example, in 1928, the Local Appointments Commission advertised for a trainee nurse. She was to be paid £75 a year, with 'rations, fuel, light and accommodation'.[7] The rations may not have been impressive given that some nurses sought money instead.[8] The one advantage of State employment was the promise of a pension, which could be transferred if one moved from one local authority to another.[9] Given these benefits-in-kind, some nurses were better off financially than teachers. But their salaries did not increase significantly with service. Public health nurses were better paid than most: in 1923, two public health nurses in Louth received between £150 and £200 per annum. Meanwhile, in County Cork, they were paid between £140 and £150. Many of these nurses would also have had midwifery qualifications, as well as being registered.[10]

Midwives needed to be medically meticulous in their work. They could be struck off for failing to keep proper medical records.[11] The profession thought their reputation had to be safeguarded, partly because they had to contend with 'handy women', who worked as midwives but did not have any qualifications. Maternity cases accounted for about 70 per cent of Dudley work and 'handy women' were a big problem as some of them brought midwifery into disrepute by their methods. The *Irish Nurses' Union Gazette*, in 1925, vowed to keep agitating against 'quacks'.[12] In 1928, the Department of Local Government and Public Health pointed out that 'while there had been substantial progress in the elimination of the activities of handy women, it had not been easy, in rural areas, to break through the tradition of using untrained persons.'[13] Eventually legislation was introduced, in the 1930s, to eliminate the unqualified. An examination was introduced for those who did not have the State certificate and, as an indication of the need to encourage all to sit the examination, Annie Smithson (who was a qualified midwife) assured her readers that it was, 'a simple qualifying one, and need not frighten anyone.'[14] Yet many, especially in rural Ireland, relied on 'handy women' in the absence of trained medical practitioners.

Where nurses were established their work was usually greatly appreciated by the local population. The need for district nurses was clear. Bishop Fogarty of Killaloe requested a nurse for the district of Kilbaha, in County Clare. 'The local priests tell me that a district nurse would be a great boom to the poor people and be much appreciated by them.'[15] Both patients and nurses endured grim conditions: one nurse on a maternity case spent the night in a freezing room without a fire.[16] But they were appreciated. Fr McHugh, the parish priest at Carna, in County Galway, commented on Nurse Wills. 'She is an excellent person, fond of her work, kind and nice to the poor. She is an ideal nurse.'[17] Nightingale suggested that district nurses should be 'Health Missionaries.'[18] This phrase further emphasising the link between medicine and an evangelical desire to help others. As Fox remarked, the district nurse is 'supposed to exert a generally uplifting influence on her community.'[19] Sometimes this was quite a challenge. For example, in Carna, County Galway, the Dudley nurse reported the following incident:

> At 9 p.m. four men and a boy called to my cottage, all were under the influence of drink. The boy's hand was badly injured, he becoming entangled in the spokes of a moving cart. After attending to his wounds I had much difficult in getting rid of the escort,

as they were scarcely able to maintain their balance, and I feared
they would fall asleep in my kitchen, where they waited while I
dressed the boy's hand. [20]

Communication with patients in the congested districts, many
of which were in the Gaeltacht (Irish-speaking areas), must have
been severely strained given that some of the district nurses could
not speak Irish. A classic example of this is Nurse B.M. Herderman,
whose memoir of her time spent nursing on the Aran Islands has been
carefully assessed by Nellie Ó Clérigh. Nurse Herderman arrived on
the Aran Islands in 1903, just as these photographs were being taken,
and remarkably, 'found it hard to be accepted'. Perhaps her inabil-
ity to speak the language of the islanders was a factor. She said that
her patients would be 'her silent instructors', her 'teachers'. However,
Herderman admits that she 'could not grasp much of what they were
saying'. One of the local schools offered to take her 'ashore in all the
"Bearla" (English language) he could command'. She admitted that
Irish was a 'beautiful and expansive language'. Her appearance, especially her coiled hair, intrigued the young girls on the island. Cultural
conflict was inevitable between Hederman and the local ('handy')
women who traditionally tended to childbearing women. She wrote,
'I had promised to visit a newly-made mother, because lactation had
not been established, and well-meaning neighbours have a habit of
giving babies many fearful abominations. I dreaded interference,
and had some doubts as to the treatment the baby would receive if
entrusted to these ignorant women.' Despite her disdainful attitude,
she praised the islanders since they were 'inured to every conceivable hardship, with the result that their power of endurance is greater,
strengthened perhaps by the compelling influence of having to earn
a livelihood under almost the worst conceivable conditions of soil
and climate'. Given their hardiness and the almost complete absence
of formal medical care, it is hardly surprising that the local dispensary
was seen as 'a kind of guillotine or death trap – a tribunal from which,
if they entered, they were never to emerge.' Hederman's 'dissertations'
on infections and temperance were not appreciated by these islanders, who had few avenues for entertainment. She realised that the
'responsibility of a district nurse in such a spot is truly great, and more
exhausting than the heaviest hospital work'. [21]

The photograph by W.J.D. Walker, a CBD inspector, which indicates a young man 'Waiting to Guide Nurse' suggests that the locals

were intent that the nurse would be guided around the area and that she was valued.[22] Another photograph which displays, in all its frugality, the nurse's cottage in Annagry, County Donegal, was taken by 'Miss Bradshaw', of 30 Molesworth Street, Dublin.[23]

While jobs were scarce for Irish women, status was still sought. Clothing was one indicator of status. It has been argued that uniforms 'indicate social distance', and the nurse's uniform was not dissimilar to a maid's uniform.[24] This was to ensure 'that nursemaids and untrained women [could] ... no longer usurp the nurses' uniform.' To nurses' horror, 'chemists would sometimes readily supply drugs to women in a nurse's uniform'.

Meanwhile, registered nurses, and midwives, would be refused in the chemist's shop, if they were not in uniform.[25] Uniforms, then, had a double role; they conferred a certain authority, yet, simultaneously they suggested an inferior position. Uniforms summed up the dual nature of nursing, with its ambivalent mixture of respectability and subordination. Another important symbol of the profession was the wearing of a badge, which was bestowed upon nurses on the completion of their studies and was considered an important acknowledgement to be worn as part of the daily attire.

This focus on uniforms is particularly relevant when assessing the photographs provided in the annual reports of the Lady Dudley scheme. When the nurse arrived at her patient's home, her uniform was an immediate symbol of middle-class authority and respectability, hence she stood out from her patients, some of whom were shoeless. The Dudley's authority was hidden but evident in subtle ways. Nurses were on a par with teachers and priests in that they wielded considerable authority in small communities, the result of a cooperative venture on the part of both nurse and priest: clergymen sought nurses for their areas; when repairs were performed to the nurse's cottage in Carna, Revd O'Hara (a CDB board member) was thanked.[26] In a photograph where the nurse is smiling at the camera while the Arranmore family in County Donegal look at the ground, her respectable clothing ensures that she stands out. The fact that she is the only one looking directly at the camera suggests that this photograph was more for her benefit than for the family's sake (see p. 80). They do not make any eye contact with the camera: the two barefoot children have their heads turned away, while their mother is laden with a baby and a basket. She too is barefoot and focused on her youngest child (see p. 80). The man is beside a small pile of turf

and he is staring at the ground, perhaps an unwilling participant.
What did they think of this nurse? We may never know.

Teachers

The other female professionals who feature in these photographs
are teachers. The mode of entry to that profession varied from
region to region. There were several routes: monitorship, pupil-
teachership or by competitive entry to one of the training colleges.
But many teachers received their initial training as teenagers (at
about fifteen or sixteen) in a local primary school. It was not unusual for fully trained teachers, after two years at college, to begin his
or her (usually the latter) professional career at nineteen. As early as
1911, 63 per cent of teachers were female.[27] Students were selected
by their teachers or inspectors to become candidate monitors. After
extra study, and an examination, they could then be appointed as
monitors. The 'model schools' (there were twenty in Ireland) were
used as training institutions for future teachers. As Marshall has
noted, the effectiveness of the training received in these institutions
'depended greatly on the efficiency, interest and enthusiasm of the
staff of the school, in particular of its headmaster: the size of the
school and its location might also be influential.[28] Healy suggests
that the 'higher prestige which was attached to the pupil-teachership (they would have attended secondary school) was reflected in
their salary'. Monitors received £5 per annum, while female pupil-
teachers, in their first year, received £14; males were paid £18.[29]
The pupil-teacher system was also dependent on links between
primary and secondary schools. Starkie argued that poor links
between the two militated against the development of the system.
Students in urban areas were at an advantage. Religious orders,
such as the Christian Brothers, and the Mercy and Presentation
Sisters, managed primary and secondary schools (which frequently
did not charge expensive fees), so pupil-teachership were available
for students from modest backgrounds.

Monitors, in a sense, were like apprentices, in the education
system. It was not unknown for teachers to be 'apprenticed' to certain schools. Teachers were instructed to serve their masters and 'their
secrets keep, their lawful commands every where gladly do'.[30] The
most common entry route for teachers remained the monitorship
system[31] which suggests that most primary teachers came directly
from primary school to the training colleges. As Clear has noted, the

'girl who attended the free school could, if she was encouraged at home, become a paid monitress and eventually a teacher'.[32]

The introduction of the Queen's scholarship (later known as the King's scholarship, and then the Easter scholarship) examinations in 1855 provided monitors with the opportunity to qualify for a training college place. Pupil-teachers also sat this examination. These candidates usually went to an intermediate (second-level) school. If they had done sufficiently well at the intermediate examinations, they could be selected to practise teaching in a model, or in an ordinary, school. They would then proceed to a training college. In 1919-20, there were 1,400 monitors and 500 pupil-teachers.[33] It was also possible to enter the training college without any previous experience, once one passed the King's scholarship examination.

Teachers, like the Dudley's, were supposed to set an example by their scholarliness and standards of hygiene in the classrooms. Inspectors did not only note academic faults: they also commented on the cleanliness and 'moral tone' of the classroom.[34] This emphasis can be seen in the photographs of the students. Where the students are lined up outside the school, many are wearing smocks or over-garments to protect their clothes and give a semblance of cleanliness (see p. 81). These young girls in Connemara, County Galway in the early twentieth century, would almost certainly have been familiar with lice. Students from a much later period, the 1940s, have distinct memories of head lice falling from students' hair onto copies[35] though teachers were supposed to present clean students to all-seeing eye of the inspector. It is revealing, as in one of the nursing photographs, that most of the children in the picture are studiously avoiding the camera. A few confident, smiling children, four out of a total of twenty-nine, are actually looking at it. These children were not used to being the centre of attention and, like their Donegal contemporaries, are barefoot.

The young boys pictured outside a school, possibly the same school, are also barefoot, but seem more cheerful (see p. 81). One child, fourth from the right, is positively beaming at the camera. Others are gazing skywards: perhaps they were told to 'look up' and interpreted this literally. All of these young boys are in dresses. Local folklore suggested that young males were seen as more valuable than young females and it was hoped that if they were 'disguised as girls' they would not be abducted by fairies or other supernatural beings. A photograph of the older boys outside a school suggests that they

too wore dresses, though at least two students were in trousers. Again, all bar one are barefoot but several seem happy to smile for the camera. Unusually, most of the boys are actually looking in its direction. Perhaps they anticipated a day off school for good behaviour! What their school experience was like is difficult to surmise. After the 'adoption of a compulsory attendance policy in 1892 (just before these photographs were taken) only 50 per cent of the children attended the required seventy-five times in each half-year – schools were open a minimum of 200 days – and attendance was dreadful in depressed urban areas and in the western counties.'[36] Further changes in the early twentieth century made an impact on their learning environment.

By 1910, the Irish language movement was making an impact on the curriculum, with Irish examinations being introduced for the first time for students who wished to teach in a bilingual school.[37] It is also likely that fewer and fewer local teachers were employed in the congested districts given the gradual professionalisation of primary teaching. Two photographs show a teacher in action (see p. 81). In one, a young woman, possibly a teenager and almost certainly a monitor, is watching a semi-circle of children who are possibly playing an instrument. The monitor is, relatively speaking, well dressed with a shawl on her shoulders and a full skirt. She also appears to be wearing shoes. The other photograph obviously shows a teacher demonstrating conkers to young children. Was this a game they played or was there a more serious pedagogical intent? We can see the children in this photograph. Most, whether male or female, have short hair, perhaps to prevent head lice. Yet again, while the teacher is quite well dressed with an apron over her full-length dress, shoes or boots on her feet, the children are bare footed. Was she a local woman? We cannot tell, but there were serious concerns about nepotism in education, particularly at primary level. Given that most of the teachers were probably elevated locals, they would not have been as respected as the nurses, who were invariably, at this stage, better-trained outsiders. Even in the twenty-first century the triumph of proximity over performance is still an issue.

The local dimensions of the teaching profession are all too evident in the correspondence between the Roman Catholic Archbishop, William Walsh, and Sr Evangelist Forde (Principal of Baggot Street Training College for Catholic women from 1883 to 1888). She 'implored' him to 'use his influence' to ensure that her graduates were employed. Forde told Walsh that parish priests (managers of local national schools) were filling vacancies with untrained teachers instead of trained teachers. Dr Walsh 'promptly contacted the Bishops, asking them to point out to parish priests the unacceptability of their behaviour.'[38] He noted, 'apart from this injustice to the young teachers, there was also an injury done to her college as payment for the students' board and lodging was not made till evidence of efficiency as teachers – after a probationary number of years – was supplied to the Commissioners by Inspectors.' Walsh wrote a letter to one bishop who, it seems, attended retreats and was able to influence the clergy. He explained that sixty-one Baggot Street students had yet to find employment.

In a comment that reflects the local nature of school appointments, Sr Evangelist Forde wrote:

> In many cases local circumstances and influence prevent Parish Priests (who are usually the managers) from appointing a stranger; and they are often obliged, even against their own judgement and inclination, to get an untrained teacher (because a parishioner) appointed. It strikes me that what a P.P. [Parish Priest] cannot do, without, perhaps, giving offence to his parishioners, the Bishop of the Diocese could effect, without any such inconvenience, by expressing his wish that in making appointments to their schools, the Managers should, as far as possible, give the preference to those candidates who have regularly trained in a Catholic Training College.

Forde further argued that having trained teachers was a 'great advantage' to the school. She wanted Walsh to be aware of the danger of

'bankruptcy to the College'.[39] As the capitation grant per student
was lower for females, the all-female college would have been under
more financial pressure if their students did not obtain jobs after
qualifying. The correspondence between Forde and Walsh suggests
that Catholic networks were used in order to guarantee the survival
of Catholic institutions. Given the minimum fees at the training colleges, this profession was attractive for those who could not afford a
university education.

Ironically, the sectarian nature of Irish society benefited teachers
in some respects. Just like the Roman Catholic Church, the Church
of Ireland thought it was 'of the utmost importance that the children
committed to the spiritual care of our church should be early and
earnestly taught in schools whose managers and teachers belong to
one commuion'.[40] This policy ensured the proliferation of Protestant
small schools and, consequently, more jobs for teachers. The Board
recognised schools with as few as fifteen students.[41] Many of the
schools in the congested districts would have been small, one-teacher
institutions and by 1909, 70.7 per cent of students were being educated in mono-denominational schools.[42] In rural areas, this would
have affected Protestants more than Catholics, as they were scattered
throughout the country. For example, only forty-three Protestant
schools had an average attendance of over seventy pupils, while 171
had an average of less than fifty pupils.[43]

The link between female teachers and kindergarten education
was further reinforced in 1905 by the Commissioners of Education,
Rule 127(b). This decreed that 'boys under eight are ineligible for
enrolment in a boys' school where there is not an assistant mistress,
unless there is not a suitable school under a mistress in the locality'.[44]
This meant that small one-teacher schools were under threat, and
females would teach the younger students in a larger school. This
rule was changed after criticism from the Roman Catholic Church
who thought that it would lead to co-education. It was also felt that
males were less likely to opt for a teaching career, so needed every
encouragement.[45]

The inspector greatly affected one's progress in the profession.
Utilitarian educational philosophies, so wonderfully exposed by
Charles Dickens in his portrait of Mr Gradgrind, the facts-obsessed
teacher in *Hard Times*, would have been a familiar picture for many
in the Irish educational system. Concentration on rote work, and
memorisation without comprehension, were the direct results of

the inspection system. Prior to 1900, primary teachers were paid according to performance of their students. This approach won particular support from Patrick Keenan, one of the Commissioners of the National Board of Education, and the only Catholic on the Board.[46] His influence was so far-reaching that his sister, Mother Ligouri Keenan, used his connections in establishing the college in Baggot Street for training Catholic females.[47] However, payment by results had come under a sustained attack and in 1900 the system was changed. From then, primary teachers were to be inspected, and their schools examined. One of the Head Inspectors complained, in 1896, that 'one of the defects of the results system, as carried out, is that it makes no provision for directly rewarding a teacher whose school, by its good organisation, order, discipline and cleanliness merits such an award'.[48]

The visit of the inspector spelled an important day. Perhaps women would have preferred the more objective examination system, rather than the assessment of male inspectors. Very little escaped the inspector's gaze. If he gave a poor report, then the teacher would not be promoted; in fact, she could even be demoted. He (they were invariably male, though women were recruited as junior inspectors in the 1920s) commented on the cleanliness of the room. It was not unknown for teachers to be criticised for having 'cheerless' rooms. The number and variety of maps, as well as the type of seating, were also noted. However, the most important comments were reserved for the performance of the pupils and their teacher.[49] Inspectors were frequently seen as unhelpful: they were employed as a result of a competitive examination and no prior teaching experience was required.[50] The arrogance displayed by some inspectors was not conducive to good relations with the teaching profession.[51]

From 31 March 1900, with the abolition of payment by results, teachers were allocated to various categories, depending on the report of the inspector: grade three, grade two and grade one. All grades were divided into class two and class one.[52] Only a certain number were admitted into each grade, so it was not a strictly meritocratic system. This introduction of categories meant that the inspector made pivotal decisions regarding the future prospects of primary teachers.

It is difficult to ascertain whether or not inspectors were harsher towards female teachers. Judging from their comments, it is clear that many had no concept of diplomacy. Students were, on occasion, described as 'extremely dull'; we are not told if any students were bright. Nonetheless, some teachers indulged in highly unusual behaviour, if the inspectors' reports are to be believed.[53]

The Killanin Committee,[54] in 1918, noted that 'three-fourths of the schools are rural ones scattered over a country of sparse but general inhabitancy; and a teacher, as a factor in social life, fills a very prominent and influential position in such surrounding'.[55] Photographs suggests that school buildings were quite basic in structure, but clearly the teacher had a position of authority in that environment. The difficulty for teachers was that poor pay paradoxically coincided with social status. A 'respectable' lifestyle was assumed, if not always financially possible. The Committee was critical of the 'lowness of the salary'.[56] But the report also suggested that, of the 'large supply of women candidates … many … [were] not up to standard'.[57] 'Special qualifications' could be 'recognised financially'. A Higher Certificate should have been awarded if a primary teacher had passed a university examination. However, the Commission did not believe that male and female teachers should be rewarded equally. 'We have made a man's salary somewhat higher than a woman's, because his expenses are greater; and in fixing all remunerations we have taken into account the degree of security of income and tenure which a teacher enjoys'.[58]

Teachers' pay was dependent on attendance, and poor attendance was attributed to poor teaching, regardless of social circumstances. 'The good school is nearly always well-attended, and it is quite appropriate that the principal teacher in it should benefit accordingly.'[59] Arguments regarding local illness or social disadvantage were brushed aside. Attendance on a particular day was often dependent on the state of the roads. The radical conclusion of the report was that 'no difference in salary should be made between rural and urban schools, or between schools for boys and girls and those for the one sex only.'[60] It did, however, favour females in recommending that a normal salary scale be introduced in schools with an average attendance of thirty for male, and twenty for females, recognition that girls' schools tended to be smaller. The maximum salary maintained sex differentials, with £200 for men, as compared to £170 for women. Male teachers, 'with an average attendance of 20 to 29 pupils, should receive the scale of salaries assigned to women teacher,' the report suggested.[61]

The concentration of small schools in female hands was encouraged. Most of these would have been in the West of Ireland. 'Trained teachers of schools under twenty average, should always be women, and should receive remuneration at the normal commencing rate for women teachers, £90 per annum, and should be eligible to rise by ten annual increments of £4 to a maximum of £130 per annum,' the Killanin Committee suggested. Furthermore, it recommended that 'teachers of mixed schools of 35 pupils or under should, as a general rule, be women'. This policy meant that female teachers would receive less pay, but they enjoyed better job prospects. However, 'untrained women teachers appointed in future should leave the service on marriage, or on attaining the age of 30 years'.[62] This encouraged teachers to see their job as a 'filler' prior to marriage. In the event of non-marriage, they would be replaced by a fresh supply of poorly-paid young females.

Conclusion

The one advantage of State employment was the promise of a pension, which could be transferred if one moved from one local authority to another.[63] Given these benefits-in-kind, some nurses were better off financially than teachers, but their salaries did not increase significantly with service. Public health nurses were better paid than most. Many of these would also have had midwifery qualifications, as well as being registered nurses. While they were recognised in the community, these nurses frequently lived alone. A circulating library was established to ward off loneliness. This is hardly surprising given that there would have been very few professional women in the congested districts and language difficulties would only have exacerbated the isolation. While teachers and nurses were both working professionally in depressed parts of Ireland, they were likely to be considered of higher status. The nurses were invariably outsiders, therefore they were likely to be considered of higher status in small communities than the teachers who were usually locals, so their status was lower.

The lives of nurses and teachers in the congested districts do not always intertwine. While much is revealed in State and professional sources regarding the opportunities and impediments faced by professional females, we know so little about the lives of those they served. Photographs can tell us a little about the attitudes and even socio-economic environment of the families who endured harsh lives in the congested districts of the West of Ireland in the late-nineteenth and early twentieth centuries.

Chapter 9

Dr Kathleen Lynn and Maternal Medicine

Introduction

In 1928, Sir James Craig, Professor of Medicine at Trinity College, Dublin wrote a reference for Dr Nora Stack who had recently graduated in medicine. He declared: 'Dr Stack represents the qualities which in my opinion should attach to a lady medical practitioner – she is quiet, earnest, conscientious and kind.'[1] A particular view of women and their suitability for medicine was to define their involvement in the profession. They were seen as possessing attributes which would facilitate their access to the profession, but they were not expected to radically change the face of medical care. It is not surprising, then, that women should turn to medicine. Increasing interest in public health and women's traditional role as carers facilitated their entry to the medical profession. This paper will demonstrate that women were predominant in particular areas of medicine and their relations with their patients were conditioned by perceptions of female characteristics. Dr Kathleen Lynn personifies the link between women and maternal medicine. Female physicians' work in the Women's National Health Association (WNHA) and St Ultan's give us a picture of the way they approached their patients (usually women and children) and dealt with medical issues.

Women and Welfare

Why were female doctors so prominent in paediatrics and public health? They were very adept at creating their own niches, especially in maternity and child welfare work. Women capitalised on their increasing interest in public welfare as new positions such as health inspectors and school medical inspectors were created.[2] This included reducing infant mortality rates. Along with a national movement for improved public health, the 'family became subject to social management in the nineteenth and twentieth centuries.'[3] This is precisely where the role of women in medicine becomes pertinent. They were seen to be the appropriate channel through which State policies could be transmitted to individual families. Women working in welfare medicine became part of the increasingly strong arm of the State backed up by social legislation which dictated the way in which people led their lives.

Why females were seen as particularly important in the drive towards better hygiene was articulated by Lady Aberdeen, the foundress of the WNHA. Her 1911 presidential address to the Royal Institute of Public Health was entitled 'The Sphere of Women in Relation to Public Health'. In order for new medical ideas to be successful, she argued, the 'confidence of the housewives' had to be sought. Women would help to 'popularise' new ideas regarding health as they were the people who 'moulded' ideas in the home. She wanted to have household science made compulsory for women in university and she argued that placing domestic science on the curriculum would raise the status of the subject.[4]

Nonetheless, the links between medicine and women were contradictory. As Magill has argued 'women were censured for the inadequacies of personal and domestic diet, and accused of colluding in their own ill-health and self-neglect.'[5] Yet, it was perceived that women were the best people to deal with the ill-health of females and children. Women were the alleged carers in society, but they rarely had an impact on legislation which affected women's health. They were expected to put into practice the aspirations of social legislation.

Female doctors were particularly appreciated in paediatrics. Just as the Babies' Clubs in Ireland were dominated by female doctors, like Dr Alice Barry, so the Children's Bureau in United States also attracted females. The American, Dr Florence Sherbon believed that women doctors were uniquely qualified to work with children. She argued: 'being women as well as physicians we share with our sex in the actual and potential motherhood of the race ... and being women and mothers, our first and closest and dearest interest is the child.'[6] However, like the Belfast Health Society, the Children's Bureau claimed that infant mortality was a socio-economic, not a medical problem. Unlike the Belfast public health activists, the Children's Bureau doctors did not see infant mortality as a moral problem.[7] Though medically trained, many women sought socio-economic solutions to the health difficulties of women and children. This approach could lead to a patronising attitude towards those most in need of welfare initiatives. Nellie Healy, a trained nurse and assistant superintendent of the Dublin Maternity and Child Welfare Centre, in an article on 'Child Welfare Nursing' suggested that when giving health talks to impoverished mothers it was important to remember that 'this poor mother has not been accustomed to value time or to be punctual or regular in any of her habits.'[8] It is difficult to ascertain the views of working-class patients who were being told by middle-class women how to have a healthy life. For example, maintaining a clean home must have been a considerable challenge when most homes were without running water. Improvements in public health were only possible when environmental factors, such as poor housing, were tackled.

Welfare developments should not be seen as medico-social revolution. The State continued to depend on voluntary groups for welfare initiatives. Ireland, both pre- and post-independence, was not noted for the emphasis it placed on social policy.[9] Political issues predominated. Meanwhile, in the words of Susanne Day, a philanthropist in the 1910s, 'slow murder by infection' was the fate of many.[10] In France, because of Church control of welfare and education the 'impetus for a public policy explicitly aimed at the family' was, ironically, reduced.[11] The same argument could be applied to Ireland, particularly in relation to medicine, where the willingness of religious orders to provide a range of welfare institutions let the State off the hook, in the short term, at any rate. These institutions provided work for female medical practitioners but their environments were rarely subjected to State scrutiny. The willingness of many to remain quiet, one of the 'qualities of a lady medical practitioner', was to have long-term implications for the inhabitants of these institutions.

Women's National Health Association

Given their involvement in public health it is not surprising that female doctors were prominent in the Women's National Health

Association (WNHA). Primarily concerned with reducing the frightening TB death rate, it wished to educate the public, particularly women, on health matters. Its interests ranged from hygiene, to the distribution of milk and the lowering of infant mortality rate. The WNHA established dozens of local branches and travelled the country with medical experts delivering lectures on public health. Their local branches ultimately linked up with nursing groups and child welfare schemes. They established Babies' Clubs (nine in Dublin city alone) and TB dispensaries.[12] The WNHA exerted political pressure to have public health legislation (for example the 1907 and 1915 Notification of Births Acts) implemented. Furthermore, they sought funding for child welfare. Sanatoria in Newcastle, Co. Dublin (Peamount) and Rosslare Co. Fermanagh were established by the WNHA to cater for T.B. patients. As their golden jubilee report noted, in 1957, much of the work 'pioneered by the WHNA has been taken over by local and government authorities.'[13]

The work of the WNHA in reducing infant mortality was noted by William Lawson, who commented on the co-operation sought between the Infant Aid Society, the WNHA and the Public Health Department of Dublin Corporation. He referred to the reports on the physical welfare of mothers and children by Drs Ella Webb, Marion Andrews and Alice Barry who discussed what was being done respectively in Dublin, Belfast and Cork.[14] It has been suggested in relation to child welfare that the First World War brought to Ireland the 'language but not the reality of social reform.'[15] In a sense, the WNHA was filling this gap between rhetoric and reality in the medical world. They initiated a nation-wide campaign to spread the gospel, the word is appropriate since their travels from Donegal to Waterford with their health caravan and its motto 'War on Germs' took on the appearance of an evangelical crusade. The WNHA also produced a journal, *Sláinte*, from 1909. Through it, they advertised their varied activities from lectures to establishing a pasteurised milk depot. The WNHA brought both the language, and the reality, of sanitary reform to many parts of Ireland.

There were several female doctors at the first annual meeting of the WNHA, in 1908, including Dr Lily Baker.[16] She was to make her mark nearly two decades later when she was appointed to Bristol Royal Infirmary in charge of the ante-natal department. During the First World War, she had worked in the Women's Royal Air Force where her speciality was the 'management of colonels' many of whom saw women in the RAF as 'one of the minor horrors of the war'. It is unlikely that the colonels saw much of Dr Baker as she worked in the gynaecological and obstetric departments and apparently made herself indispensable.[17] Possibly the female doctor most associated with the WNHA is Dr Alice Barry. Between 1912 and 1929 she was in charge of the nine Dublin Babies Clubs' which were run by the WNHA. They were launched the following manner, according to one Dublin wit:

> So the Babies' Club was started in a real viceregal way with a feast
> o' cakes from Scotland and a mighty flood o' tay
> An Mrs Aberdeen was there in her disinfected best, an swallowed
> with her tay as many microbes as the rest.[18]

In 1929, the Babies' Clubs were taken over by Dublin Corporation. Dr Barry became Resident Medical Officer at Peamount which had been established WNHA.[19]

Peamount Sanatorium was set up in 1912. It expressed in institutional form the aspirations of the WNHA with its emphasis on fresh air, sunshine, cleanliness, wholesome food and its local industries for able-bodied patients. It even had an open-air school for the younger patients. A former patient remembered Dr Barry as 'full of kindness and gentleness, but … a strict disciplinarian when the occasion required it.'[20]

As an indication of the social stigma attached to TB when patients complained about the food in Peamount, they were told that 'if the food in their houses was good they would not then be in Peamount.'[21] In addition to setting up sanatoria, the WNHA continued to lobby for improved facilities. In 1919 their advisory committee on 'Legislation affecting Child Welfare and Public Health' included Dr Ella Webb and Dr Alice Barry.

St Ultan's: A Women's Hospital for Infants[23]

In the same year, Dr Kathleen Lynn Madeleine ffrench-Mullen established St Ultan's Hospital for Infants. Kathleen Lynn was probably the most famous of the pre-1900 female medical graduates.[24] The daughter of a Church of Ireland rector, Revd Robert Young Lynn, she was born in 1874, near Cong, Co. Mayo. Kathleen's maternal grandfather was Revd Richard Wynne of Drumcliffe, Sligo while Revd Wynne's wife, Catherine, was the daughter of Colonel Richard

Beaver Brown. Kathleen Lynn's grandfather was a younger son of Owen Wynne, a Member of Parliament for Hazelwood, and Anne Maxwell, the Earl of Farnham's sister.[25] Despite these aristocratic connections, she never associated herself with the privileged, and her later career was primarily concerned with the less well off. During her childhood, Co. Mayo was noted for its immense poverty. The suffering wrought by the bad harvests of the late-1870s stimulated intense political activity, particularly in the Land League, which sought to improve the lot of tenants. These two strands, the poverty of so many people and political activity, which sought to eliminate the causes of that poverty, were to be continually intertwined in Dr Lynn's professional career. After education in Manchester and Dussledorf, she attended Alexandra College.

This school was to educate many female doctors. Dr Ethel Bentham, the first female physicians to sit in the House of Commons, attended Alexandra School and College. In keeping with the welfare interests of so many female doctors, she choose to study medicine. Therefore, she would have greater access to the poor. Bentham had been involved in a 'Sunday club for girls,' while a student at Alexandra. Dr Bentham studied at the London School of Medicine, but had to obtain a statutory qualification from Scotland, qualifying, in 1894, with the Licentiate of the Royal College of Physicians and Surgeons in Edinburgh.

Her public life was intertwined with her professional interests. Bentham was chair of a court which dealt with non-attendance at school, and she was also a member of the Metropolitan Asylums Board. Her contemporary, Dr E. Honor Bone, felt that Dr Bentham's 'most important contributions to the social welfare of her time was the inception of the baby clinic … [Dr Bentham] realised in the course of her practice that the start in preventative medicine should really be made in the earliest months of a child's life, and that it should therefore be possible for mothers to bring their children to some centre where they could get advice about diet and hygiene.' This practice was to be emulated in St Ultan's Hospital for infants in Dublin. Dr Honor Bone described Dr Bentham as one who had little patience 'with palliatives. She wanted to get to the root of all social troubles.' Her Dublin childhood was vital in this respect. As a child, she had been sent on an errand and saw an impoverished group of children standing around a child's coffin. Dr Bentham's pragmatism motivated her to seek preventative cures for illnesses, especially those of children. The Babies' Clubs were her legacy. There were many similarities between Bentham and Lynn.[26]

Lynn graduated from Cecilia Street in 1899 and became a Fellow of the Royal College of Surgeons in 1909. Additionally, she did post-graduate work in the United States. Dr Lynn was refused a position in the Adelaide Hospital, as the other doctors objected to a female colleague, even though she had been elected as a resident doctor. It was not until May 1913 that the medical board allowed female students to apply for residence at the hospital.[27] Lynn eventually joined the staff of Sir Patrick Dun's Hospital, and she also worked at the Rotunda between 1902 and 1916, according to an obituary of her friend Madeleine ffrench-Mullen.[28] Between 1910 and 1916, she was a clinical assistant in the Royal Victoria Eye and Ear Hospital, but was not allowed to return after the 1916 Rising. Another female doctor, Dr Georgina Prosser, was appointed to replace her.[29] It has been suggested that Dr Lynn was the first female resident doctor at the Eye and Ear hospital.[30] Her private practice, at 9 Belgrave Road, Rathmines was her home for over forty years. An active suffragist, and an enthusiastic nationalist, Lynn was a friend of James Connolly, the labour activist who established the Irish Transport and General Workers' Union.

When the Irish Citizen Army (ICA) was set up in 1913, Dr Lynn was asked by Connolly to teach first-aid. Dr Lynn went on to become a captain and chief medical officer in the ICA. This would bring her into close contact with the families of unemployed, or poorly-paid, workers in Dublin. She worked with Countess Markievicz, Constance Gore-Booth (they were distantly related, as a Wynne had married a Gore-Booth) in the soup kitchens which were established during the 1913 Lock-Out of workers. A photograph of women involved in the 1916 Rising shows Dr Kathleen Lynn and Madeleine ffrench-Mullen at the front. During the Rising, her medical training was vital. From her post in St Stephen's Green, Lynn organised the medical needs of the ICA. She also established a temporary surgery. After the Rising, Lynn, like many women, was imprisoned, and her diaries include interesting comments on conditions in Kilmainham and Mountjoy prisons. She mentioned receiving gifts of fruit and flowers, but the lice in Kilmainham were not to her liking. One officer was 'quite civil', and he cleaned out the lavatory.[31] Dr Lynn was later Surgeon-General to Sinn Féin and a member of the Sinn Féin executive in 1917. She was 'on the run' between May and October 1918. When arrested, she was sent to Arbour Hill Detention Barracks. The Lord Mayor of Dublin,

Laurence O'Neill, 'made representations to the authorities with a view to having her professional services made available during the influenza epidemic'. The authorities agreed to release her.[32] Because of her republican activities, Lynn was still monitored carefully. When she visited the Red Cross in Switzerland, in 1923, her house was searched.[33] In the same year, Lynn was elected to Dáil Éireann on the anti-Treaty side but did not take her seat. Her nationalist/social-ist principles remained undimmed. This is clear from an election poster of Lynn's. Dr Lynn declared that she was a follower of Wolfe Tone and James Connolly and sought the 'abolition of privilege of every kind'. In 1925, she wrote in her diary 'Hogan's [Patrick Hogan, Minister for Agriculture] new Land Bill in, all landlords must sell, good.'[34] She was also a very religious woman and a regular attender at Holy Trinity Church, Rathmines. However, she was not afraid to be critical. When her relative, Canon Wynne, who was to establish the Samaritans in Ireland asked her, 'why is the Church not pacifist?' she replied, 'because it is not Christian.'[35] Dr Lynn is remembered, primarily, for her work in St Ultan's. She worked there until her death in 1955.

The hospital was fortunate from the very beginning in having an excellent matron in Nan Dougan, a native of Co. Derry, who had trained at Sir Patrick Dun's Hospital. She did not retire until 1945.[36] But why was this infants' hospital established in the first place? The people associated with St Ultan's such as Dr Ella Webb, Dr Elizabeth Tennant, Dr Katherine Maguire, Dr Alice Barry, Madeleine ffrench-Mullen and Dr Lynn were all interested in children's health. The first meeting of the committee (held at 25 Kildare Street) which estab-lished the hospital, was primarily concerned with venereal disease. Many political figures were present at the meetings such as Mrs Kathleen Clarke and Mrs Jennie Wyse-Power. Wyse-Power had a long career in public life from the Ladies Land League to Cumann na mBan. She was to become a senator in the 1920s.[37]

At the meeting, Dr Lynn, who read a paper on venereal dis-ease, declared her desire to educate the public on the matter. Dr Alice Barry proposed, and Miss Lucy Griffin (later secretary of St Ultan's Committee) seconded the motion that 'this conference of Irishwomen note with appreciation that the Corporations of Dublin and Belfast have taken up the question of venereal dis-ease, and urge those bodies to see that every soldier who lands at Irish ports is guaranteed free from disease.'[38] There was a Royal

Commission on venereal disease sitting in 1918. Dr McWeeney, Professor of Pathology and Bacteriology at Cecilia Street Medical School, and bacteriologist to the Local Government Board, had asked to present a paper with slides to the Statistical and Social Inquiry Society of Ireland on the subject. He gave the paper in January 1918. It was subsequently published, regrettably without the slides.[39] At the same time, the *Irish Journal of Medical Science* had several pieces on the subject.[40]

Additionally, given the nationalist outlook of the committee, they were particularly critical of British soldiers infecting Irish women and children. The St Ultan's committee possibly saw this in a wider political context. British rule was affecting the health of the nation. T.P.C. Kirkpatrick, in an article in the *Irish Journal of Medical Science*, referred to a leaflet issued by the 'Sinn Féin Public Health Department', in which it is stated that at the close of the war probably 15,000 soldiers will return to Ireland suffering from syphilis.[41]

The St Ultan's committee was also part of a group known as Sláinte na nGaedeal which was interested in the health of the nation. They were part of a national movement which sought the cultural, moral, physical and intellectual regeneration of the Irish people through organisations such as the Gaelic League and the Gaelic Athletic Association (G.A.A.). The committee feared for the health of the nation's children.[42]

St Ultan's recommended that 'local authorities under the Children's Act … [should] have such infants [suffering from syphilis] immediately removed for treatment to hospitals on diagnosis of their disease by the medical officer of the district, and that copies of this resolution be sent to Boards of Guardians and local authorities.' They also asked whether there was provision for syphilitic infants in any hospital.[43] By May, the committee had sent Miss Lucy Griffin to see Mr P.T. Daly of Dublin Corporation regarding health facilities. These early issues underline a number of different developments, which affected female doctors. The increasing role of the State (including local government) in medicine, and the growing importance of paediatricians and public health (the two were closely linked), provided a focus for female doctors who, by this stage, had been part of the medical profession for over three decades.

By July 1918, arrangements were being made to buy 37 Charlemont Street, the eventual site of the hospital. When the influenza pandemic reached Dublin in November 1918, the committee appealed directly to the public. Dr Lynn and ffrench-Mullen met Dr William Walsh, the Roman Catholic Archbishop. It was reported, in the minutes that 'the Archbishop never likes [the words 'would not' were scored out] to share in the starting of an enterprise like this for which he is not directly responsible [and] that he will be guided in his support by the advise of his medical advisers. [He also] recognises the need of such a hospital ... [and] he is sympathetic towards it.' Despite this qualified support, the committee published the Archbishop's approval in the daily papers on the 1 January 1919.[44]

A book entitled, *Leabhar Ultáin the Book of Saint Ultan* was compiled in 1920 by Katherine MacCormack and sold to support the hospital. It contained an introduction by the historian Alice Stopford-Green (the aunt of Dr Dorothy Price, who later worked in St Ultan's), poems, drawings and pictures by George Russell, Maud Gonne MacBride, Thomas Bodkin, Harry Clarke and Jack B. Yeats amongst others.[45] Every year the hospital organised a pilgrimage-cum-picnic to Ardbraccan, the site of St Ultan's well and his tiny church.[46] This multi-denominational outing usually consisted of a rosary and Evensong in Irish. Dr Lynn, along with Sean O'Casey, wanted to gaelicise the Church of Ireland liturgy. In 1921, the committee thanked President de Valera for permitting them to advertise that 'he was coming to the Derideacht' (outing), as it increased attendance five-fold.[47] Many of the St Ultan's events were advertised in Irish thus linking their activities with nationalist movements. The hospital maintained its connections with individuals associated with Irish nationalists. 'Mrs James Connolly' (*sic*) was nominated as a new member of the committee in November 1920.[48]

The connections between St Ultan's and the Women's National Health Association (WNHA) were obvious, given that both were concerned with the elimination of tuberculosis and the health of children. When the WNHA organised a conference on public health in November 1921, they sought delegates from the hospital and St Ultan's gladly complied. The WNHA was concerned that health visitors had to train in England. They wanted to have a course in Dublin, and they sought the co-operation of St Ultan's.[49] The hospital's concern for the health of mothers extended to running a holiday home for them in Baldoyle.[50] One of the aims of the hospital was to be 'a university for women'. The staff strongly encouraged mothers to attend lectures at the hospital. Welfare workers also attended; the hospital declared that one of their main aims was to 'spread knowledge.'[51] They were therefore part of an international movement to train mothers. Dr Newman, the Chief Medical Officer to the Board of Education in England, pointed out that infant mortality was due to the 'ignorance of the mother and the remedy is the education of the mother.'[52] At St Ultan's the patient practitioner encounter was based on the mother of the child being advised by the 'Lady Medical Practitioner'. The careers of the female doctors associated with the St Ultan's were remarkably similar.

Dr Elizabeth Tennant received her licentiate from the Royal College of Physicians and Surgeons, in 1894, and practised in Harrington Street, Dublin, between 1894 and 1937. She was an honorary visiting physician to St Ultan's where she was a 'valued member' of staff and was also medical officer to St Catherine's School and Orphanage in Dublin. Her large general practice in Dublin specialised in midwifery. As a student in the Meath Hospital, she made life-long friends, including Sir John Moore, MD, in an obituary, *The Irish Times*, wrote that 'her devotion to her work and to the hospital [St Ultan's] is acknowledged by all those connected with it to have been one of the biggest factors in the success of the institution.'[53]

Isabella Webb was the eldest daughter of the Dean of St Patrick's Cathedral. Like many doctors, she was educated at Alexandra College, though she also studied at Queen's College, Harley Street, London and at Gottingen, in Germany.[54] Although Webb wanted to study medicine, she first graduated with a natural science degree from the Royal University of Ireland. In 1904, she graduated with first place in her medical degree from Cecilia Street to the delight of 'Speranza' from *St Stephen's*. The magazine pointed out that it 'was a record to gain it over the heads of so many competitors of the sterner sex, which, until recent years, regarded medicine as exclusively its own ground.'[55] Webb was awarded her MD in 1906. Like, Dr Katherine Maguire, she won the prestigious travelling scholarship and went to Vienna. After her marriage to George Webb, a Fellow of TCD, she combined raising a family (she had two a son and a daughter) with private practice and a free evening dispensary in Kevin Street. Her busy professional life also included working as a demonstrator of physiology in the Women's Department of the TCD Medical School, as well as election to the visiting staff of Adelaide. She resigned, in 1927, but continued to run a children's dispensary.

Her work in the WNHA and St Ultan's established her reputation as a paediatrician. It is not surprising that she worked in the Stillorgan Children's Sunshine Home. In 1924, Dr Webb had written a paper on 'Sunshine and Health' for the Alexandra Guild Conference. This interest coincided with her research on rickets. Subsequently, a committee of women 'interested in child welfare had been formed to provide an open-air convalescent home.' Ultimately, this led to the development of the Sunshine Home.[56] Her work with Drs Lynn and Price further enhanced the reputation of female doctors in the prevention of diseases, particularly those which were exacerbated by socio-economic deprivation. Dr Webb did not lose her Alexandra links, and was an honorary commandant in the Alexandra College St John's Ambulance Brigade Nursing Division, where she taught first aid. Her friend, Letitia Overend, was commandant in the brigade. Like Dr Lynn, Webb saw action during the 1916 Rising as the brigade was on duty at the Emergency Hospital at 14 Merrion Square (the St John's headquarters). Dr Webb 'cycled continuously through the front line to visit hospitals. She was later made a Lady Grace of then Order of St John of Jerusalem in recognition of her services,' and awarded a medal for gallantry.[57] In 1918, Dr Webb was awarded an MBE. Noted for her 'strong personality' and her toughness, she had, according to Mitchell, 'a rugged sense of honour, a charming smile and a deep contralto laugh'.[58]

Another colleague of Dr Lynn's at St Ultan's was Katherine Maguire. Dr Maguire was the youngest daughter of Revd John Truelock Maguire, a rector at Boyle, Co. Roscommon. One of the first two women students admitted to the Adelaide Hospital, along with Isabella Harper, Maguire won the Hudson scholarship at the Adelaide (the first woman to do so) in 1881, after studying at Alexandra College and the Royal University of Ireland. She graduated in first place in her final medical examinations.[59] In 1878, twenty-eight Adelaide students had complained that they could not study certain subjects with females present. Hence, the decision to admit two females was unexpected.[60] Maguire had already obtained first place, first-class honours and an exhibition in the BA examination in biological science, the first woman in RUI to do so.[61] Dr Maguire was noted for her interest in social medicine. In 1898, her paper, to the Alexandra Guild on 'Social Conditions of the Dublin Poor', motivated the guild to establish model tenement houses.[62]

Dr Maguire's work in St Ultan's Hospital exerted a powerful influence on Dr Dorothy Stopford-Price. Dr Price noted:

It was from Dr Katherine Maguire that I learnt to take an interest in clinical observations; or rather renewed an interest inculcated in my student days by Professor William Boxwell ... For about nine years I had imbibed wisdom from her in St Ultan's Hospital, making a point of doing her round with her, and she would pause at the last cot, with the baby clutching her fingers whilst she drifted off into a very interesting discourse, drawing on her great experience and her wealth of reading. She was a very clever woman and Sister Mulligan and I enjoyed these bedside talks, when she would range far and wide ... Dr Maguire encouraged any never-so-feeble evidences of an enquiring mind, and urged one to take trouble to find things out and to read and publish. During her last illness in 1930-1, I carried on her extensive practice for her which indeed she left in my hand in the end. She wrote me frequent and almost indecipherable letters about her patients up to the end. She was very indignant when I said some lady was suffering from Anno Domini.[63]

It is clear from Dr price's later career that she heeded Dr Maguire advice to read and publish.

Dr Maguire had a private practice in Mount Street, and later in Merrion Square in Dublin. She also opened a Free Dispensary at Harold's Cross. As part of her interest in alleviating the causes of ill-health, she bought four tenement houses in Tyrone Street and let them at a minimum rent. As a lecturer on hygiene at Alexandra College (her lectures on health began in 1893),[64] she was described as an 'exceptionally gifted teacher'. Although a member of the Academy of Medicine, Maguire's 'self-effacing disposition did not permit her to speak or to show cases.' Enthusiastic about women's rights, she was described, somewhat oxymoronically, as a 'non-militant suffragette.''After her death in 1931, a 'bronze tablet' was erected in her memory at 27 Grenville Street.[65]

Probably the most dynamic female doctor who worked in St Ultan's was Dr Dorothy Stopford-Price. Her originality and energy were rewarded by improvements in the TB mortality figures.[66] While working in Kilbrittain, West Cork as a dispensary doctor, she met her first case of TB. Price's comments reflect the backward nature of Irish medical research, something she tried to rectify through research and publication: 'a woman was dying of pulmonary tuberculosis, and alongside of her in the cottage her nine months old baby was fading away; repeated physical examination revealed no signs in the lungs, and when he died, in puzzled ignorance I certified the death as 'Tuberculosis Diathesis'. Quite incorrectly, there is no such thing; but, in 1921, we in Ireland were not taught that infants died of miliary tuberculosis,[67] and I for one had not heard of the tuberculin test, although it was discovered in 1907 by von Pirquet.'[68]

Her nationalist outlook led to an appointment as medical officer to a Cork brigade of the IRA. She mentioned that she had instructions from the Headquarters of Cumann na mBan to lecture on first aid to the Kilbrittain branch which 'was closely caught up in the activities of the West Cork Brigade of the IRA and its Flying Column.'[69] Price resigned from the Kilbrittain Dispensary in 1923. However, she stayed in contact with the Crowley family from Kilbrittain. Over twenty years afterwards, she remembered the 'warm west Cork feeling' and the 'warm-hearted spot'. She asked if Kilbrittain has seen any more 'Doctoresses … They are as common as pebbles on a beach now.'[70] This was an exaggeration. In 1948, she mentioned she was 'trying to push this new BCG vaccination against tuberculosis' and that they were 'lucky' with the new Minister of Health, 'he is a splendid young fellow and doing a lot for tuberculosis'. She remained committed to the anti-Treaty side, as she 'still voted for Dev. however.'[71]

Her husband, Liam Price, wrote that it was 'only after several years' experience in dealing with diseases of infants in St Ultan's that she commenced to take a special interest in tuberculosis.' A visit to Vienna, in 1931, provided further stimulation. Her investigations eventually became her 'life work'. Not one to depend on tradition or old wives' tales, 'she tested everything out for herself in a thoroughly critical scientific spirit'. At one stage, she was moved to declare that 'the blood stream does not obey nuns' rules' when trying to explain how children infected each other in hospitals.[72]

The influence of Dr Katherine Maguire has already been mentioned, but others played a role in Dr Price's work. Professor William Boxwell was important in her professional development as he emphasised the importance of post-mortem examinations. She was his clinical clerk for six months in the early 1920s. Boxwell suggested she had a 'shy personality' and 'took life seriously'.[73] Dr Ella Webb was another influence. Dr Price enthused, 'she lets me go down and help her in her slum dispensary on Tuesday evenings and shows what simply wonderful things a person can do besides doctoring'. Dr Price described Dr Lynn as follows: 'she is a lady of an old-fashioned

type, if you can imagine the exact reverse of Dr Webb, who, indeed, is
much more the Sinn Féin sort, you'd think.'[74] She was to work with
Drs Barry, Lynn and Webb in St Ultan's. Additionally, her enthusiasm
for Dr Webb's work was enhanced further when they both worked
in the Sunshine Hospital for Children.

Her appointment as House Surgeon to St Ultan's, in 1923, provided the progressive environment for her researches into TB in
childhood. Dr Alice Barry began 'tuberculin testing as a routine on
entry' to St Ultan's, in 1934. Dr Price also benefitted from the medical research of Dr Bob Collis. He had, like Dr Price, studied under
Dr Wassen, who introduced BCG, with great success in Sweden.
Price was so impressed with Dr Wassen's work that she determinedly
told him she would 'brandish' his 'decreased mortality figures in
the faces of authorities.'[75] Price's interests did not focus purely on
medical research and she was a member of the Irish Clean Milk
Society. However, she was frustrated at the lax attitude towards those
who were convicted under the legislation against dirty milk.[76] Dr
Price's thesis on 'Primary Tuberculosis of the Lungs of Children' was
accepted as an MD by TCD, in 1935. It was subsequently published
in the *Irish Journal of Medical Science*.

Eventually, in 1936, she was given permission by the Department
of Local Government and Public Health to import the BCG vaccine.
It arrived at St Ultan's Hospital on 26 January 1937. In the same year,
she was appointed consultant physician at Newcastle Sanatorium.[77]
By the 1940s, St Ultan's had drastically reduced its TB mortality rate
from 77 per cent to 28 per cent.[78] But, Price was to be frustrated by
the lack of accommodation at St Ultan's. Their plans for an extension came to naught as the Catholic Children's Hospital was built in
Crumlin. Nonetheless, her work was recognised by Dr Noel Browne
when the National BCG Centre was located at St Ultan's. Her 1942
book, *Tuberculosis in Childhood*, had enhanced her 'international reputation.' Such was its success that a second edition was published in
1948.[79] Internationally, Price was nominated for the World Health
Organisation Leon Bernard prize for contribution to social medicine.

Price's hectic schedule, as well as her many hospital appointments (consulting physician to the Royal National Hospital for
Consumptives in Ireland, as well as Baggot Street, St Ultan's and
Sunshine Home commitments and a private practice), plus involvement in the Baggot Street Linen Guild caught up with her. In the
late-1930s, she got an attack of 'muscular rheumatism'. Despite ill-

health, her enthusiasm never waned. In a letter to Dr Wassen: 'I had the Minister [Dr Noel Browne] here twice and finally persuaded him to do what I wanted.' Seeking a scientific approach to the prevention of TB ensured the success of BCG vaccination will be given to all infants (irrespective of contact) at an early age, thus affording protection from nurse, milk, casual contact and unknown source.[80] Thanks to Dr Price, that day has come. Dr Harry Counihan, a younger colleague, believed 'she fulfilled herself more completely, and used her talents to greater effect than any physician I have known.'[81] Although she claimed that 'doctoresses were as common as pebbles on a beach', the ripples of this particular pebble were felt long after her passing in 1954. Her career encapsulated many of the interests pursued by Dr Kathleen Lynn and St Ultan's Hospital with its focus on prevention.

The hospital's concern for the health of mothers extended to running a holiday home in Baldoyle.[82] During the 1920s in England, classes in 'mothercraft' were organised and, according to Jane Lewis, a 'series of rhymes helped drive the points home':

> Baby thrives at Mother's breast
> That's the food he likes best
> Give when his meal hour strikes
> Not at any time he likes [No demand feeding here]
> ... If healthy children you would raise
> Open windows nights and days.[83]

Dr Lynn also preached the virtues of cleanliness and fresh air. She was heavily involved with *An Óige* (a youth organisation which promoted outdoor activity) and her cottage at Glenmalure in Co. Wicklow was given to them after death. In 1928, she gave a talk on breast-feeding where she pointed out that 'breast milk is the baby's birthright' and it was 'nourishment provided by God'. St Ultan's, with its focus on mothers, realised that breast feeding was difficult for many. They introduced special breast pumps for mothers who had difficulties producing milk.

As well as educating mothers, St Ultan's had a school for its patients and Dr Lynn's interest in education was given a further impetus in 1934 when Dr Maria Montessori (the first woman to take a medical degree at Rome University in 1896) visited the hospital. Dr Montessori was noted for advocating a child-centred approach to education.[84] This view did not meet with the approval of Dr

Timothy Corcoran, Professor of Education in University College, Dublin and a forceful advocate of a rigid educational curriculum. He devoted several articles in *Irish Monthly* to Montessori education which he described as 'braggart blasphemy'.[85] One of the striking things about the St Ultan's Archives is the amount of photographs devoted to young patients. Unusually we are only given the names of the children, not the staff. The Montessori Method is child-centred education, and as St Ultan's offered child-centred medicine. St Ultan's most important legacy was its pioneering research in relation to the prevention of tuberculosis.[86] This was particularly associated with Dr Dorothy Stopford-Price, whose career has been discussed.

Dr Price and Dr Lynn had two totally different approaches to the care of infants. At a medical board meeting Dr Lynn declared that the patients needed love. Dr Price, on the other hand, wanted them to be tuberculin tested on entry and TB patients segregated for fear of infection.[87] Both of these approaches (the scientific and the maternal) were combined in St Ultan's. Patients came from all over the country. In keeping with the social outlook of the hospital, annual reports contain detailed records of the background of the patients, including the proportion whose father was unemployed. In 1924 this was 44 per cent. The report also noted that fifteen per cent of the patients were 'illegitimate'.[88] St Ultan's sought to support families and, in the 1930s, the St Ultan's Hospital Utility Society was to establish model tenement homes in order to break the cycle of poverty and ill-health.[89]

What was the role of St Ultan's for female doctors and their patients? It was yet another example of female doctors creating their own niche, in this case paediatrics. Its staff read like a who's who of prominent female paediatricians with Drs Maguire, Lynn and Price gaining valuable experience there. The hospital provided these professionals with the freedom to run an institution as they saw fit. Thus, patients were given a higher priority and mothers were seen as part of the medical process. This could be a double edged sword, as an ill child was seen as a reflection on his/her parents. If mothers were educated in health care, then they were obliged to ensure that their children received proper care, regardless of their social circumstances.

Conclusion

Despite the success of the first generation of female doctors, not everyone was convinced that women were needed in medicine. In his 'Ode to the Lady Medicals' Mac Aodh questioned the Lady Medicos.

Though all the world's a stage and we are acting,
Yet still I think your part is not dissecting
To me the art of making apple tarts
Would suit you better than those 'horrid parts.
And as for learning chemistry and that,
Twould be a nicer thing to trim a hat.
I known your aims in medicine are true
But tell is there any need of you?'[90]

Female practitioners, by extending domestic ideals into professional life in their relations with their patients, managed to vindicate
their professional position and did not upset the medical apple cart.
Perhaps the personification of the female doctors' attitude towards
their patients is Dr Angela Russell.[91] The product of a comfortable
background (her father was a senior inspector of schools) she graduated in medicine from UCD in 1921, and completed a Diploma in
Public Health in 1928. However, after marriage in the mid-1920s
she never worked professionally. Nonetheless, she spent the rest
of her long life (she died in 1991) promoting public health. This
included writing on socio-medical matters in the newspapers and
giving radio talks. She was also heavily involved in the Cheeverstown
Convalescent Home for the Children (which provided facilities for
deprived children), Save the Children (which sought greater protection for children at risk), the Irish Society for the Prevention of
Cruelty to Children, the WNHA and St Ultan's. Her aim, she once
said, was to create 'an enlightened public'. Furthermore, she argued
that 'home-making' was a woman's 'most important job' and females
should be trained in 'mothercraft'. All of this reinforced the view that
women were responsible for the health of their children.

Female doctors' focus on mothers ensured that the patient-practi-
tioner relationship centred on women advising women. In this way, a
broader approach to medicine, which included a focus on the socio-
economic causes of ill-health, was achieved. Through her work with
both patients and practitioners, and her focus on social or maternal
medicine in St Ultan's, Dr Kathleen Lynn made a major contribution to Irish medicine, and, indeed, to Irish life.

Chapter 10

Dorothy Stopford-Price and the elimination of childhood tuberculosis[1]

> It is probably inevitable that a small nation which has just achieved self-government should be preoccupied with its own affairs to the almost total exhaustion of what is happening in the rest of the world.[2]

This view of 1930s Ireland has pervaded and it is presumed that few international influences impinged on Irish life. However, public health and, more particularly, the fight against childhood tuberculosis, benefited greatly from research conducted during the 1930s by one of the lesser-known Irish doctors. Much of the credit for the elimination of Tuberculosis in Ireland has gone to Dr Noel Browne, Minister for Health between 1948 and 1951.[3] Yet there has been a tendency to exaggerate his role. The groundbreaking efforts to prevent TB in children prior to his term in office have been largely neglected. This required a vaccination known as BCG (Bacillus Calmette Guerin, named after the two French scientists who discovered its properties). It was already being used on the Continent in the 1920s, and although its introduction to Ireland in the 1930s encountered much opposition, the fact that it predates its introduction in the UK illustrates an openness not generally perceived as characteristic of the period.

This lack of awareness of the outside influences on medical practice in Ireland can be explained by the limited attention public health has received from historians until recently. With the exception of brief biographies by Coakley and Lyons[4] we know very little about public health professionals in the twentieth century. Even less is written about the treatment of TB before the tenure of Noel Browne. The autobiography of Dr James Deeny, who was very interested in tuberculosis and published widely on the subject, fails to mention the introduction of BCG in the 1930s. Instead he concentrates on his activities as Chief Medical Officer in the newly formed Department of Health in the 1940s and 1950s.[5] This paper will try to address this gap by analysing the impact of the BCG vaccination campaign of Dr Dorothy Stopford-Price.

Career of Dr Dorothy Stopford-Price

Born in 1890, Dorothy Stopford was the third child of Constance and Jemmett Stopford, a Dublin accountant. Her maternal grandfather, Evory Kennedy, was Master of the Rotunda Lying-in Hospital.[6] Her aunt was the famous historian Alice Stopford-Green. Stopford's early upbringing in Ireland was comfortable with a governess brought over from Britain to educate the young Stopfords. However, when her father died from typhoid fever in 1902 the family moved to London to live with relatives. As a foundation scholarship student at the newly established St Paul's Girls' School in London, Dorothy Stopford benefited from the progressive atmosphere there. Dr Barbara Stokes, later a colleague of hers at St Ultan's Hospital for Infants and at the Royal City of Dublin Hospital, Baggot Street, Dublin, was also a student at St Paul's. She recalled that the students were not encouraged to think about whether they would have a job but 'what kind' of job they would seek.[7] At school Stopford's 'steady enthusiasm for social work' was noted.[8] After school Stopford worked with the Charitable Organisation Society, which provided social services in London and she hoped to become an almoner (social worker). Although passing the entrance exam for Regent St Polytechnic, she returned to Dublin to begin her medical studies in TCD in 1916. At twenty-five years of age she entered Trinity with 'flying colours in oral Euclid – [and] a squeak in Algebra'.[9]

At Trinity she encountered the discriminatory attitude towards women which permeated the profession at the time. The Dublin University Biological Association for instance refused her membership because they did not admit women. Considering the content of the papers delivered to the society it is not surprising that the

Biological Association was unwilling to allow females to become members. In 1912 Mr J.N. Armstrong, in a paper on 'Women's Work and its relation to the Race', suggested that the:

> Sudden and dominant importance of the brain in guiding both nat-
> ural & sexual selection probably marked the advent of men ... True
> women [he continued] display their sex in two long recognised
> varieties–the Mother, the wealth of the nation, and the Courtesan,
> the latter varying in her pose according to the taste of the age.

Women who worked were acting contrary to the interests of the race because they bore no children, were willing to take lower wages and therefore deprived mothers of the 'necessities of life'.[10] This superficially economic argument was, in fact, based on views of what was appropriate for females. It was a familiar one at the time and was often used to deprive women of employment.

Dorothy Stopford was particularly keen to get involved in the scientific side of the association. There is an envelope addressed to the secretary of the women Medical Students' Committee in the Price papers so it is probable that Stopford had assumed this position. Dr Euphran Maxwell, a sister of the historian Constantia who began lecturing in ophthalmology at TCD in 1915, is also mentioned so perhaps the female medical students sought her support in gaining admittance to the Biological Association.[11] Her efforts were to no avail. In 1930 the association decided that women should be excluded from its annual dinner altogether. The association eventually accepted women as full members in 1941.[12] Despite these restrictions she was to get plenty of clinical experience as a student in Trinity during the 1918-19 influenza epidemic. Professor William Boxwell was particularly important in her professional development. Stopford was his clinical clerk for six months in the early 1920s, when he described her as taking 'life seriously' and having a 'shy personality'.[13] His emphasis on the importance of post-mortem examinations, later proved useful in her work on TB for which it was vital to ascertain the exact cause of death.[14]

In 1921 after 'trying without success for various posts in Dublin and being quite penniless by this time ... [she] decided to apply really for the Kilbrittain dispensary, in west Cork'.[15] During her appointment at Kilbrittain dispensary Dr Stopford met Dr Alice Barry[16] who had also worked there and whom she described as 'great on babies'.[17] The local government files reveal that Dr Stopford was very concerned about sanitation in Kilbrittain village. Poor hygiene had led to an outbreak of diphtheria in Kilbrittan village. She agued that with some 'simple reforms' the conditions could be improved.[18]

While working in Kilbrittain she met her first case of TB. Her comments regarding the patient reflect the backward nature of Irish medical research at that time something she later tried to rectify through research and publication:

> [A] woman was dying of pulmonary tuberculosis, and alongside of her in the cottage her nine months old baby was fading away; repeated physical examination revealed no signs in the lungs, and when he died, in puzzled ignorance I certified the death as 'Tuberculosis Diathesis'. [Diathesis is a pathological tendency to get certain disease.] Quite incorrectly, there is no such thing; but in 1921 we in Ireland were not taught that infants died of miliary tuberculosis, and I for one had not heard of the tuberculin test, although it was discovered in 1907 by von Pirquet.[19]

The latter had published widely on childhood tuberculosis in the 1910s and 1920s and miliary tuberculosis derives its name from the 'little white spots that are found in the human organs attacked by tuberculosis which are very like millet seeds'.[20] During the 1930s Dr Stopford and Dr Barry were to administer the tuberculin test in St Ultan's Hospital in order to ascertain the presence of tuberculosis.

Dr Stopford's nationalist outlook led to her appointment as medical officer to a Cork brigade of the IRA. She mentions that she had instructions from the headquarters of Cumann na mBan to lecture on first aid to the Kilbrittain branch which:'was closely caught up in the activities of the West Cork Brigade of the IRA and its Flying Column'.[21] A student at Alexandra College, where Dr Price subsequently was appointed as the school doctor, remembered her wearing a man's gold watch given to her by the IRA.[22] She resigned from the Kilbrittain Dispensary in 1923 but over twenty years later she still remembered the 'warm west Cork feeling' and the 'warm-hearted spot'.[23] Dr Price's subsequent career was spent primarily in St Ultan's Hospital for Infants and Royal City of Dublin Hospital (known as Baggot Street), where in the 1930s she made use of the radiological facilities to survey children who were susceptible to TB. In 1925 Dr Stopford married Liam Price, a barrister and district justice in Co.Wicklow, who published widely on the local history of his native county.[24] In a reflection on the relative status of either profession he would have earned £1,200 a year, while dispensary doctors (who admittedly could also have a private practice) earned £300 a year in the late 1920s.[25] Liam Price wrote that it was 'only after several years' experience in dealing with diseases of infants in St Ultan's that Dorothy commenced to take a special interest in tuberculosis.'[26]

In one of her letters to the Crowley family from Kilbrittain, with whom she had kept contact, she asked if Kilbrittain had seen any more 'Doctoresses [they are now] as common as pebbles on a beech'.[27] However, this was quite an exaggeration: while the number of female doctors in the Free State doubled from 208 to 430 between 1926 and 1946, they still constituted less than 10 per cent of all medical practitioners.[28] Women physicians were particularly attracted to paediatrics and public health, and both specialities were combined at St Ultan's Hospital. Female doctors capitalised on the increasing interest in public welfare, and were active in Babies' Clubs, which were established in order to cater for the health of children, and to instruct mothers in childcare.[29] By the 1930s, this innovative hospital for infants, which had been established by Dr Kathleen Lynn and Madeleine ffrench-Mullen in 1919, provided female doctors with an institution which encouraged research in the hope of reducing infant mortality.[30] St Ultan's actively sought to improve the daily lives of children in the newly independent State, and was very open to outside influences. As early as 1922 the hospital's bacteriologist, Miss Jones, visited Berlin to carry out research, establishing a tradition in the hospital of continental research.[31] Dr Price was to enhance that tradition through her tuberculosis and BCG research in Germany and Sweden.

The Introduction of the BCG

The advantages of the BCG vaccine were not universally accepted from the outset, and as a result its introduction was controversial worldwide. Although the vaccine was given successfully to infants in Paris as early as 1923 and Dr Price noted that Professor Wallgren had achieved good results with BCG in a children's hospital in Gothenburg, Sweden in the 1920s,[32] it was not until the 1950s that it was generally accepted by the medical profession. In Northern Ireland BCG vaccination only began in 1949. By the end of 1953 just 22,000 vaccinations had been given, while another 24,000 were administered in 1954. This suggests that Dr Price's use of the vaccine in 1937 was all the more radical.[33]

Why did it take so long for the vaccine to achieve acceptance? Medical historian F.B. Smith has suggested that its acceptance was delayed by 'insularity, ignorance and innuendo'. He reports that the French had adopted the vaccine in 1924, but that 'British doctors dismissed the information and blocked lay attempts to act on it'.[34] British doctors were engaged in a mini Anglo-French war and were instrumental in discouraging New Zealand and Australia from introducing the 'French' vaccine in the 1930s. This resistance within the medical profession was exacerbated by the 'impenetrable' figures and 'gimcrack statistics' presented by Calmette, one of the vaccine's discoverers, to prove its effectiveness. Some of the early sample groups of infants 'disappeared', so it was difficult to calculate mortality rates accurately.[35]

Given the strong connections between British and Irish doctors the determination of the British to dismiss French science delayed Dr Price's work. She believed that tuberculosis was 'closed book' in Ireland due to 'the fact that doctors in Ireland did not read or visit German-speaking centres, and took everything via England'.[36] For example, in 1933 (when Dr Price was attending post-graduate course in Germany on childhood TB) Professor William Mervyn Crofton of University College, Dublin declared that BCG was 'beset with dangers' and furthermore, he maintained that it led to mortality. However, he did not provide any evidence for his assertions.[37]

Dr Price studied under Dr Wassen, who had introduced BCG in Sweden, with great success, and was so impressed with his work that she determinedly told him she would 'brandish' his 'decreased mortality figures in the faces of the authorities'.[38] They were worth brandishing. In Gothenburg the death rate for infants declined from 3.4 per hundred between 1921 and 1926 to 0.3 per hundred in 1933.[39] In the same year, the infant mortality figures in Ireland were frightening: the national rate in 1933 was 6.5 per hundred but 12.6 and 8.3 per hundred respectively for Limerick and Dublin County Boroughs. Figures for England and Wales were not much better with an infant mortality rate of 6.4 per hundred.[40] If one compares the proportion of deaths among Scottish males under one year of age caused by TB (55.92 per cent) with their Swedish counterparts (14.78 per cent), then the effect of BCG is clear. The figures for children between the ages of one and four are even more striking with 53.68 per cent for Scotland and 10.61 per cent for Sweden.[41]

Yet as late as 1953 there were still those who doubted the value of BCG. The authors of a new book, *The White Plague: Tuberculosis, Man and Society*, which Dr Price was asked to review, rejected the role of BCG in reducing mortality rates. She felt the book failed to 'make a good case against' the vaccine, while the statistics cited on page 165 actually made its effectiveness quite clear. When BCG was introduced 'tuberculosis mortality in Japan fell from 280 per thousand in 1945 to 181 in 1948.'[42] Yet the authors declared: 'this does not prove that BCG played any significant part in the control of the disease for expertise has repeatedly shown that tuberculosis increases during wars and revolutions and recedes rapidly when social conditions return to normal'. Furthermore they argued, in a passage which was highlighted, probably by Price, that 'tuberculosis will recede as it has always done spontaneously when life has become easier and happier'.[43] These social explanations, while partially accurate, provided yet another barrier to the introduction of BCG.

BCG in Ireland

The medical care of infants was not given a high priority in Ireland in the first half of the twentieth century. The scientific approach in medicine was relatively new and there was still much research to be done particularly in paediatric medicine. Dr Price's investigations into childhood tuberculosis became her 'life work'. Not one to depend on tradition or old wives' tales, 'she tested everything out for herself in a thoroughly critical scientific spirit'. The resistance that the application of new knowledge encountered led her at one stage to declare: 'the blood stream does not obey nuns' rules' when trying to explain how children infected each other in hospital.[44] At this time it was not uncommon for healthy children to walk through tuberculosis wards in Irish hospitals despite the risk of infection.[45]

Dr Price's approach to TB was influenced by a number of other Irish doctors. Dr Katherine Maguire's work at St Ultan's[46] had a powerful effect. It 'was from Dr Katherine Maguire that I learnt to take an interest in clinical observation; or rather renewed an interest inculcated in my student days by Professor William Boxwell.' In a wonderful vignette she described learning from Dr Maguire:

> For about nine years I had imbibed wisdom from her in St Ultan's Hospital, making a point of doing her round with her, and she would pause at the last cot, with the baby clutching her fingers

whilst she drifted off into a very interesting discourse, drawing on her great experiences and her wealth of reading. She was a very clever woman and Sister Mulligan and I enjoyed these bedside talk, when she would range far and wide … Dr Maguire encouraged any never-so-feeble evidences of an enquiring mind, and urged one to take trouble to find things out and to read and publish. During her last illness in 1930-1 I carried on her extensive practice for her which indeed she left in my hands in the end. She wrote me frequent and almost indecipherable letters about her patients up to the end. She was very indignant when I said some lady was suffering from Anno Domini.[47]

It is clear from Dr Price's later career that she heeded Dr Maguire's advice to read and publish. As a lecturer on hygiene at Alexandra College since 1893, Dr Maguire was described as an 'exceptionally gifted teacher'.[48] However, she was reticent to promote her work to her fellow professionals. Although a member of the Academy of Medicine, her 'self-effacing disposition did not permit her to speak or to show cases'.[49] Dr Price, however, used these professional meetings to introduce continental research on TB to Irish doctors.

Dr Ella Webb, a former student at Alexandra College, Dublin, who had been medical inspector at St Paul's Girls' School between 1904 and 1923[50] while Dorothy was a student there, was another influence.[51] Dr Price enthused about her work in Dublin: 'she lets me go down and help her in her slum dispensary on Tuesday evenings and shows what simply wonderful things a person can do besides doctoring'. She contrasted Dr Webb, who, indeed, is much more the Sinn Féin sort, you'd think.'[52] Her enthusiasm for Dr Webb's work was enhanced further when they both worked in the Sunshine Home for Children in Stillorgan, sharing an interest with Katherine Maguire in diseases which were exacerbated by socio-economic deprivation.

Dr Price's interest in tuberculosis can be attributed to her colleague, Dr Nora O'Leary. She recounts how the disease was not foremost in her mind: 'until 1932 when Nora O'Leary came as house-physician to St Ultan's'.[53] Dr O'Leary had a 'very good analytical brain and an inquiring turn of mind', and once they began testing the patients both Drs Price and O'Leary read as much as they could about TB.[54] Dr O'Leary was to travel to Germany with two St Ultan's patients, who were cured there. Her visit helped immensely as Dr Price was warmly welcomed in Germany subsequently. She felt that 'Dr O'Leary must have written to every one and asked them to be nice.'[55] Another influence was Dr Bob Collins, who had worked with Professor Wallgren in Gothenburg.[56] When Dr Collins founded the Irish Paediatric Club in 1933 (it later became the Irish Paediatric Association), its first meeting was held at Dr Price's home in 10 Fitzwilliam Place.[57]

As stated earlier, the scale of the TB problem in Ireland was enormous. While the tuberculosis rate in Ireland was declining, the Irish Free State still had the 'highest incidence of tuberculosis mortality in young adults among twenty-four European and North American countries'.[58] Evidence that Irish and Welsh nurses were 250 per cent more likely to 'develop lesions' than their English colleagues suggested that Celtic nations seemed to be far more likely to suffer from the disease.[59] While the tuberculosis death rate continued to decline gradually in the 1930s with the lowest rate ever being recorded in 1938 (1.09 per thousand), it remained a major killer of young people.[60] This state of affairs was likely to continue as long as the Irish medical profession remained aloof from continental research on tuberculosis.

Dr Price played an extremely important role in the changing this situation by gaining experience on the Continent. She completed a postgraduate course in Bavaria in 1934 where her colleagues were 'mostly Danish, German and Swiss'.[61] Given the increasing tensions prior to the outbreak of the Second World War it was rare to see English-speaking doctors benefit from continental ideas, particularly in Germany. Her international experience continued and in the summer of 1935 she represented St Ultan's with Dr Rose O'Doherty in Rome at an International Hospitals Federation Congress. She inspected Italian hospitals and noted that, like Ireland, they did little to prevent TB. All of this research and activity ultimately led to the introduction of BCG in 1937 by Dorothy Price.

Given the amount of international scepticism regarding BCG, the need for clinical testing of the vaccine was paramount in order to convince the medical establishment prior to introducing it in Ireland. As a physician in the Royal City of Dublin Hospital, Baggot Street in the 1930s and 1940s Dr Price was able to conduct these tests. She also tuberculin tested healthy students from Coláiste Moibhí, a Protestant preparatory college for primary teachers. As medical officer at the college she 'knew the family and personal history of each pupil' which facilitated her work. Dr Alice Barry who had come to work at Peamount Sanatorium, which was established by the Women's National Health Association to cater for TB patients, also contributed by introducing the tuberculin test, which could diagnose the presence of TB. They actually discovered that contrary to the original diagnosis some of the patients at Peamount were not suffering from TB at all.[62]

A further discovery during these tests indicated that it was vital to locate tuberculosis patients as early as possible to avoid further facilities. Dr Price noted:

Our success with the diagnostic employment of tuberculin allowed us further to differentiate between curable and incurable cases; treatment proved most successful in primary lesions, but [was] completely ineffective where the disease had already progressed to a later stage.[63]

She further argued that 'early recognition of the primary infection followed by immediate treatment would do more to lower the death-rate from tuberculosis than perfectly equipped sanatoriums dealing with the established disease.[64] This waste of sanatorium space could therefore have been prevented by wider use of the tuberculin test, but it was treated with 'scepticism'.

While she was a student at TCD the tuberculin test had been considered to be 'faddy and useless'.[65] In the mid-1930s Price noted:

… some slight interest in the subject [tuberculin testing] was evinced, but in general I do not think anyone regarded it as having any relation to reality and certainly the Department of Health and the local authorities showed no enthusiasm for skin-testing as a public health measure by their TB officers.[66]

Nonetheless, aided by her republican connections and those of St Ultan's, the hospital received funding from the hospitals' sweepstakes which went, in part, towards providing tuberculosis costs.[67] Her efforts to combat the disease did not focus purely on medical research. She was a member of the Irish Clean Milk Society, which sought to prevent infections through milk consumption. However, she was frustrated at the lax attitude towards those who were convicted under the legislation against dirty milk, and people continued to be infected with TB from contaminated milk.[68]

Dr Price's thesis on 'Primary Tuberculosis of the Lungs of Children' was accepted for an MD degree by TCD in 1935 and was subsequently published in the *Irish Journal of Medical Science*. However, her views, though widely endorsed on the Continent, were not immediately accepted by Irish doctors. The *Irish Journal of Medical Science* was not read by many GPs who were the front-line troops in the fight against tuberculosis, but even academics did not take her work on board.

To counteract medical ignorance, Dr Price invited Dr Pagel, a childhood tuberculosis expert whom she had befriended on the Continent, to come to Ireland in 1937 to give a talk to the Royal College of Physicians. According to Dr Price, his talk 'marked an advance in the development of modern views on tuberculosis among Dublin doctors.' Furthermore, Pagel examined specimens in St Ultan's which provided further illuminations for Dr Price, and taught her how to recognise TB. Her published work also brought others in contact with her work on tuberculosis. For example, in 1938 she published a paper in the *British Medical Journal* based on the seventy-eight cases who had received BCG in St Ultan's, and she wrote on the 'Hospital Treatment for Tuberculosis Children' for the *Journal of the Irish Free State Medical Union*. This publication was received by all members of the union therefore her views finally reached a wide medical audience. In this article she argued that a provision for paediatric beds should be a priority in the spending of funds allocated towards the elimination of tuberculosis.[69] This would ensure that the disease was treated in its early stages, thereby increasing the changes of eliminating it.

As well as medical intransigence, she faced the woolly thinking of those whose approach to medicine was not as scientific as her own. Part of her task was changing the perceptions of the medical profession and, according to her husband, her 'work in producing statistical proof of the value of tuberculosis testing and of the correctness of the continental views helped to convert the Dublin medical schools'.[70] This was a slow process however, and was not complete until a decade after she conducted her tests in St Ultan's and elsewhere.

Dr Price also took practical steps to combat the disease in Ireland. In 1935, she started a weekly tuberculosis clinic at St Ultan's and by 1936 its TB unit had ten cots. However, this was insufficient, as there was big demand for tuberculosis infant beds.[71] In the same year, she was granted permission by the Department of Local Government and Public Health to import the BCG vaccine. It arrived at St Ultan's hospital on 26 January 1937.[72] This made St Ultan's the first hospital in Great Britain and Ireland to use it. [73] As a result of the vaccine St Ultan's drastically reduced its TB mortality rate from 77 per cent to 28 per cent.[74] Between 1933 and 1936 she treated seventy-eight tuberculosis patients, sixty of whom died, whereas between 1937 and 1942, 169 were treated and 132 were cured.[75] In 1942 she declared: 'our whole effort is directed towards early diagnosis'.[76] Price wished to inoculate children before they had the chance to contract TB, hence her emphasis on early diagnosis. Poor facilities for paediatrics, which were not a high priority in medicine anyway, retarded her work.[77] She was particularly frustrated by the continued lack of accommodation at St Ultan's. In 1937 she noted: 'our infant hospital is very crowded with pneumonias and gastro-enteritis'. This was, however, not wholly unjustified as the latter was the biggest killer of infants in the hospital throughout the 1930s.[78]

Realising that more space was required in order to implement a full paediatric medical service and to fulfil the need for a fully equipped children's hospital, St Ultan's sought to amalgamate with the National Children's Hospital at Harcourt Street. The architect Michael Scott had drawn up plans for the site of a new children's hospital alongside St Ultan's. However, greater powers were at work. The fact that neither of these two hospitals were under the control of the Roman Catholic Church raised some worries in that quarter. In December 1935 St Ultan's received a letter from Dr Byrne, the Roman Catholic Archbishop of Dublin. He expressed his fear that 'in such a united institution the faith of Catholic children (who will be 99 per cent of the total treated) would not be safe'.[79] He also outlined his suspicion that sterilisation might take place in the hospital. These objections were passed on to Dr Price, as secretary of the medical board of St Ultan's, by the hospital's administrator, Madeleine ffrench-Mullen.[80] The Roman Catholic Church managed large Dublin hospitals like St Vincent's and the Mater and was keen to control medical activity particularly where it involved children.* St Ultan's plans for extension came to naught and instead a large children's hospital was built in Crumlin with the Church's blessing. The implementation of Price's plans were thus put on hold for a decade, and St Ultan's remained too small to cater for all childhood tuberculosis cases.

Despite this setback, Dr Price continued to promote continental approaches to the elimination of childhood tuberculosis. In March

1939 Professor Wallgren was in England and Dr Price invited him to speak to the Irish Paediatric Club, hoping his voice would influence the reluctant government. She wrote: 'childhood Tuberculosis is as yet untouched here by the Government, and when they start to do something I hope that it will be on Gothenburg lines and not on English'. Dr Price wrote to Sean T. O'Kelly, the Minister for Local Government and Public Health, and invited him to Walgren's talk. He declined. Wallgren visited St Ultan's and his lectures were published in the *Irish Journal of Medical Science* in 1939.[81] In the same year Dr Price spoke in Belfast on tuberculosis in adolescents and her talk was reported in the national papers. The process of educating both the profession and the public was a long one but dividends were gradually becoming evident. Dr P.F. Fitzpatrick, a regular correspondent of Dr Price and the Cork tuberculosis officer, began 'routine tuberculin testing' in the late 1930s. Meanwhile the physician at Crooksling (the Dublin Corporation Sanatorium) finally forbade infants and children on visits thereby diminishing the risk of infection.[82]

Final Success

Dr Price's work was interrupted by the Second World War when it was impossible to obtain BCG. However, in 1942 her book *Tuberculosis in Childhood* was published which enhanced her 'international reputation' and such was its success that a second edition was published in 1948.[83] Subsequently she was nominated for the World Health Organisation Leon Bernard Prize for contribution to social medicine. After the war her campaign for the treatment of TB was finally successful. The BCG vaccine again became available and records indicate that Dr Wallgren supplied St Ultan's with it three times a week via airmail. Dr Price noted that in Ireland BCG was used exclusively at St Ultan's.[84] By 1946 the TB unit at St Ultan's had finally been extended to thirty cots and Dr Price reported 'remarkable progress in the prevention and cure of tuberculosis in children up to five years'. By the late forties her work was accepted by others working with infants. Dr Alan Browne, the Master of the Rotunda between 1960 and 1966, noted:

> O'Donel Browne [master 1947-1952] supported the introduction
> of BCG infant vaccination as prophylactics against tuberculosis,
> which was initiated as a public health measure in the Rotunda in

1949, under the supervision of Sr Pearl Dunleavy. It *gradually* [my emphasis] became widely accepted with long term benefits that still prevail in Ireland.[85]

Her work in researching BCG and propagating the results in Ireland paved the way for 'official recognition' of the value of the vaccine from the State. This became clear when the new Minister of Health, Dr Noel Browne, located the new National BCG centre at St Ultan's in 1949. In a letter to her Crowley friends from Kilbrittain, Co. Cork, she mentioned she had been 'trying to push this new BCG vaccination against tuberculosis', and that they were 'lucky' with the new Minister of Health: 'he is a splendid young fellow & doing a lot for tuberculosis'. Despite her appreciation for the new Clann na Poblachta minister she remained committed to the anti-treaty side as she 'still voted for Dev'.[86] Dr John Cowell, the medical director of the new national BCG scheme, pointed out that 'the energetic work of Dorothy Price … [may be seen] as a landmark in the history of Irish preventative medicine'.[87] The first report of the National BCG Committee stated:

> The initiation of BCG vaccination will always be linked with the name of Dr Dorothy Price. Due to her conviction of the value of this preventative measure and to her individual endeavour sufficient clinical evidence was made available to her work at St Ultan's Hospital to warrant the adoption of BCG vaccination on a larger scale in Ireland.[88]

Dr Price's hectic schedule, her many hospital appointments (she was consulting physician to the Royal Hospital for Consumptives in Ireland as well as Baggot Street, St Ultan's and Sunshine Home commitments) and the demands of her private practice had caught up with her. In 1939 she got an attack of 'muscular rheumatism', which continued to affect her over subsequent years. Despite her ill health her enthusiasm never waned. In a letter to Dr Wassen she admitted that she did not obey the doctor's orders to stop work at five o'clock 'but it was worth it to get the BCG across'. Determined to have her methods adopted, she reported to Dr Wassen: 'I had the Minister [Dr Noel Browne] here twice & finally persuaded him to do what I wanted.' In 1948 Dr Price said she was looking forward to 'the day when BCG vaccination will be given to all infants (irrespective of contract) at an early age, thus affording protection from nurse, milk, casual contact and unknown source'.[89] That day finally arrived in the 1950s. The nation-wide BCG vaccination programme ensured that 100,000 vaccinations were administered by 1955 while the target was half a million.[90] Subsequently the incidence of TB in Ireland was reduced to an absolute minimum. It is easy to be critical of the human wastage which resulted from the slow acceptance of BCG. However, Ireland was not unique in its tardy attitude to medical research. In 1971 the editor of *Tubercle* remarked in reviewing fifty years of BCG that 'future historians will find the story of BCG vaccination a strange mixture of endeavour, inertia and ineptitide'.[91] By 1950 there was a worldwide acceptance of the value of BCG. Mass vaccination under the auspices of the World Health Organisation (WHO), which had been established in 1948, was begun internationally in the late 1940s and early 1950s.[92] In Ireland the experience gained as a result of Dr Price's endeavours paved the way for a relatively speedy introduction. When vaccination was instituted on a nationwide basis in Britain in the 1950s as well, some medical staff there benefited from her work when they came to Ireland in order to train.[93] The State-driven BCG campaign in Ireland also benefited from the co-operation it then received from Church leaders who gave access to schools and allowed local clergymen to announce the arrival of the vaccination team in the locality. This facilitated the dissemination of information and the ultimate acceptance of BCG by both the profession and the public.[94]

Dr Price's efforts show that while 1930s Ireland appeared increasingly self-obsessed and stagnant there was still room for energetic and determined individuals to make their mark. Her travels abroad, her international reputation as well as the vital part she played in the elimination of childhood TB indicate that the insular Ireland of the popular consciousness is not entirely valid. Furthermore, the focus on Church-State relations and the Noel Browne saga have clouded the achievements of lesser known and possibly more quietly effective individuals such as Dr Dorothy Stopford-Price. The State programme of BCG vaccination was part of 1950s and '60s Ireland, but the crucial process of gaining medical acceptance for the vaccine was begun in the 1930s. Although Dr Price claimed that 'doctoresses' were 'as common as pebbles on a beach', the ripples of this particular pebble were felt long after her passing in 1954.

Chapter 11

Flower power and 'mental grooviness': nurses and midwives in Ireland in the early twentieth century

> It requires a woman's hand to settle flowers. The flowers are ...
> a symbol. They are friendly, they are colour, they are silent. So I
> ... have found my nurses. (*Irish Nursing News*, September 1927,
> p. 627.)

Many would associate Florence Nightingale with the foundation
of professional nursing, though she would have been aghast at the
term 'professional nurse'. Her legacy was an ambivalent one, as she
focuses on the vocational aspects of the occupation to the detriment
of professionalisation. While nursing was not a desirable occupation, religious orders in the nineteenth century, such as the Sisters
of Charity of St Vincent de Paul founded in 1633, were possibly the
largest nursing organisation in the world. Their legacy of a 'pious
motive' in the care of the ill was also to affect the status of the emerging profession of nursing.[1] If Nightingale wished to make nursing
attractive for 'gentlewomen', the nursing orders wished to make it
part of Christian philanthropy; neither emphasised the professional
preparation of nurses and proper working conditions.

The preparation of Irish women in philanthropic endeavour has
been discussed by Luddy.[2] This included hospital work, where nuns
were prominent as carers for the ill. St Vincent's hospital in Dublin,
established in 1834 by the Sisters of Charity, and hospitals in Cork
(1857) and Dublin (1861) run by the Sisters of Mercy consolidated

the female presence in Irish hospitals.[3] However, a century earlier, voluntary hospitals, such as Jervis Street, and the House of Industry hospitals and Sir Patrick Dun's, had been established in Dublin, under the auspices of Protestant philanthropic endeavour. These institutions were to train professional nurses in the nineteenth and twentieth centuries, though their historical background often meant that nurses were trained in Victorian, if not Georgian, institutions (both in terms of décor and discipline). Nuns, with their willingness to provide inexpensive care, established a tradition of poor pay and arduous hours for nurses. Additionally, lay women found it difficult to 'compete with the resources, commitment, sense of authority and religious spirit shown by the nuns'.[4] In a sense, their legacy was similar to that of Nightingale's, as vocational commitment, not professional preparation, was emphasised.

This essay will focus on the training and working conditions of nurses which suggest that nursing was not a high-status profession. Furthermore, the relationship between the emphasis placed on Christian ideals in the profession and the subservience of nurses will be examined in addition to the role of the religious orders in nursing.

Training and Working Conditions

In a lecture to the Statistical and Social Inquiry Society of Ireland in 1920, Dr Ninan Falkiner, formerly a lecturer at the Dublin Metropolitan Technical School for Nurses, which was founded in 1893, and later a Master of the Rotunda, discussed the position of nurses. Appropriately, he quoted Shakespeare who described a page as 'kind', 'duteous', 'diligent', 'so tender over his occasions true', 'so Nurse-like'. This image of nurses was to persist. However, Falkiner glided over the conflicts between nurses, and he was unaware of Nightingale's unpopularity. A prominent matron, Alice Reeves of Dr Steevens' Hospital, commented on Falkiner's lecture. Reeves thought that much needed to be done 'before the public … [could] feel confident' in nurses. She pointed out that, prior to State registration, which had been introduced in 1919, 'nursing was the calling of the dunce of the family'. In order to prepare students properly for a nursing career, Reeves wished to establish a pre-nursing school in Dublin.[5]

Miss Vera Matheson, in response to the lecture, commented on the authoritarian atmosphere in hospital; 'no amount of ethical teaching administered by lecture and class to a group of nurses can counteract the evil effect of the example of a harsh sister or senior nurse who makes use of her privileges to speak to her juniors as if they were naughty children.' Some of the probationers were treated like a 'charwoman'. Furthermore, a lack of co-operation between probationers and staff, as well as superior attitudes, prevented many from taking up the profession. The hospitals were 'hard schools of suffering, servitude, and self-sacrifice', she argued. This 'tyrannical despotism' was not to the benefit of women in the profession.[6] However, the attraction of a respectable profession and its association with traditional female virtues encouraged many to opt for a career in nursing.

There seemed to be no shortage of females willing to begin nursing in Ireland. According to the novelist, Canon Sheehan, writing in 1917, the 'eagerness and zeal with which the profession of nursing has been taken up of late years by hundreds of young ladies throughout the land' was seen as 'proof' that nursing was the 'natural duty and calling of young girls.'[7] The fact that males could not train as nurses in Ireland, or that many occupations were unavailable for females was not considered. However, females were not always encouraged to adopt the profession for which they were allegedly so well fitted. Medical practitioner, Dr Ryan, in the *Irish Monthly*, argued that …

> … as far as possible the care of the sick and infirm poor should be given to religious orders … There is room for all … let the trained nurse supply the manual and technical skill, the nuns supply the supervision, the sympathy and the spirit of charity, which are far more important, and which their self-sacrifice and devotion render them most competent to supply.[8]

This vision of nursing care pervaded many institutions. Lay nurses worked as auxiliaries, while the nuns supervised their activities.

The emphasis on discipline in nursing was universal. Self denial, while a feature of Catholic social thinking, makes a regular appearance in the nursing journals. However, its emphasis was not confined to Catholic-run institutions.[9] In July 1929, the *Quarterly Journal of the International Council of Nursing* pointed out that the nurse's role was 'of a moral kind'. The discoveries of Louis Pasteur changed the way nurses were trained, and the author admitted that the 'nursing sisters were temporarily taken aback' by the scientific discoveries.

However, the hierarchies inherent in the preparation of nurses were made clear in the following statement. In France, the doctors and surgeons 'selected particularly intelligent members of the nursing staff and instructed them to in their methods. These sisters then gave the real nursing care and took responsibility for the patients, while the other sisters continued with their subordinate tasks as attend-ants and domestic worker'. All French nursing orders were advised to take the 'State diploma' and their schools of nursing were 'accred-ited by the State'. Additionally, the schools accepted 'well-educated young women as lay-student'.[10] Chaptal, the author of an article on international trends in nursing, believed the nuns' 'technical equip-ment' was 'on a level with their moral influence'.[11]

However, difficulties also arose in France in the 1920s between the Daughters of Charity and Dr Anna Hamilton, an Irish doctor involved in nursing reform in Bordeaux in France. The introduction of a nursing school was seen as a 'veiled and ill-conceived attempt by politicians to squeeze the nursing sisters out of hospitals'. Nuns were not allowed to care for pregnant patients or change the nappies of male infants. But the doctors were wary of giving qualifications to lay nurses as they might usurp the medical profession's authority. Nuns, by preserving the status quo, were, therefore, more acceptable to the doctors. Eventually, the nuns and the lay students trained in separate institutions.[12] Dr Hamilton was very critical of the religious orders in nursing as they were, she argued, 'devoid of all training.'[13]

At the Hôtel Dieu hospital in Beaune, France, the nursing nuns faced a similar situation as the French medical profession was begin-ning to place increasing emphasis on State qualifications. Soeur Jacques, the superioress of the Hôtel Dieu, pointed out that when the State diploma for nurses was introduced in 1922:

> The governing board of the Hôtel Dieu took the necessary steps to secure the hospital nurse diploma for their nursing sisters. Their claims having been proved by the records the sisters received [in] the equivalent [of the State certificate] granted during the transi-tion period; they are thus virtual holders of the State certificate'

Virtual reality reigned in Beaune. Soeur Jacques felt the 'spiritual vitamins' available in Beaune helped refine and elevate the minds of the patients. The patients' minds were also diverted by the frescos on the wall. They could perhaps have done without these diversions given that the frescos frequently depicted scenes of hell. Finally, the superioress argued that 'the regulation of the Hôtel Dieu, first drafted over five centuries ago, do not require the sisters to obtain a State diploma.'[14] The fact that medicine might have changed in half a millennium was not considered. Hence, despite the increasing encroachment of the State, tradition still held sway. The State, in both Ireland and France and indeed Italy, was heavily dependent on religious orders for the provision of health services.[15] It was not surprising, therefore, that in some cases when nursing nuns came under pressure to professionalise their experience, they received support from the local community.

Kelly's study of Irish workhouses in the period up to 1921 reveals in Thomastowm, county Kilkenny, the bishop was told by one nursing nun that, 'nuns require no special preparation except the instructions they receive from their Reverend Mother on nursing'. This perspective was not unique. The *Freeman's Journal* asked: 'what is a trained nurse? A chit of a girl with a paper certificate from some Dublin hospital … or, a devoted nun'.[16] Clearly, nuns were seen as superior to lay nurses, regardless of qualifications. Not surprisingly, therefore, characteristics associated with nuns such as piety and self-discipline were present in the training of women for the nursing profession.

Sr Catherine Black, who came from a Presbyterian background, suggested, in her autobiography, that nursing 'demands the most constant self-sacrifice'.[17] While Annie Smithson, editor of the *Irish Nursing and Hospital World*, stressed the close monitoring of probationers; 'living out is considered unsuitable for probationers, as the training is ethical as well as practical, and she has to study as well as work, and needs supervision to secure proper rest'. Somewhat optimistically, she suggested that trainee nurses enjoyed 'all the amenities of a comfortable and sometimes luxurious home'. Smithson then asked: 'what other profession costs so little-feeds, part clothes, gives laundry allowance and pocket money during the course of training?' Given that one's accommodation was catered for and there was very little chance that one would be led astray in large cities, where rural probationers trained, nursing was also designed to ensure that nurses put patients first. Smithson noted 'a keen nurse generally likes to see her patient through the crisis of an illness with little thought of the strain upon herself'.[18]

Nonetheless, some criticism was articulated. Percy Brown of the Red Cross argued that 'mental work done by those in training for a

profession was not ideal form of discipline'.[19] Gender was a vital element in obtaining most nursing positions. Many jobs were specific
for female nurses. For appointments as a public health nurse, one had
to be 'of the female sex' and unmarried, or a widow.[20] Male nurses
(there were less than ten in the Irish Free State in the 1920s) were paid
more that their female colleagues.[21] The absence of male competition
was seen as advantage by Margaret Huxley who was influential in
establishing training for nurses. As they were entering a labour market
virtually devoid of the opposite sex, women had opportunities in
nursing which they were denied in other professions.[22]

One view on nurses' education suggests that nurses were trained,
rather than educated. In the words of one matron, training was a
question of 'survival of the fittest'.[23] If the application forms for
training in maternity hospitals are examined, then the endurance
required by nurses was substantial. One form for an Irish hospital stated 'all nurses and students are required to be total abstainers
during the time they are working and another for the Manchester
Maternity Hospital included the question: 'are you strong and well?'
The matron of Belfast Maternity Hospital had to check that all
nurses took the 'proper amount of rest and exercise'.[24]

The nursing reformer, Dr Anna Hamilton, had a vision of nurses
which, ironically, complied with a religious view of the profession.
All nurses, she suggested should lead a 'life of celibacy, sacrificing
marriage and family to devote themselves body and soul to caring
for the sick and poor.' Even more paradoxically, considering that she
was a female doctor, Hamilton declared: 'it is extremely ridiculous
for a nurse who possesses neither the knowledge nor the rights nor
the sex of the doctor, to try to imitate his way of interacting with
the patient and to try to use his language'. She believed that 'character' and 'proper feminine behaviour' remained the primary criteria
for admitting students, and grading their performances during the
two-year training period'. Students were examined in fifteen areas.
Two of these could be described as technical skills; the remaining
thirteen related to social skills. Dr Hamilton stressed the importance
of 'punctuality, calmness, docility, reflection, [the State of one's] uniform, cleanliness, patience, kindness, coiffure, discipline, conscience,
manners, and voice'.[25]

The training of nurses reflected the desire to provide competent
and compliant medical help. With the emphasis on long hours and
obedience, it prepared nurses for the conditions they would face as

fully-trained professionals. The long working day of nurses was the subject of considerable discussions. While nurses sought an eight-hour day, hospital authorities repeatedly pointed out that they could not afford it.[26] Another argument suggested that nurses should accept suffering, whether it arose from their own fatigue or patients' ill health, as it was an integral part of the profession's underlying philosophy. Such belief were heavily influenced by Christian idealism which saw suffering as a means to gain access to God.[27] In an address by Revd J.H. Farrell, at the fifth annual congress of the Irish nursing profession, in early 1929, medical care was linked to Christianity:

> Death is inevitable, and so are suffering and disease. The nurse, therefore will need in the exercise of her profession, not only the divine charity to alleviate distress, but the virtue of faith which teaches her to see in human suffering a painful but a necessary part of the divine plan by which a loving God is working out of the salvation of an immortal soul at the cost, perhaps, of suffering to the merely physical frame.

There are many references to Calvary and the need for pain in order to achieve salvation. He concluded with the view that the nurse was to her patients, 'as a mother to her child'. She should 'accept joyfully the will of God'.[28] These ideas were not new in the 1920s Ireland, but doctors did not seem to be subjected to similar views. Females were seen as comforters of the sick, not alleviators of pain. That, it seems, was left in male hands.

Female stereotypes were also used, particularly by male commentators, to justify difficult working conditions. Fr Gerhard, at a monthly meeting of Irish nurses, assured his listeners, 'in your profession – which ranks among the noblest to which a woman can give her life – you will meet ingratitude from your patients often, but never from God and never from Her who will take your service to them as given to Her son'. Furthermore, he appealed to a woman whose ideal life they should emulate, 'take Mary Immaculate as your model in your profession; invoke her powerful intercession with the entire confidence'.[29] Fr McKeown reinforced this link between suffering, women and Mary Immaculate:

> … at times it would seem as if the nurse were a receptacle for abuse. Try to accept these sufferings in the proper spirit – in the

spirit of the Blessed Virgin ... by accepting your sufferings in the proper spirit you are helping Jesus to carry His cross and you are weaving your heavenly crown.[30]

Nursing was seen as a way to fulfil one's duties within the professional world. This made it acceptable as a career for women. As Cahill pointed out, 'short of the priesthood and the religious life, there is no vocation holier or in which you may advance to closer union with God than that of your own chosen profession in which Christ's brethren – and often the very least of these – is so especially in your charge'.[31] This interlinking of women, nursing and Christian duty was echoed in other religious quarters also. The Revd Potter, suggested, in a speech on the moral advantages of nursing, in early 1928, 'in other careers for women, one or two talents are required and exercised; in the nursing profession every talent given by God to woman gets fair play and is increased manifold'.[32] Women were sanctified by their profession, but their sanctity did not save them from arduous work. In a sense, it was used to deify dire conditions.

Nevertheless, due to the prevalence of beliefs about the Christian, self-sacrificing nature of Irish womanhood, those who sought access to nursing training outside of Ireland were at an advantage over women from other backgrounds. By the late 1920s, there were long waiting lists for the acceptance into nursing training and many young Irish women travelled to Britain to start their careers. In 1931, the *Irish Nursing and Hospital World*, reporting on the work of the Lancet Commission into nursing, suggested that, in England, in all Irish women who applied to hospitals for training were engaged, and the weeding out process took place later. Irish women were seen as 'more spiritually inclined'; they saw nursing as more of a vocation.[33]

The fact that some of the biggest hospitals in Ireland, such as the Mater and St Vincent's in Dublin, were run by religious orders also explains the emphasis on spirituality. Nurses in the Mater Hospital had a three-day annual retreat, but according to Miss Harold, the assistant matron, the nurses felt it was 'too short'.[34] As well as the spiritual element, the retreat was probably a welcome rest from the physical exertion of work.

Fr Fahey, who founded Marie Duce, a Dublin-based, middle-class, Catholic organisation, suggested that 'an interior attitude of full acceptance of God's plan of life is an indispensable part of a fully-trained nurse's equipment'. Nurses were supposed to be spiritually fortified. In their free time, Fahy advised nurses to avoid novels, as they had no reference to the supernatural, and they took the nurse's mind away from her 'duty'.[35] Given the constant presence of death, it is not surprising that nurses were continually reminded of their moral duties. The profession was part of the ongoing battle against, what was termed, the 'specious sophistries and arrogant theories of secularist, [and the] goddess hygenia'.[36] The military metaphor was appropriate, as medicine was often the battleground for various theories, whether theological or social. The military regime of some hospitals also reflected the origins of modern nursing in the Crimean War, and the military experience of some nurses. For example, Miss McLoughlin, the matron of Temple Street Children's hospital, had been matron-in-chief of the Irish Free State Military Service.[37] Furthermore, Irish nurses served in Queen Alexandra's Imperial Military Nursing Service (QAIMNS). Anne O'Brien, who later became matron at Peamount Sanatorium, served in QAIMNS during the Second World War, while Sir Patrick Dun's matron, Miss P.W. Northey, trained in Guy's Hospital in London, and served as a military nurse in England and India.[38]

This was not to suggest that all nurses accepted difficult working conditions. There were occasional voices who, in the words of Ruth Nicholls, honourary secretary of the Irish Guild of Catholic Nurses and a nurse in the North Infirmary, Cork, wished to 'ventilate' the disadvantages of nursing. She felt that the work was 'exacting'. Nurses ran the risks of 'spiritual slackness, of mental grooviness [expressing their own point of view, or acting as individuals], of physical overstrain, and of relative poverty'.[39] However, if anything, the sanctification of the profession was supposed to compensate for any material disadvantages. 'Mental grooviness', or individual expression, was also on the mind of Miss A. M. Fitzgerald, assistant matron at Cork Street Fever hospital. She lamented the lack of 'social intercourse' between hospitals. Rugby was the only inter-hospital game, and nurses could not take part. She asked why there were not inter-hospital competitions in tennis, hockey and swimming as she pointed out that 'mental grooviness and physical overstrain would probably disappear if we had'.[40] The long working day may have made it difficult to organise these extra activities. However, mixed tennis matches between nurses and doctors at the Royal Victoria Hospital in Belfast were greatly enjoyed by all.[41]

At the quarterly meeting of the National Council of Trained Nurses, held in Dublin, in 1928, with Alice Reeves, the Matron of Sir Patrick Dun's presiding, the conditions of nurses in county homes and county hospitals were discussed.[42] Later in the year, a deputation from the Irish Nurses' Association met Richard Mulcahy, Minister for Local Government and Public Health, to discuss the poor condition in county homes and other 'institutions under the several Boards of Health'. Issues such as salaries, rations, accommodation and hours on duty of 'trained temporary nurses and the inadequacy of nursing staffs in some of the institutions were aired'.[43] Louie Bennett, general secretary of the Irish Workers' Union of which the Irish Nurses' Union was a member, summarised the nurses' predicament. They were seen as 'heroines whose mission it is to live in poverty, and wear themselves out in long hours of hard toil, so as to bring ease to the sick and help the government and general public practice economy'.[44]

Complaints by nurses of their conditions were not always appreciated. Annie Smithson, secretary of the Irish Nurses' Union, 'heartily' agreed with Alice Reeves who felt that 'the grievances of the nursing profession mostly belonged to the misfits'.[45] Hence, there was little support from female colleagues despite the difficulties. Would the presence of males in the profession have made a difference? The most unionised nursing group was the mental nurses, where males predominated. Yet, male nurses faced discrimination because they could not train in the Irish Free State.[46]

Part of the difficulty about working conditions lay with the matrons who were in charge of the nurses. Miss Musson, matron at the Royal Victoria in Belfast, articulated a view which was shared by many matrons. She argued that the shortage of candidates in the United Kingdom was due to the profession being 'judged by the conditions of the past and not by those of the present … an erroneous idea of overwork, under-feeding, and under-pay exists, and exaggerated reports of treatment of seniors remain in the minds of possible candidates and parents'. In a reference to recently introduced legislation which stipulated a forty-four hour working week, she asked: 'we know many things in our conditions of service need improvement, but would legislation be in the best interests of the profession? Would a farseeing nurse not rather evolve a code through their organisation and from within, as all professions have done before them.' Nurses, however, did not have the necessary autonomy to decide their own working week. Musson believed that strikes were totally unacceptable, 'we have

seen some hospitals tragedies of down tools encouraged by publicity.'
As regards general conditions, she pointed out that there was much
talk of 'the lack of freedom, excess of discipline, and a good deal of
unnecessary talk about aching feet and stretched nerves.' However, this
was partly because students entered the profession with little preparation. Grievances, she argued, were 'more fancied than real'. Those who
complained of 'unjust treatment by sisters are usually not conscientious
in the discharge of their duties'. Any dissatisfaction, then, was seen as
an indulgence. Reinforcing the subservient, if not servile nature of the
profession (excluding matrons, of course, who had a lot of authority),
Musson pointed out that 'courtesy required from probationers should
not be mistaken for servility, recognition of senior members is only
good breeding'.[47]

This attitude was no consolation to the nurses employed by the
Sligo Board of Health whose working day began at 7 a.m. and finished at 9 p.m. They had two hours off duty, with meal times when
they could 'be fitted in'.[48] In St Vincent's Hospital, in Dublin, the
nurses attended Masses at 6.30 a.m and were expected on the wards
at 7.30 a.m. They finished work at 8 p.m., with a two-hour break
during the day, and time off for meals. Night duty was often obliga-
tory where nuns were present. In Sligo, the Mercy nuns would not
do night duty, and the Roman Catholic Bishop of Elphin thought
that lay nurses could be employed for night work. Similarly in hospitals in counties Mayo, Leitrim, Limerick and Galway, the burden of
night duty fell on lay nurses. Nurses had one day off a month, and a
half day once a week, when they began work at 3.30 p.m. Such hours
seemed to have prevailed generally in Irish hospitals.[49]

When nurses sought an eight-hour day, practices in other nations
were surveyed. The *Irish Nursing and Hospital World* noted in 1931, that
nurses in Australia worked on a forty-eight hour week, in Denmark
fifty-four hours on day duty, and seventy-two on nights. In Britain,
fifty-six hours was the norm. Consequently, the working day of Irish
nurses differed little from their international counterparts. Anne
Smithson concluded that an eight-hour day was not pragmatic.[50]

Nurses endured such conditions because their complaints would
have fallen on deaf ears. Indeed keeping silent also formed part of the
ideal nurse's character and was encouraged by hospital authorities.
Sydney Gifford writing under the *nom de plume*, 'John Brennan', suggested in 1909 that nurses in uniform should not be allowed to speak
to males in a public place.[51] Meanwhile, in St Vincent's Hospital, stu-

dent nurses were not allowed to speak 'to a house officer or student in the hospital except in the line of professional business.' Nurses were sent home if they disobeyed this rule.[52] Nursing, therefore, was regarded as a respectable occupation because of these strict regulations. It was also viewed as particularly appropriate for females to be involved in a caring profession.

Nurses and the Irish Free State

In the early 1920s, the Irish Free State government, led by William T. Cosgrove, faced the problem of an unwieldy health service. There were Catholic and Protestant voluntary hospitals in the cities, an infirmary in each country and 130 workhouses located throughout the country. Although this system appeared impressive, the new government immediately moved to improve it. Workhouses were either closed or converted into county homes and county, and district and fever hospitals.[53] Other hospitals were amalgamated, much to the disappointment of rural communities which faced the possibility of losing their local hospital which, as well as providing a medical service, was regarded as a source of local patronage. Nurses became entangled in some of the inevitable conflicts which developed particularly where staff changes resulted. Power struggles between lay and religious nurses developed within hospitals and also involved local communities.[54]

In Manorhamilton, County Leitrim, controversy arose in 1922 over appointments to the local hospital. A Mrs O'Malley was elected to the position of matron by the county council but three nuns applied for two positions of nurses on the grounds that they had been nursing in Manorhamilton for decades. The council, however, found it impossible to appoint only two nuns because three was the required minimum number to form a religious community. All of the nuns had to be appointed. A Miss Cox also applied for a position as a nurse, but she was not employed. The chairman 'protested against the underhand way Miss Cox had been treated' and said that he was 'ruling against his wishes'. But he admitted that the council would not be 'worth their salt if they did not give the nuns a chance.' Miss Cox was promised the next vacancy.

This was not the end of the saga. Difficulties arose between the lay matron and the nuns. The nuns sought a definition of their duties. They apparently refused to recognise the matron's authority. Being part of a religious community, they did not appear to come under this secular label. It seems that the matron had threatened to put the nuns on alternate day and night duty. The nuns argued that they had had complete charge of the hospital under the British government and under the new arrangements they felt their roles were being downgraded. The matron responded, 'I don't like to be rude to the nuns, yet I have got to hold on to my own, and you know no matter where they are, they want to reign supreme.' The Minister for Local Government and Public Health felt the 'trouble ... did not come exclusively from one side.[55]

These difficulties were not unique to Ireland in this period. In France, Dr Anna Hamilton noted in 1929, that in hospitals managed by a religious order, 'there were two masters, the director (usually male) and the superior (who was in charge of the nuns)'. They were often 'at daggers drawn' as 'she alone has authority over the nuns ... he rules it over the lay employees, who work under the nuns' orders'. Consequently, there was 'constant friction'. Hamilton's antagonism towards the nuns seems to have been motivated, in part, by snobbery. Nurses, she thought, should be 'refined and womanly', but some religious orders drew their members from the 'servant class'.[56]

The difficulties in Ireland were not confined to one region. In Mayo, the county council decided in the early 1920s not to appoint the Sisters of Mercy to manage the county home as it was felt to be unfair 'to the lay nurses' profession'. Not everybody agreed with this explanation. A hospitals' inspector declared that 'were the nuns to get the running of the [county] home it would in my opinion cut out a whole lot of wire pulling that is going on and would make for decided improvement in the whole management'. The decision was subsequently reversed and the nuns were appointed by a unanimous vote.[57]

In county Limerick, in 1921, a local priest, Fr Lee, 'expressed the desire that nuns might be appointed at Croom [hospital]'. He explained to W.T. Cosgrove, Minister for Local Government and Public Health, 'this ... is a test of your faith, and of the religion of Sinn Féin, and I beg of you to act the part of a Catholic administrator and don't allow the scandal of expelling the nuns from the care of the sick and dying poor and replacing them with lay people'. Lee felt the nuns were a 'boon' in the management of hospitals.[58] In Clifden, county Galway, when the new district hospital was opened in 1931, the county council decided that it would be run by the Sisters of Mercy.[59] Also, in Galway city, there was continuity of hospital man-

agement by the religious before and after independence. In the early
1900s, there were differences between the Poor Law guardians, who
wished to keep Sr M. Bernard Ryan as lady superintendent of the
county infirmary, and the medical faculty at University College,
Galway (UCG), who were unhappy because she was not certified.
Sr Ryan remained in the position following the intervention of
Alexander Anderson, president of UCG. Whereas, the first matron
appointed by the county board of health (which replaced the board
of guardians in 1925), at Galway Central Hospital in 1925 was also a
Mercy nun as were most who followed her. Furthermore, the religious dimension of nurses' training was consolidated in the latter
hospital, with the establishment of a training school for nurses in
1927.[60]

    This lay/religious conflict in nursing was continued into the 1930s.
In 1933, Annie Smithson, secretary of the Irish Nurses' Union, wrote
to Dr Byrne, Roman Catholic Archbishop of Dublin, in order to
explain the difficulties between religious and lay nurses. She indicated that the annual council meeting of the Irish Nurses' Union had
devoted 'a rather long debate' to reports in the press which had 'given
offence to some of the Orders engaged in nursing, especially the Bon
Secours nuns'.[61] An article in the *Irish Press* noted first, that 'nuns in
hospitals were taking work from lay nurses' and the evidence offered
was that 'lay nurses … had never been so busy as when the nuns went
on retreat'. Secondly, the newspaper informed its readers that 'a French
order [the Bon Secours] in the south were doing work that should be
done by the Irish girls whom they displaced'. Thus, not only was there
a problem about the employment of nursing nuns above lay nurses but
the French order, of which there were many in Ireland, was accused
of depriving Irish women of employment. Subsequently, Smithson
asked the archbishop to consider the position of lay nurses. At a time
when new hospitals and sanatoria were being opened, Smithson asked
that lay staff be allocated 'a certain percentage of the positions' in these
institutions. She reassured Byrne that the Irish Nurses' Union did not
'want to appear in anyway [*sic*] anti-Catholic for the vast majority of
our members are Catholics'. She also raised the thorny issue of night
duty, pointing out that in an institution under religious control, the lay
nurse was forced to do all the night duty.[62]

    The re-organisation of the provision of medical services by the
authorities in the Irish Free State embroiled nurses in controversies.
Yet, opportunities for nurses continued to expand. By 1929 school

nurses were employed.[63] By the mid-1920s the Department of Local Government and Public Health conceded that all nurses in county homes and hospitals would be 'fully trained and registered' and it would not 'in future, sanction [the employment of] matron or charge nurses' without qualifications.[64] In other words, the untrained or partially trained nurse was to give way to the professional nurse. However, tradition and custom remained a strong argument and both local and national aspirations played their part in the selection of staff.

Conclusion

In Ireland, and elsewhere, nursing had an 'almost completely feminine face'.[65] This female image restricted the development of the profession while conferring respectability on those who chose this 'caring career'. In many senses, the semi-professional nature of nursing with its poor pay, indifferent status and lack of autonomy ensured that nurses would find it difficult to improve working conditions.

In the early twentieth century, the Nightingale influence retained its potency. Despite the registration of midwives and nurses in 1918 and 1919, the persistent presence of the unregistered in the profession militated against full professional development. In Ireland, as in France, the tradition of religious orders in nursing posed particular barriers to professionalization. Nuns, as noted earlier, were very willing to provide inexpensive care. Lay women had to comply with their outlook, as religious orders ran many institutions. Furthermore, Catholic social teaching inculcated, or at least attempted to inculcate, an acceptance of suffering as God's will. This was sometimes used to justify very difficult working conditions. Furthermore, the authoritarianism of nursing leaders also affected the profession. This was not confined to Ireland. However, given the difficult economic conditions of the 1920s, it meant that nurses were not encouraged to unify in the pursuit of increased pay.

Furthermore, women were expected to fill the nursing ranks, while men monopolised the medical jobs. It is not surprising, then, that nurses were seen as flowers, ideal for brightening up their patients' lives but the real work of healing was in male hands. While many nurses would have wished to nullify Florence Nightingale and the image of a decorative medical aid, her ambivalent influence in nursing remains prevalent even to the 1990s.[66]

Chapter 12

Women, politics, and public health: The Babies' Clubs in Ireland and the Children's Bureau in the US

This paper will examine the the Babies' Clubs in Ireland and the Children's Bureau in the United States. Many female physicians were attracted to paediatrics and public health. Why? First of all, it is necessary to examine women's access to the medical profession in Ireland, then the links between women and public health will be discussed. The Women's National Health Association in Ireland and the Children's Bureau in the United States will be discussed. Finally, it is suggested that through the activities of these organisations public health was placed on the political agenda.

The gradual professionalisation of medicine paved the way for the entry of women. Magill has attributed the development of the medical school in Belfast to commercial growth and Presbyterian influence. As dissenters, Presbyterians were unable to aspire to landed status, so they turned to medicine, law, and the Church.[1] The same argument was applicable to females, who were also excluded from the law and the Church. They turned to medicine as it was a respectable profession which was open to them.

Rossiter has argued that the professionalisation of science excluded many gifted amateur women scientists. With the establishment of learned scientific societies, women were excluded from the profession.[2] However, with the passage of the medical acts in 1858 and 1876, and the recognition of the qualifying institutions, once women gained access to these institutions, and had passed their examinations, they could not be excluded from the profession. But qualifying was only the first step towards becoming a professional. It was necessary to obtain employment in one's chosen profession. In an oversupplied profession like medicine, this was often a difficult task. In the late-nineteenth century, medicine became a science. New institutions were established, and, unlike many of their American counterparts, aspiring Irish female doctors trained with their male colleagues. The all-female medical schools in the United States may have aided women's entry to the medical profession, but they probably placed their graduates at a disadvantage once they tried to obtain work. Frequently, women 'lacked the needed medical connections'.[3]

In 1858 the first significant medical act was passed. It introduced a degree of uniformity into the training of medical practitioners. The Royal College of Surgeons in Ireland was recognised as a qualifying institution for medical practitioners.[4] With the passing of the 1876 Act, which prohibited any distinction of sex for medical registration, the profession became open to women. In 1877, the Royal College of Physicians in Ireland gave women permission to sit for its licentiate. The Royal College of Surgeons of Ireland was the first institution in the United Kingdom of Great Britain and Ireland to admit women to its lectures. Agnes Shannon was the first female student to register there in 1855.[5] The professionalisation of medicine is associated with these medical Acts, and the development of university medical faculties. While opportunities were gradually opening up for women, some reticence remained. Females were provided with separate dissecting rooms. As late as 1930, Trinity College, Dublin, would not allow women to study physiology or anatomy until they were at least eighteen years old.[6]

The pioneering female doctors benefitted most from the 1876 Act. Licentiates of the Royal College of Physicians in Ireland include some of the women closely associated with the early years of the profession in Britain and Ireland. The first Irish women doctors qualified in the late 1870s and early 1880s. Sophia Jex-Blake, one of the earliest licentiates of the Royal College of Physicians, said the women 'met in most quarters with an extremely cordial reception' in Ireland.[7] She became a Licentiate in 1877, and a Member in 1880. She was to die in 1912, aged seventy-one, after a long career in medicine.[8] Dr Jex-Blake pointed out as early as 1869 that female doctors would cater for female patients: 'perhaps we shall find the solution to some of our saddest social problems when educated and pure-minded women are brought more constantly in contact with their sinning and suffering sisters, in other relations as well as those of missionary efforts.'[9] Like female teachers, female doctors were supposed to cater for their own gender.

In a speech to the Alexandra Guild Conference in Dublin, Professor Winifred Cullis, the president of the British Federation of University Women, argued that women could affect legislation in relation to health and child welfare. They had a 'big responsibility' for these matters, she argued.[10] The Alexandra Guild had been established by Dr Katherine Maguire in 1898, in response to the dreadful conditions of the Dublin tenements.[11] She presented very detailed information on wages, rents, and dwelling conditions, and challenged the guild to begin 'at the beginning of their [the poor's] misery.' The well-off were responsible for the poor, Maguire argued. 'We are to blame ourselves, so long as we, of the so-called better classes are contented to live our own lives in good houses, without even asking how our neighbours (many of them very near neighbours) are living in thier houses. So long as we ignore our individual responsibility for the condition of the working classes, who else can we call to account for this?'

At the Aberdeen Conference of the National Union of Women Workers, a paper regarding women on medical boards came to the conclusion that it was 'essentially a woman's work to look after the sick.'[12] By a remarkable coincidence, or perhaps, it is possible to argue that the entry of women speeded up the process, as women gained access to the medical profession, welfare work expanded.

As part of the drive towards greater awareness of public health, the Women's National Health Association was established in 1907 by Lady Aberdeen, the wife of Ireland's viceroy. Its aim was to educate the public on health matters. The WNHA was part of an 'International philanthropic movement of National Women's Associations then active in North America and Europe.' The organisation attracted funding from the United States, and its message was spread through catchy slogans such as 'Public Health is Purchaseable'.[13] Hence, its focus was primarily educational. Unhealthy habits were the focus of many WNHA lectures. In Cork, during 1907, talks were given on 'School Hygiene' and 'The Public Health Act' by Miss O'Sullivan and Dr Alice Barry.[14]

By 1911 there were 155 branches of the organisation and nearly 18,000 members.[15] 'Public opinion, women, public health – around this nexus the campaign was to swirl and flow. The public, but particularly women, were to be energised and activated in the fight against tuberculosis.' Hence, there was a concentration on women and children in the home. Schools and religious communities were vital avenues which helped spread the good news of good health. The WNHA, therefore, became involved in the provision of school meals.[16]

Links between the WNHA and District Nurses were inevitable, given the nature of the work, particularly with infants. The WNHA infant mortality sub-committee of Dr Marion Andrews and Dr Elizabeth Bell (two Belfast doctors) reported that they attended the Babies' Clubs, for an hour, on the days they were open. The clubs were run by nurses for the rest of the time.[17] The WNHA helped to established female doctors as part of the Irish medical scene. Furthermore, the association helped to put public health on the political agenda. Nonetheless, much of the work remained voluntary. Female doctors were the vital link between voluntary and professional philanthropy. Public health and paediatrics provided physicians with a niche in the medical profession.

Possibly the female doctor most associated with the WNHA is Dr Alice Barry. Between 1912 and 1929, she was in charge of the nine Dublin Babies' Clubs which were run by the WNHA. They were launched in the following manner according to one Dublin wit:

> So the Babies Club was started in a real viceregal way with a feast
> o' cakes
> from Scotland and a mighty flood o'tay
> An Mrs Aberdeen was there in her disinfected best, an swallowed
> with her tay
> as many microbes as the rest.[18]

In 1929, the Babies' Clubs were taken over by Dublin Corporation. Dr Barry became Resident Medical Officer at Peamount which had been established by WNHA.[19]

Peamount Sanatorium was set up in 1912. It expressed, in institutional form, the aspirations of the WNHA with its emphasis on fresh air, sunshine, cleanliness, wholesome food, and local industries for able-bodied patients. It even had an open-air school for the younger patients. A former patient remembered Dr Barry as, 'full of kindness and gentleness, but ... a strict disciplinarian when the occasion required it.'[20] In addition to setting up sanatoria, the WNHA continued to lobby for improved medical facilities. In 1919, their advisory committee on 'Legislation affecting Child Welfare and Public Health' included Dr Ella Webb and Dr Alice Barry. The latter was the representative of the Irish Medical Committee on the Report of the Irish

Public Health Council on the Public Health and Medical Services in Ireland. It recommended greater institutional care for TB patients.[21]

The activities of the WNHA can be compared to the Children's Bureau in the United States, which was established in 1912. This bureau gave advice on children's health and, according to Ladd-Taylor, it 'designed and administered the first federal and social-welfare measure, the Sheppard-Towner Maternity and Infant Protection Act of 1922. During the seven years of its operation, public health workers disseminated information on nutrition and hygiene, established well-baby clinics, and provided prenatal care for pregnant women in rural areas.'[22] As in the WNHA, females predominated in the Children's Bureau. These included Dr Florence Kelley, most noted for her activities against child labour; Dr Dorothy Reed Mendenhall, medical officer of the Children's Bureau between 1917 and 1936; and Dr Josephine Baker, director of the New York Bureau of Child Hygiene. Like the WNHA, the bureau's promotion of public health 'greatly expanded women's influence in government, politics, and medicine.'[23] Both groups used local contacts with women's organisations, the press and the clergy to spread their message. In 1916, they began the Baby Week just like the Irish equivalent over a decade later.[24] The interesting difference is that most of the American legislation relating to material and infant care dates from the 1920s, whereas Irish legislation was enacted in the 1910s. In both cases, females were to the fore in its implementation.

How radical were these medical developments? Neither group questioned women's position in the home; in fact, they reinforced it by their insistence that only women could care for young children. The Babies' Clubs placed a lot of emphasis on encouraging women to monitor the health of their children. This included keeping a check on the baby's weight.

Women were encouraged to become paediatricians. Just as the Babies' Clubs in Ireland were dominated by female doctors, like Dr Alice Barry, so the Children's Bureau in the United States attracted female doctors. Dr Florence Sherbon believed that women doctors were uniquely qualified to work with children. 'Being women, as well as physicians, we share our sex in the actual and potential motherhood the race … and being women and mothers, our first and closest and dearest interest is the child.'[25] However, like the Belfast Health Society, the Children's Bureau claimed that infant mortality was a socio-economic, not a medical problem.[26] Though medically trained, many women sought socio-economic solutions to the health difficulties of women and children.

The most illuminating evidence of the association between female doctors and welfare is in the evidence of the National Council of Women in Ireland and the Joint Committee of Women's Societies and Social Workers to the Irish Commission on Vocational Organisation in the 1940s. The National Council of Women consisted of groups such as the WNHA, the Irish Save the Children Fund, Saor an Leanbh [Save the Child], and the Irish Matrons' Association. The National Council of Women promoted reform 'with special reference to women and children.' They also sent a delegation, in 1926, to the 'Paris Congress of the International Alliance, and submitted a report on Maternal Mortality in Ireland.' The National Council of Women participated in the 1928 annual congress of the Royal Institute of Public Health. The Joint Committee of Women's Societies and Social Workers was another group which linked women and welfare. Their member societies included the Irish Nurses' Association and *St Patrick's* Guild, whose objects centred around the care of expectant mothers and the training of probationers in infant welfare work.[27]

These links between welfare and medicine were strongly advocated by professional women. In 1902, an ode, by Mac Aodh, challenged the readers of *St Stephen's*, the magazine of the Catholic University in Dublin, to 'vindicate the Lady-Medico.'[28]

Ode to the Lady Medicals
Though all the world's a stage and we are acting,
Yet still I think your part is not dissecting.
To me the art of making apple tarts
Would suit you better than those 'horrid parts.'
And as for learning chemistry and that,
'Twould be a nicer thing to trim a hat.
I know your aims in medicine are true,
But tell me is there any *need of you*?

Increasing opportunities in public medical service, as maternity and child-welfare officers, school inspectors and medical officers of Health provided female medical practitioners with opportunities. In this way, many women justified their presence in a male-dominated profession.

Dr Louisa Martindale, whose sister Hilda made such an impact as an inspector of factories in Ireland, wrote a history of the woman doctor in 1922. She claimed that 'professional isolation' was the 'chief disability' for female doctors. It is not surprising, therefore, to see that she was an Honorary Surgeon in the new Sussex Hospital for Women and Children where there were other females employed. Given, as she said herself, the 'glacier like evolution of the adult mind', women naturally turned to positions where they were more acceptable. Dr Martindale noted that there were 146 hospitals staffed entirely by women in India.[29] Canadian doctors also duplicated the trends of their Irish counterparts, with their interest in social reform and religious activity.[30] Likewise, a study of the career paths of graduates of the University of Buffalo in New York noted that women in medicine 'carved a niche for themselves in providing services to their own.'[31]

In both Ireland and the United States, women involved in the Children's Bureau and the Women's National Health Association were part of the generation of the suffragette and they helped shape the politicisation of a dynamic group of women. Despite this, women colluded, perhaps, in their exclusion from certain medical specialities by their emphasis on nurturing qualities. They also managed, however, to obtain a footing in the profession, and thereby vindicate the 'lady Medico'. However, their emphasis on women's maternal qualities defined and confined their role. It placed the responsibility for children's health firmly on women's shoulders and this burden has remained.

Chapter 13

'Is there any need of you?': women in medicine in Ireland and Australia

This paper will examine two hospitals, one in Ireland and one in Australia, which were established by women. It was not unusual for women to establish hospitals. This was done in the nineteenth century to facilitate women's access to the medical profession. In 1896, Victoria Hospital, Melbourne, was founded by women. The first venereal clinic for women and children was set up in the hospital in the 1920s just as St Ultan's Hospital for Infants in Dublin, which was founded in 1919, was expressing concerns about the problem. Women justified their position in medicine by their work in paediatrics and public health.

> Ode to Lady Medicals
> Though all the world's a stage and we are acting,
> Yet still I think your part is not dissecting.
> To me the art of making apple tarts
> Would suit you better than those 'horrid parts.'
> … And as for learning chemistry and that,
> 'Twould be a nicer thing to trim a hat.
> I know your aims in medicine are true,
> But tell me is there any *need* of you?

In 1902, this ode, by Mac Aodh, challenged the readers of *St Stephen's*, the Catholic University (later University College Dublin) Medical

School, to 'vindicate the Lady Medico'.[1] It is the argument of this paper that increasing awareness of public health and high rates of infant mortality provided a justification for female physicians. Furthermore, female health professionals were seen as the ideal people to deal with women and children. Why was there a perceived need to establish hospitals for children? Late-nineteenth and early twentieth-century public health and sanitation reform impulses were not unique to Ireland. Internationally, the increasing prominence of political women and the focus on citizenship had placed the spotlight on those whose needs the State had neglected. In France, for example, there was a call to provide 'social protection' for all mothers. Furthermore, in the aftermath of a devastating world war, there were increasing concerns about poor population growth. Inevitably, infant mortality became a focus for governments who wished to rejuvenate the nation. Population growth, then, was placed on the political agenda and it forced nations to assess the public health of its people. For instance, in Australia, 'home and family were placed under the microscope, and a new range of experts made their recommendation'.[2]

Ireland was not immune to those concerns. Mokyr has argued that 'the idea that children were worth protecting and nurturing became central to late-nineteenth and early twentieth-century reformism'. Furthermore, the entry of women into the medical profession in the late-nineteenth century coincided with the bacteriological revolution. The discovery of germs and their role in the spread of infection in the late-nineteenth century impacted on the lives of medical professionals. Many female doctors were fortunate that their careers bridged the gap between the sanitation and vaccination movements. However, vaccines were not widely used until after the Second World War. Hence, great stress was placed on the elimination of dirt.[3] This greater awareness of disease and germs and the belief that illness could be prevented through maternal vigilance placed grave responsibilities on women.

Moreover, women's presence on health committees was encouraged. For example, in Ireland, the 1915 Notification of Births Act gave the power to appoint a committee that was 'to include women'. In response to this, the Pembroke Urban Council in Dublin appointed a maternity and child welfare committee, which included Poor Law guardians, members of the Women's National Health Association, and a Medical Superintendent Officer of Health.[4] This link between women and health was not unique to Ireland. The Scandinavian Women's Sanitary Association, which was founded in 1896, and the 'Siamese triplets' of the National Association for Women's Suffrage, the Association for Women's Rights, and the Women's Sanitary Organisation worked together to improve both the health of the nation, and women's rights.[5] Progressive schools were quick to latch onto the connection between hygiene and women. Alexandra College, the *alma mater* of several Irish doctors such as Kathleen Lynn, Ella Webb, and Katherine Maguire, linked with Trinity College in establishing a course on Sanitary and Applied Hygiene, in 1908. Maguire and Webb, who were later to work in St Ultan's, both taught on the course that sought to prepare students for work under the Department of Agriculture and Technical Instruction.[6] Tuberculosis committees also tended to have female members.

Women were seen as particularly important in the drive towards better hygiene. This was articulated by Lady Aberdeen, the Viceroy's wife. She founded the Women's National Health Association in 1907 in order to lower tuberculosis rates. Her 1911 presidential address to the Royal Institute was entitled, 'The Sphere of Women in Relation to Public Health'. In order for new medical ideas to be successful, she argued, the 'confidence of the housewives' had to be sought. They would help to 'popularise' new ideas regarding health as they were the people who 'moulded' ideas in the home. Lady Aberdeen wanted to have household science made compulsory for women in university. She suggested that placing domestic science on the curriculum would raise the status of the subject.[7] Given their involvement in public health, it is not surprising that female doctors, such as Alice Barry, Ella Webb, and Marion Andrews, were prominent in the Women's National Health Association.

The Women's National Health Association brought both the language and the reality of sanitary reform to many parts of Ireland. It was not unusual for the aristocratic and professional women to combine their resources in order to improve public health. The infant mortality rate of New Zealand was reduced from eight per cent in 1902 to five per cent in 1912, largely through the efforts of the 'Plunket Society', a health society established by Lord and Lady Plunket.[8] Australian Edith Cowan was a noted politician, feminist, and social worker. In 1906, she was one of the founders of the Children's Protection Society. Her involvement in Red Cross activities during the First World War conceived her of the need for

reforms in the treatment of women and children.⁹ This period also
saw the gradual transformation of aristocratic philanthropy into professional philathropy.

In the late-nineteenth century medicine became a science. New
institutions were established and, unlike many of their American
counterparts, aspiring Irish female doctors trained with their male
colleagues. The all-female medical schools in the United States may
have aided women's entry to the medical professions, but probably
placed their graduates at a disadvantage once they tried to obtain
work. Frequently, American women 'lacked the needed medical
connections'.¹⁰

The first significant medical Act was passed in 1858, which
introduced a degree of uniformity into the training of medical
practitioners. The Royal College of Surgeons in Ireland was recognised as a qualifying institution for medical practitioners.¹¹ With
the passing of the 1876 Act, which prohibited any distinction of sex
for medical registration, the profession became open to women.
In 1877, the Royal College of Physicians gave women permission
to sit for its licentiate. The Royal College of Surgeons was the first
institution in the United Kingdom to admit women to its lectures.
Agnes Shannon was the first female student to register there in
1885.¹² The professionalisation of medicine is associated with these
medical acts and the development of university medical faculties. While opportunities were gradually opening up for women,
some reticence remained. For example, male and female students
used separate dissecting rooms, and, as late as 1930, Trinity College
Dublin barred the study of physiology or anatomy to women
under the age of eighteen.¹³

The pioneering female doctors benefited most from the 1876 Act.
Licentiates of the Royal College of Physicians in Ireland include
some of the women closely associated with the early years of the
profession in Britain and Ireland. The first women doctors would
therefore have qualified in the late 1870s and early 1880s. Sophia
Jex-Blake, one of the earliest licentiates of the Royal College of
Physicians, said the women 'met in most quarters with an extremely
cordial reception' in Ireland.¹⁴ She became a licentiate in 1877 and
a member in 1880. She died in 1912, aged seventy-one, after a long
career in medicine.¹⁵ Dr Jex-Blake pointed out as early as 1869 that
female doctors would cater for female patients:

perhaps we shall find the solution to some of our saddest social problems when educated and pure-minded women are brought more
constantly in contact with their sinning and suffering sisters, in other
relations as well as those of missionary effect.[16]

Like female teachers, female doctors were supposed to cater for their
own gender.

The Royal College of Physicians was not the only institution in
Ireland to welcome aspiring female doctors. Such was the reputation of the Rotunda Hospital, Europe's oldest lying-in hospital that
students from Britain came to train in midwifery. They possibly
influenced Irish women who saw it was possible to study medicine.[17]
Additionally, by 1900, the Royal University of Ireland provided
medical degrees for women through the medical schools in Belfast,
Cork, Galway, and Cecilia Street in Dublin, the home of the Catholic
University School of Medicine. The history of Cecilia Street suggests that its first female students arrived in 1895. Frances Sinclair
was the first female medical student and she graduated in 1898.[18]
In 1890 Eleanora Fleury was the Royal University of Ireland's first
medical graduate. She qualified with first-class honours, having stud-
ied at the London School of Medicine for Women and the Royal
Free Hospital. She subsequently graduated with an MD from the
Royal University of Ireland in 1893, winning the gold medal. Dr
Fleury worked in the Richmond Asylum, Dublin.[19] Dr Ambrose
Birmingham, Professor of Anatomy and Registrar of the Catholic
University School of Medicine, suggested female medical students
were 'hard-working, earnest and most conscientious'. He also noted
that 'several ladies appear to dissect in the general room', and that
the admission of women was 'productive of nothing but good to
the institution'.[20] This support should not be underestimated.
It facilitated women's access to the profession in an era when women
did not have the vote. In Cork, there were also male supporters of
women who desired to pursue a medical career. Dora Allman and
Lucy Smith were the first two female students to be admitted to
Queen's College Cork medical school, thanks to pressure exerted
by Professor Maurice Hartog and T.P. O'Sullivan of the college.
Drs John O'Mahony, Theodore Dillon, and Richard Crosbie also
wanted women to gain access to medical lectures. After admittance
in 1892, both women sat their final examinations in 1896.[21] Both
Allman and Smith allegedly disguised themselves as men in order to

work in the hospital clinics. Dr Allman specialised in mental illness
and was chief superintendent of Armagh mental hospital for many
years.[22] Dr Smith who worked in the Cork Lying-In Hospital, was
described as the 'first lady doctor to practice in Cork'.[23] In 1920 she
was appointed as an examiner for the Central Midwives Board of
Ireland, having been recognised as a lecturer in midwifery by the
Central Midwives' Board in England.[24]

Harriete Rose Neill was reputedly the first female medical graduate of Queen's College Belfast in 1894, but Dr Elizabeth Gould-Bell
graduated a year earlier, having entered the medical school in 1889.[25]
Hester Dill Smith (*née* Russel) graduated with her MB, BCH, BAO,
in 1891 and an MD in 1898, hence she is the first femail Queen's
graduate in medicine. Two decades later Belfast students were debating the motion, 'The Role of Women in Medicine is a Failure'.
One male student, who later became a gynaecologist, remarked
that women students were 'like mustard plasters, very irritating'.[26] In
1916, Teresa Walsh became University College Galway's first female
medical graduate. Although not as well known nationally as Dr Ada
English, who was lecturing in mental diseases in University College
Galway at that time, Dr Walsh was interned under the Defence of
the Realm Act.[27] Dr Eva Jellet, the daughter of the Provost, was the
first female to graduate in medicine from Trinity. She had previously
been a student at Cecilia Street since women did not gain access to
Trinity College Dublin until 1904.[28]

The early female doctors, such as Elizabeth Garrett-Anderson,
facilitated the careers of others by endowing institutions, which
then had to accept female entrants. For example, the Johns Hopkins
Medical School in the United States was opened to women as a condition of Dr Anderson's gift of $350,000.[29] Women also established
institutions such as the Women's Hospital in London, thereby providing employment opportunities for female professionals.[30] In a study
of the New York-based Blackwell Medical Society, Ellen More argues
that the medical women's society functioned as an 'effective instrument of professional integration and legitimation'. Once the women
were well-established professionally, the society disappeared.[31]

Additionally, women on missionary activities in India and China
established hospitals for the locals. In 1896, Victoria Hospital in
Melbourne, Australia was founded by women. Eleven female doctors set up the hospital in a Sunday school hall. In the first three
months they saw 2,000 female patients. The hospital was renamed

Queen Victoria for Women and Children in 1897. It employed the first woman pharmacist in the state of Victoria. The first venereal clinic for women and children was set up in the hospital in the 1920s.[32] Like St Ultan's the 'Queen Vic was ahead of its time in such areas as nutrition, diet and social services because its management and medical staff had always insisted on considering the needs of the patients over and above the expansion of departments, staff and equipment'.[33] Although the Ulster Hospital for Women and Children was established in 1873 by men, they provided employment for female doctors. The first female doctor appointed to the Belfast Hospital for Sick Children was Mary Slade in 1919, while Dr Marion Andrews was honorary gynaecologist between 1902 and 1914, and Dr Elizabeth Robb was a house surgeon in the Ulster Hospital.[34] Revealingly, Dr Andrews was also the honorary secretary of the Belfast Eugenics Society.[35] The potent mix of race, hygiene, public health, ecclesiastical paranoia, and reproductive politics would shatter the plans for expansion at St Ultan's in the 1930s. However, in its earlier manifestation, St Ultan's staff drew inspiration from a variety of sources. International developments motivated the doctors, as they noted that Dundee, Manchester, and London had opened hospitals for women.[36] However, St Ultan's was unique in Ireland as the only hospital run entirely by women.

In May 1918, at the first meeting that was to lead to the establishment of the hospital, Kathleen Lynn read a paper that declared her desire to educate the public about venereal disease. Dr Barry proposed, and Lucy Griffin seconded, the motion that:

> This conference of Irishwomen note with appreciation that the corporations of Dublin and Belfast have taken up the question of venereal disease, and urge those bodies to see that every soldier who lands at Irish ports is guaranteed from disease.[37]

This concern was not solely the preserve of *Cumann na dTeachtaire*. There was a Royal Commission on venereal disease sitting in 1918. Given the nationalist outlook of the committee, they were particularly critical of British soldiers infecting Irish women and children. The committee possibly saw this in a wider political context: British rule was affecting the health of the nation.

The founders of St Ultan's, and Lynn in particular, were part of a group known as *Sláinte na nGaedheal*, which was interested in the health of the nation. They were part of a national movement that sought the cultural, moral, physical, and intellectual regeneration of the Irish people through organisations such as the Gaelic League and the Gaelic Athletic Association. The committee feared for the health of the nation's children and recommended that:

> … local authorities under the Children's Act…[should] have such infants [suffering from syphilis] immediately removed for treatment to hospitals on diagnosis of their disease by the medical officer of the district, and that copies of this resolution be sent to Boards of Guardians and local authorities.

They also asked whether there was provision for syphilitic infants in any hospital.[38] By May, the committee had sent Lucy Griffin to see P.T. Daly, a nationalist member of Dublin Corporation, regarding health facilities. These early issues underline a number of different developments that affected Lynn and her colleagues. The increasing role of the State, including local government, in medicine, and the growing importance of paediatrics and public health (the two were closely linked), provided a focus for Lynn to express her political beliefs and professional concerns. She was a particularly strong advocate of breastfeeding and wrote in the periodical, *Old Ireland*, that 'nature made no mistake when she designed that mammals should suckle their young.'[39] The importance of milk in reducing maternal and infant mortality was emphasised elsewhere. In Britain, an editorial in the *Medical Officer* suggested that a reduction in maternal mortality would be achieved 'by a herd of cows than by a herd of specialists'.[40] The link between reducing infant mortality through breastfeeding is still being promoted in South America and the Caribbean in the twenty-first century.[41]

St Ultan's concern for the health of mothers extended to running a holiday home for them in Baldoyle. One of the aims of the hospital was to be 'a university for mothers'. In 1917, Edward Coey Bigger, the Medical Commissioner of the Local Government Board for Ireland, declared that Irish women were 'not fitted for motherhood'. The 'great evil is lack of good mother-craft', he surmised.[42] Lynn and her colleagues agreed with this assessment. The staff strongly encouraged mothers to attend lectures at the hospital, and welfare workers also attended; the hospital declared that one of their main aims was 'to spread knowledge'.[43] They were therefore part of an international

movement to train mothers. Dr Newman, the Chief Medical Officer
to the Board of Education in England, pointed out that infant mortality was due to the 'ignorance of the mother and the remedy is the
education of the mother'.[44] Educating women was a particular interest of many physicians and St Ultan's attempted to spread the gospel
of cleanliness. This focus on education reflects the middle-class bias
of many physicians whose intention was to instruct mothers. In her
work on tuberculosis in Belfast, Isabel Magill suggested that:

> ... hygiene which concentrated upon moral and domestic reform
> was seen as part of the process by which the poor were to be sub-
> dued, modified, improved and moulded into a cogent economic
> force.[45]

On occasion, this focus on education dampened the social radicalism
of St Ultan's. Without the political will at a national level to improve
the living conditions of patients and their parents, the infant mortality rate would not be radically reduced. The need for the hospital was
obvious: of the fifty-three infants treated in the first year, twenty-
three died, a shocking mortality rate. It is worth noting that in 1925
'more than half (281) the total number of deaths of illegitimate
infants occurred in Dublin county and city'. These infants were six
times more likely than their legitimate contemporaries to die before
the age of one.[46] Given the high number of illegitimate infants at the
hospital, the high mortality rate is not surprising.

Clearly St Ultan's was providing a service for those who badly
needed it, but they were unable to prevent mortality in most cases.
In October 1922, it was proposed by Dr Elizabeth Tennant and seconded by Dr Alice Barry that:

> Cases of infant girls should not be admitted while there are cases
> of vaginal discharge in the house-subsequently girl infants admit-
> ted should be kept under observation for a time before being
> admitted to the ordinary wards. All cases of vaginal discharge now
> should be discharged as soon as possible.[47]

The following January, when Lynn was not at the medical committee meeting, it was decided that the infants with vaginal discharge
should not be treated in the hospital and 'the child with no parents can be sent to the Lock Hospital'[48], suggesting a considerable

move away from the hospital's original concern with venereal disease. However, the original concerns about the socio-economic conditions of families persisted. While little could be done about a child infected with venereal disease, there was a sense that improved medical care might alleviate distress. In 1926 it was suggested that an antenatal clinic might be established. Like the Babies' Clubs, they sought to give advice to expectant mothers and, crucially, given the poverty of so many families, to provide meals or supplement the home diet with milk and eggs and clothing 'where necessary'. The medical committee also planned to have a consulting gynaecologist and a trained nurse at the clinic. However, these great plans would come to nothing without funds.

Likewise, it had been suggested in relation to infant aid in Australia, that we should be 'sceptical about what can be achieved through advice-giving that is not accompanied by supportive public policies'.[49] Clearly there was a perceived need for Babies' Clubs, infant aid centres, and children's hospitals. In New Zealand, children were seen as a 'social asset' and a school medical services was introduced in 1912, while Dr Elizabeth Gunn established the first health camp for vulnerable children in 1919.[50] However, the onus of responsibility was placed on voluntary effort. While states were aware of the need to improve the health of the nation, frequently this was an aspiration rather than a reality in children's lives in the western world until after the Second World War.

Chapter 14

A medical appointment in Meath: controversy in Kilskyre

A controversy which erupted in Kilskyre concerning the appointment of a dispensary doctor in 1927 serves to illuminate the difficulty, in the early days of the Irish state, of ensuring the independence and integrity of professional appointments, particularly in medicine. The medical profession was seen as a particularly sensitive one, since medical ethics, on occasion, disguised local aspirations and ambitions.

Health workers have been described as the 'chief architects of the institutional welfare state.'[1] In this role, they were dependant on the State for employment, like many of their fellow professionals, such as teachers. Furthermore, employment of this nature could depend on political factors. In Ireland, particularly after the establishment of the Irish Free State in 1922, dispensary work was seen as particularly problematic. For doctors in general practice, the steady income from dispensary work was often essential. Competition for the position of dispensary doctors was 'acute'. Bribery regarding medical appointments was not unknown.[2] It is possible that the appointment of Dr Florence Dillon, as a medical inspector to the local government board, may have owed something to her husband, William Blake-Dillon. He was a solicitor and died in 1915. Politically well connected, he was a cousin of John Dillon MP, the last leader of the Irish Party. Dr Dillon was a strict inspector, and was reputed to have a keen eye for imperfections.[3]

The first female dispensary doctor was Dr Kathleen Moran, a native of Co. Sligo, and formerly a student at University College Galway and University College Dublin. Based in Drumshambo, Co. Leitrim, she had been awarded a Licentiate in Midwifery and a Diploma in Public Health (1928) from the National University of Ireland. Dr Moran worked in England as a medical doctor. Her brother was also a dispensary doctor and her father was a JP, and a local county councillor. Hence, she was not disadvantaged in her local connections.[4] Ironically, in the local government files for Co. Leitrim, there is a letter from a Galway TD, Padraic Ó Máille, who stated that he was not 'personally … in favour of appointing lady doctors'. The doctor concerned, Dr Mary Kelly, was sanctioned as Medical Officer in Leenane, County Galway. The people of the locality were happy with Dr Kelly, he admitted.[5] Local influence was often vital, and 'a local candidate against an unknown stranger … foisted on them from Dublin' was in advantageous position.[6] Having landed a local government position, the successful candidate did not necessarily have a comfortable existence. Dr Mary Kelly, the Medical Officer of the Mullingar Dispensary District, realised this. Usually, dispensary doctors were provided with a house, at low rent. Despite the efforts of the Board of Guardians, she was not provided with a residence.[7]

Historian Joe Lee has noted that the county councils, established after the 1898 Local Government Act, 'soon became a by-word for corruption in their appointments'. Thirty years later, not much had changed. Quoting from the *Connaught Telegraph* of 1931 he explained that a 'candidate, no matter how highly qualified or widely experienced, had little prospect of securing an appointment' without the influence of a blood relation, or political pressure. Lee wittily pointed out that the establishment of the Local Appointments Commission in 1925, and the assessment of candidates based on 'professional merits … imposed intolerable strains on many an imagination.'[8] Hence, while female doctors benefited from the increased employment created by public health schemes, they had to contend with local political machinations.

Furthermore, there were particular concerns about upholding Catholic values in the new Irish state. The *Catholic Bulletin* asked: 'Is the School of Medicine, Trinity College, Dublin, a safe place for the training of doctors who are to practice, even to practice with the prestige [of] a civil appointment, among the Catholic people of Ireland, poor or rich?'[9] Protestants were seen as posing a moral threat to Catholics. Protestants were affected by these views, particularly after the 1930 Church of England Lambeth Conference which approved of contraceptives in certain circumstances. Much has been written about Letitia Dunbar Harrison, a female Protestant, whose appointment as librarian in Mayo caused a furore as it was suggested that a Protestant could not be trusted to recommend appropriate reading to Catholic children. However, the sub-text to this incident was the presence of a local candidate, Miss Burke, who had failed to be appointed.

These comments revealed the fear of Protestants and resentment over their perceived, and sometimes real, socio-economic advantages. Dr Gilmartin, the Catholic Bishop of Tuam, quoted statute 256 which enjoined the Parish Priest to see that 'the Faithful, especially midwives, doctors and surgeons, learn well the correct manner of conferring Baptism in the case of necessity.' The following statute (257) was even more emphatic and would have profound implications for Protestant doctors.

'Parish Priests and other priests are bound to prevent the impious crime by which, through the aid of surgical instruments or other means, the infant is killed in the womb. Wherefore let them use their best efforts to have deputed to public positions only those doctors and surgeons who have prosecuted their studies in school where Catholic principles in this matter are recognised.'[10]

Occasionally Catholic ethics were a disguise which hid the desire to appoint the local candidate. There were medical versions of the Letitia Dunbar Harrison case. In 1927, sectarian arguments were used in County Meath when a Catholic, Dr Eileen Brangan, was passed over for a local appointment as medical officer in Kilskyre in favour of Dr Francis O'Brien-Kennedy, a Protestant, male outsider. The Vicar General 'drew attention to the fact that religion formed an important element in the appointment of a dispensary doctor.' The debates surrounding the appointment are revealing of the anxieties felt by the emerging Irish Free State. Eileen Brangan had many advantages when she applied for the position. She had assisted her father for the previous three years when she had been medical officer in the Kilskyre Dispensary District. When he died, she continued, at the 'request of the Meath Board of Health', to act a dispensary doctor on a temporary basis. However, in line with the growing tendency of the Irish Free State to avoid localism, the Local

Authorities (Officers and Employees) Act of 1926 made clear that local authority positions requiring professional qualifications were to be filled by the Local Appointments Commission. The Act was supposed to introduce meritocracy but it did not appeal to many more parochial politicians. At the Meath Health Board meeting, the chairman, County Councillor Patrick Hopkins, made it clear that Eileen Brangan had 'done her duty well and faithfully, and to the entire satisfaction of the people, and won the confidence of all concerned regardless of class and creed.' Hopkins proclaimed that it was the 'duty of the board to assist in fighting this cause to the finish.'[11]

Meath was roused! The *Meath Chronicle* announced that 'Kilskyre is not taking the autocratic action lying down, and the people, regardless of class, creed or political affiliations, are determined to make the issue a serious one.' There were morbid mutterings about a 'dark cloud of coercion'.[12] A protest meeting took place at Kilskyre Schoolhouse on 6 November and such was the attendance that less than half of the crowd could be accommodated. Furthermore, a 'large number of women were present, which was a sufficiently unusual occurrence for the reporter to remark on it.' John Quinn, the Chairman of Meath County Council, resurrected the sectarian dimension to the appointment by referring to a letter from the Vicar General of Meath which had been published in the daily and local papers. It was suggested that religion 'formed an important element in the appointment of a dispensary doctor.' Quinn argued that the 'Vicar General had made an unassailable case for a Catholic dispensary doctor.'[13]

Despite all these complaints, the appointment was not changed and Dr Francis O'Brien-Kennedy of Newtownmountkennedy, County Wicklow, formerly medical officer in charge of the Royal National Hospital in Newcastle and a 1908 Trinity College graduate, was appointed. Nonetheless, the arguments put forward by aggrieved locals are indicative of the nature of local appointments and the resentment towards centralised authority. These anxieties have not entirely disappeared.

Chapter 15

Irish women in dentistry

Dentistry was a paramedical profession that attracted a growing number of females in the twentieth century, although it remained a resolutely male-dominated occupation until the latter part of the century.

Educational developments in the late-nineteenth and early twentieth centuries, with the establishment of the Royal University of Ireland in 1879, which became the National University of Ireland (NUI) in 1908, and the opening of Trinity College Dublin (TCD) to women in 1904, facilitated women's access to professional careers.[1] Dental schools were established in University College Dublin in 1908, and in University College Cork in 1913. Both were colleges of the NUI. By 1920, there was also a dental school in Belfast. In 1924 there were twenty females and ninety-seven males registered at the TCD Dental School.[2] As in pharmacy, the profession gradually became popular for females in the 1920s. Six women from Methodist College, Belfast, opted to study dentistry in the 1920s.[3] Despite their growing presence at dental schools, females were not prominent in the organisation of the profession. In the 1920s, the Dublin-based Miss de Sales Magennis was the only female member of the Irish Dental Association.

Irish dentists were registered in the Irish Free State under the 1921 and 1928 Acts, which ensured that only those registered could practice. The enrolment of Lilian Murray in 1899 at the TCD Dental

School meant she was the first female dentist to be admitted to the General Dentists' Register. Significantly, this was five years before women were allowed to take degrees at Trinity. By 1917, the committee of management of the university's dental hospital withdrew 'its objections to lady students becoming members of the Students' Society should the majority of members desire their admittance'. Given that females did become members, there must have been a willingness to accept the 'lady students'.[4]

A 'lady dentist' felt women were not inclined to opt for dentistry because it was perceived that great physical strength was required. She thought females were at an advantage in the profession. 'Children, for instance, are inclined to think that a women is going to do something for them, whereas a man is going to do something to them!' she argued. Nonetheless, her clients were not primarily women and she felt that 'the average man' thought 'if there's any gentleness to be got out of dentistry he'll get it from a woman.'[5] This view was echoed by an American dentist, Dr Gracia Paxson, who argued that the 'women dentist', with her feminine eye for symmetry and proportion, should be well adopted' to the profession.[6] Yet again, the emphasis on alleged female characteristics made the profession somewhat more accessible for women. It assumes, unfairly, that men are not gentle and balanced.[7]

The greatest difficulty facing women in dentistry in the early years of the twentieth century, were societal rather than educational. Women were perceived as taking jobs from traditional breadwinners. In 1926, a Kells Councillor, Mr Tully, complained that 'the modern young woman cannot be easy unless she has a man's job, and a man's trousers on.' He argued; 'It's very unfair, in ten years' time we'll have nothing in this unfortunate country but old maids and cats. It is the greatest curse in Ireland to be having women in everything ... Are we going to be bossed by petticoats? ...Woman was made for one job by God Almighty, and she is a fool in her own interests if she does not stick to it.'[8]

Because of developments in women's employment in the early twentieth century, aspiring females were still seen as taking a job from a male with a family. Women, therefore, rarely challenged the male monopolies in dentistry, medicine, law, engineering or accounting.[9]

It is difficult to ascertain the precise career paths of Irish female dentists. However, it is worth noting that when a female dentist was offered a post in a western town, during the late 1930s, the salary was fixed at £400 per annum. However, she was advised to reject the position as the profession believed it was too low.[10] By way of contrast, in 1946, during a major strike, primary teachers sought £364 per annum (a pound a day).

Like their colleagues in medicine, female dentists were inclined to opt for public service jobs, even if the pay was not as substantial as private practice. Public service work offered regular pay, and this made it attractive to those who were new to the profession. Catholic social action is now receiving attention from historians. Professional women were prominent in organisations such as the Catholic Women's Federation of Secondary School Unions.[11] The aim of the Catholic Women's Federation of Secondary School Unions was to 'promote and foster Catholic social principles and action, especially from the women's point of view, and in particular to promote and defend the interests, rights and duties of the family.'[12] The St Dominic's Social Service Club was established in 1926, but the union was set up in June 1914. Its president was Mary Hayden, Professor of Modern Irish History at UCD. The educationalist, Louise Gavan Duffy, 'proposed a social work scheme.' She advocated 'the necessity of social work amongst catholic girls.' The union organised a night school that taught technical/domestic subjects and supplied the teachers. It also organised social activities such as tennis and hockey matches. Medical inspections were conducted by female doctors involved in the college union. 'Miss Cunniffe', a dentist, was interested in establishing another club for girls. Such activities stitched together, in an intricate pattern, a wide range of social activities amongst women.[13] Dr Louisa Cunniffe was one of twenty-five female dentists listed in the Irish Free State Dental Register of 1930. She was based in Ballaghaderen, County Mayo and had graduated with a BDS from the National University of Ireland in 1926.[14]

According to the Irish Free State census of 1926, there were 31 female dentists out of a total of 536, or 6 per cent of the profession. In Northern Ireland, at the same time, there were only five female dentists and 250 male dentists. Hence, women, constituted only 2 per cent of the profession.[15] In medicine, women, were 14 per cent of the profession in northern Ireland and 11 per cent in the Irish Free State.

Female dentists may not have been prominent in Irish public life during the twentieth century but at least one achieved sporting fame. Thelma Hopkins was a dental student at Queen's University in

Belfast in 1956 when she broke the world record in the high jump. Later in the year she won a silver medal at the Melbourne Olympics. Hence, she was breaking barriers in a variety of ways.[16]

For twenty-first century dentists, rigorous preparation for a professional career forms an essential part of their development.[17] Rosemary Daly was a student at University College Cork between 1998 and 2003. Given her desire to work with her hands and with people, her choice of career is not surprising. She also liked the fact that an independent career, in one's own business, was possible. However, the actual course work was extremely demanding and extensive work in the dental hospital during the day had to be supplemented by intensive study in the evening. Colleagues were caring and one tended to know everyone in the class. Out of a total of forty-two students, eighteen were female. In some respects, it was good preparation for the professional life as one had to work nine-to-five and be prepared for all eventualities. In the final years of the course, the work was intensive and full-time in clinics. After graduation, Dr Daly decided to prepare for Membership of the Faculty of Dentistry, which is awarded by the Royal College of Surgeons. This involved undertaking a job in a recognised hospital post. The work entailed a lot of variety as well as the occasional assumption that a woman could not extract an awkward tooth, 'you'll never get that out', one elderly gentleman prophesised. He was wrong! Though women now constitute one-third of the profession, there were three female and eight male consultants in the Trinity Dental School. As of 12 September 2005, there were 1,483 male and 823 female dentists registered in the Republic of Ireland.[18] Hence, from a low of barely 5 per cent after the passage of the 1928 Dentists' Act, to 35 per cent of the profession in 2005, women in Ireland have greatly increased their representation in dentistry. Whether this increased proportion will change the symmetry of dentistry remains to be seen.

Chapter 16

Women in pharmacy in the early twentieth century

Introduction

Pharmacy is now a popular profession for women, but it was not always so. The 1926 census for both the Irish Free State and Northern Ireland do not list pharmacists. However, according to the Pharmaceutical Society of Ireland, there were 163 female pharmacists registered in 1931. In total, there were 1,407 registered pharmaceutical chemists in 1930. Hence, females constituted nearly 12 per cent of the profession.[1] This was slightly lower than the percentage for female doctors. A wide geographical spread of female pharmacists is evident, with most counties represented. A third, (fifty-eight in total) were based in major urban centres, such as, Dublin, Belfast, Cork, Galway, Derry and Waterford.

The majority of female pharmacists qualified in the 1920s. Twenty-seven, or 16 per cent, were married; but some of those listed may have married in the 1930s, as many had just qualified in the 1920s. Irish female pharmacists may have been attracted to a profession where their presence, while not encouraged, was, at least, acceptable. Family connections may have played a part, given that one had to obtain an apprenticeship. Furthermore, it was not possible to prepare for this profession without financial support.

Historical Background

The profession was established in 1875 with the passage of the Pharmacy Act. Just four years later, females in Britain were successful in their application for membership. By 1908, women in Britain constituted 1 per cent (160 females in total) of the Pharmaceutical Society. About 60 per cent of these worked in hospitals and institutions. As in medicine, the difficulty lay not in qualifying, but in establishing oneself. In 1905, the Association of Women Pharmacists was established in order to promote women in the profession.[2] In Ireland, by the 1930s, there was one female member on the Council of the Pharmaceutical Society. The male domination of the profession was evident when the Pharmaceutical Society of Northern Ireland met the Irish Council. He began his address with, 'Miss Flood and gentlemen'.[3] The first gold medal awarded by the Northern Ireland Society was won by Lavina Forrest in 1930.[4]

Typical Case Studies

To become a pharmacist in the 1900s, one had to serve four years as an apprentice to a qualified chemist and pass the examinations of the Pharmaceutical Society. The biggest initial difficulty facing aspiring pharmacists was obtaining an apprenticeship. For Christina Jessop it was essential to know pharmacists.[5] She had trained in Furlong's of Dublin. As the proprietor of the shop did not know how his customers would react to a lady pharmacist, she did much of the compounding of the medicines out of public view. Jessop had qualified before her husband. Once he qualified, they established a pharmacy in Cobh, County Cork. She had been an apothecary to the South Dublin Union, prior to her marriage.[6] Jessop worked with her husband until her children were born. Her husband died in the mid-1920s, when the youngest of her six children was two years old. She then returned to her profession (in a pre-pension age she was fortunate to have a profession to fall back on) and employed a male assistant to help in the pharmacy. She was the qualified pharmacist, however. Eventually in the 1940s her son qualified and he took over the pharmacy.[7] Jessop's career illustrates several general trends. In the higher professions it was easier to work after marriage. Nonetheless, the arrival of children usually impeded one's career. Furthermore, in her particular case, professional qualifications ensured the economic survival of the family. Not surprisingly two of her offspring also qualified as pharmacists.

Family connections were also a factor in the careers of the McGrath sisters. They practised pharmacy in Carrick-on-Suir near their native Clonmel, in Co. Tipperary. They were from a faming background, with eleven children in the family. Two of their brothers became doctors, so it is not surprising that they opted for a medically-related profession. After attending the local national school, they studied at Loreto Convent in Clonmel, and then began their pharmacy studies in the College of Pharmacy, Lower Mount Street, Dublin 2. Their father wanted the girls to be educated but their mother hoped they would stay at home. Hannah McGrath served her apprenticeship with Hayes, Conynham and Robinson. Hours were long, but she remained with the firm after qualifying. Frances McGrath, apparently the more ambitious of the two, opened her own pharmacy in Carrick-on-Suir after serving her apprenticeship in Parkes Pharmacy, Blackrock, County Dublin. Frances McCarthy had worked in pharmacies in Clare, Dublin and Waterford. She received a financial loan from a drug company which helped her establish McGrath's Medical Hall. Her decision may have been influenced by the strict monitoring of pharmaceutical apprentices, akin to those endured by nurses. It was difficult, on occasion, to get time to go to the toilet and McGrath attributed subsequent health problems to earlier discomforts endured as an apprentice. McGrath later married and transferred to Cork, so her sister took charge of the pharmacy in Carrick-on-Suir. The business dealt primarily in veterinary supplies, as it was situated in the heart of an agricultural area. Hannah McGrath was fortunate in that another sister, Kit, who also remained unmarried, worked at the shop counter, and as general factotum. Frances McGrath, except for occasional locum work, did not work professionally after her marriage.[8] The McGraths' careers suggest that single women had more professional freedom and the opportunity to establish an independent lifestyle.

Marriage was no impediment to the career of Patricia Rogan. Her marriage to another pharmacist, Jim Moran, made it easier for her to continue practising her profession. Both Rogan and her sister, Mamie, were pharmacists. They were the daughters of a publican and a school teacher, who was devoted to the education of her daughters. After being educated at the Dominican Convent, Muckross Park in the 1910s, the six girls in the family had professional careers. They were divided equally between nursing, pharmacy and medicine. Rogan had served her apprenticeship in French's Pharmacy, Ranelagh, in Dublin city. She met her future husband at the Pharmaceutical College, and, once they had qualified, they married immediately. While her children were young, the family employed domestic staff. Hence, she could work full-time in the family business in Bray. Patricia Rogan loved working there. The shop operated as a mini-dispensary with children being weighed and wounds dressed there. Frequently female customers asked Mrs Rogan for advice, and her activity mirrors the activism evident in the Women's National Health Association.[9] Furthermore, many women were shop assistants, so the working environment of pharmacists was not unknown to females.

Conclusion

It is clear that, by the 1920s, the profession was becoming popular for females. It was considered appropriate for females to cater for the ill health of children, and pharmacy gave them the opportunity to do this. As noted earlier, most of the females listed as registered pharmacists by 1930 had qualified in the 1920s. In 1934 Ruth Barry was one of the first students to graduate with a degree in pharmaceutical science at Queen's University, Belfast.[10] Hence, the profession was gaining academic respectability and this raised its status. Up until the 1950s, pharmacy education in the Republic was provided by the Pharmaceutical Society of Ireland. Then it became a degree awarded by the National University of Ireland. As a result of rationalisation of third-level education in the 1970s, Trinity College became the sole centre for the education of pharmacists. Subsequently the Royal College of Surgeons in Ireland and University College Cork began pharmacy degrees in 2002 and 2003 respectively. Pharmacy is now extremely popular as is evident from the high demand, amongst leaving certificate students, for pharmacy courses in Irish universities. However, unlike the beginning of the twentieth century, where men predominated in the profession, females now outnumber males by about two to one. This change is mirrored in the medical profession where two-thirds of undergraduates are female. Over the course of the last century, pharmacy has been transformed.

Chapter 17

The early years of female veterinary surgeons in Ireland, 1900-30

Between 1900 and 1930, there were only three women working as veterinary surgeons in Ireland. One of these ladies, Aleen Cust, had the remarkable distinction of completing a long and distinguished career as a veterinary surgeon before she was eventually allowed to register as a member of the profession. Born in Co. Tipperary in 1868 to a land agent and an aristocrat mother, Aleen's background did not suggest a future career as a veterinary surgeon. When she was ten her father died, and the family moved to England, where she was educated privately. Aleen was reputed to be 'good with animals' and in 1894 she went to Edinburgh to take up veterinary studies. Though her mother disapproved of her choice of career, she supported herself from a family inheritance. In later years, Aleen pointed out that her student years were a time of frugality and sacrifice. Whilst studying at the New Veterinary College in Edinburgh, a fellow student described her as 'most diligent ... an extremely brilliant practitioner and student, being first in all her classes.' However, despite excellent results, it seems that as a young woman Aleen was ineligible for college awards. Similarly, although Aleen was qualified to sit her professional examinations, the reluctance of the veterinary profession to admit a female meant that she wasn't allowed to do so.

By 1900 Aleen had finished her studies and had begun working in Roscommon, as an assistant to veterinary surgeon William Byrne. It is thought that, initially, Aleen and William worked together, possibly as husband and wife. He was favourably disposed towards women in the veterinary professions. In 1897, he pointed out, 'why any woman who loves a horse or a dog – or, as many of them do, all dumb things – will not be allowed to acquire a knowledge of their diseases, is a thing I cannot understand. Nor can I comprehend the mental attitude of those who insist there is no world for a woman veterinary surgeon except castration and obstetrics.' In 1900, the Dublin Veterinary College was founded and William Byrne was elected as President of the Irish Central Veterinary Society. This worked to Aleen's advantage, as she virtually ran the practice in Roscommon, despite the fact that she was not on the register. By 1905, she moved practice and was based in Ballygar, south of William's practice but still in the same county.

Aleen's love of horses was a big advantage in practise. After attending the International Veterinary Congress in Budapest, she gave a paper on horse-breeding in Hungary and Serbia, to the Irish Central Veterinary Association. In 1905, Aleen was selected by Galway County Council for the post of veterinary inspector. It was to be a controversial appointment, given that she was still not a member of the Royal College of Veterinary Surgeons (RCVS). She was eventually given the title of inspector, with the word 'veterinary' removed, in order to satisfy the RCVS.

In 1909 William Byrne died and Aleen Cust took over his practice, buying a house near Castlestrange, Co. Roscommon. Apparently quite well-off by this stage, she had four household staff and her professional activities included visiting cases on horseback and castrating colts. The local priest did not approve, but he was happy to avail of her services when his own cow became ill.

During the First World War, with its huge demand for horses, Aleen moved to France to help contribute to the war effort. She was based in the north-east of France, and her fluency in both French and German languages was a great advantage. She returned to Ireland after the First World War only to face the War of Independence and the inconvenience of having her car stolen by the IRA.

After the passage of Sex Disqualification (Removal) Act in 1919, the Dublin Veterinary College admitted female students. Despite this, the London and Scottish colleges were much slower in accepting women and it wasn't until 1922, that Aleen was finally given her diploma by the RCVS. However, by 1924 she had left Ireland permanently, to retire in Hampshire, England and she never practiced professionally. When commenting on her career in the 1930s, she attributed her success to 'fate, luck, tenacity, heredity: the last by no means least for one of my grandmothers had the same undying passion for animals and a way with them'. She died in 1937.

In the 1920s, three more women qualified as veterinary surgeons, all in Dublin. Olga Bligh-Woodward was from Sandymount in Dublin and graduated in 1926. Like many professional women, Olga emigrated in order to practice her profession. Initially, she was an assistant veterinary surgeon at Westcliff-on-Sea in Essex. Later, she moved to Burton-on-Trent, and was registered as Mrs Phillips. Even though she was not the first woman to practice veterinary surgery in Ireland, Olga Bligh-Woodward was the first woman to qualify in Ireland.

Hilda Bisset graduated in 1927. Originally from Scotland, Hilda probably came to Dublin as she could not study in her home country. Straight after graduation she moved back to Edinburgh and later based herself in Glasgow. Born in 1889, Hilda would have been in her late thirties by the time she qualified. She became a fellow of the RCVS in the 1940s and in the 1930s she settled in Bray, Co. Wicklow and remained there, it seems until her death in 1974.

One of her classmates was Katherine Hueffer, who also graduated in 1927. Katherine was born in 1900, in Hastings, England. Her father emigrated to the United States, where he lectured on literature at Cornell, when his children were quite young. The rest of his family remained in England and Katherine studied at the Holy Child Convent at St Leonard-On-Sea. During the First World War, she worked on a farm as part of the war effort and developed an interest in agriculture. As the London college would not accept female veterinary students, she came to Ireland in 1920. However, she had to spend a year learning Latin (which she had dropped in favour of music at school) so she could be accepted by the veterinary college. While a student in Dublin, she met her future husband, the painter Charles Lamb (1893-1964). They married and moved to Carraroe, an Irish-speaking area in Co. Galway. Katherine did not speak Irish, so she learned the language. As secretary of the local Irish Countrywomen's Association guild, she wrote the minutes in Irish and was involved in Gaeltarra Eireann (a group which helped to established local industries in Irish-speaking areas). Katherine was particularly interested in horses, which were a vital means of transport in Carraroe during the Second World War. Her veterinary practice, which she maintained until 1947, was known as 'humanity Dick', after the Galway hero who was concerned about animals. She died in 1978.

How do the experiences of Irish veterinary surgeons compare with their American counterparts? The first female graduate from the United States was Mignon Nicholson, in 1903. In 1910, two more female vets graduated. Elinor McGrath, who graduated from Chicago Veterinary College in 1910, specialised in small animals and retired after thirty-seven years. Whilst Irish veterinarians, with the exception of Aleen Cust, arrived on the scene about fifteen years later than their professional colleagues from the US, they had more varied careers. Given that it was rare to have more than one veterinary surgeon in the locality, females had the opportunity to work with a range of animals rather than specialising in the more feminine area of small animals.

Full sources for this article are available in the author's PhD. See chapter 8 of *Far from Few: Professional Women in Ireland, 1800-1930* (University College, Dublin, History Doctorate, 1999)

Chapter 18

Shedding their 'reserve': Camogie and the origins of women's sport in Ireland

Ireland's first camogie club was based in Navan Co. Meath and was established in 1898. Tomás Ó Domhnalláin described his family's involvement in the game in *Ríocht na Midhe* 2003. His mother, Máire Ní Cheallaigh (Mary Kelly), was a member of the first camogie team ever. The club, not surprisingly, was linked to the Gaelic League which had been established in 1893 in order to promote Irish language and culture. These pioneering camogie players were part of what was described as 'a ladies' hurling team'. The club was established so that they could play an exhibition match as part of the commemoration of the 1798 rebellion. The game was played at Tara, the historic inauguration place of ancient Irish kings and one of the flash points of the insurrection in 1798. An excellent photograph of these early camogie players which was taken in 1904 has been provided on page 142 of *Ríocht na Midhe* 2003. The original photograph is in the excellent GAA museum at Croke Park.

The links between the Irish language and Camogie were strengthened with the involvement of Agnes O'Farrelly, Úna Ní Fhaircheallaigh (1874-1951) in the promotion of Camogie at third-level. A Cavan woman, she was one of the early graduates of the Royal University of Ireland, having received her BA in 1889 and her MA in 1900. She was appointed a lecturer in modern Irish in UCD in 1909 and, in 1932, she became the professor of Modern Irish Poetry on the retirement of Douglas Hyde. Like the early Camogie players she was closely involved in the Gaelic League. A popular teacher in UCD, she had, according to Dr Marie Coleman, the author of her entry in the *Dictionary of Irish Biography*, which is published by Cambridge University Press, 'a reputation as a social figure and entertained frequently at her homes in Dublin and the Donegal Gaeltacht.' Most importantly, she founded the UCD Camogie club in 1914. Winners of the intervarsity Camogie Championship receive the Ashbourne Cup because Agnes O'Farrell managed to convince the 2nd Lord Ashbourne, William Gibson, to donate this cup. Not only that, O'Farrelly was president of the Camogie Association of Ireland in 1941-2. Camogie was part of the general gaelicisation programme of the late-nineteenth and early twentieth centuries in Ireland. When the Tailteann Games were held in Dublin in 1924, Camogie was part of the programme. Dr Michael Cronin is currently researching the activities surrounding the Games and he has unearthed an *Irish Times* report (4 August 1924) of the Camogie match at the Tailteann Games. The 'international match' was played at University Park, Terenure. Ireland won easily, beating England eight nil. Furthermore, 'the weather was most adverse and the ground sodden after the morning's downpour.' Some things never change! This was August after all. The teams were as follows; Ireland: R. Cannon, A. Cunningham, Kelly, Cullen, McDonald, Thackabery, N. Byrne, Cairn, Rowden, O'Brien and Glynn; England: T. Rice, E.A Berkeney, E. Raywood, A. O'Rourke, M. Ballesty, K. Coffey, T. Glenworth, E. Donnelly, K. Furling, K. Grant, A. Mulholland and K. Halligan. Such was Ireland's superiority that they led seven nil at half time. The fact that they were playing at all may have caused surprise in certain quarters. Women were excluded from all track and field events at the Olympic Games until 1928 when a mere five events were open to female athletes. In the same year, Pope Pius XI declared that sport was 'irreconcilable with woman's reserve'! This comment was in keeping with the views of certain commentators who did not relish the sight of sportswomen. Ironically, the very devout students at Mary Immaculate College of Education in Limerick also indulged in Camogie playing the 1920s and '30s. They also played other sports as the Mary Immaculate Training College Annuals, published between 1927 and 1954, and available in the National Library of Ireland, make abundantly clear. The traditional picture of female restrictions in the sporting arena may have to be modified, when one looks at training colleges. Trinity historian, Dr Maryann Valiulis, has made much of the Mary Immaculate Modest Dress and Deportment Crusade. This sought to eliminate immodest dress amongst prospective primary teachers. She links this with the restrictions on mixed-athletics, and its ban by John Charles McQuaid, then president of Blackrock College. Sr Loreto O'Connor, the historian of Mary Immaculate Training College, points out that the crusade 'attracted thousands of members from all walks of life.' Their fashion guidelines were as follows: 'dresses to be worn not less than four inches below the knee' and 'sleeves to be not more than one inch above the elbow for day wear, not more than two inches above the elbow for evening wear and sleeves to the wrist for Church wear.' Furthermore, members of the deportment crusade were to abstain from 'loud talking and boisterous laughter in public.' However many students in Limerick also played basketball (hardly a sport noted for its sedate pace), baseball and tennis, as well as the aforementioned Camogie. Hence, despite restrictions in many aspects of their lives women had some opportunities to enjoy outdoor activities. Camogie was part of this development and its importance should not be underestimated.

Chapter 19

Internal tamponage, hockey parturition and mixed athletics in Ireland in the 1930s, '40s, and '50s[1]

In 2004, Brian Griffin published a revealing article titled 'The popularity of cycling for both men and women in counties Louth and Meath' in *Ríocht na Midhe*, Vol. XV, pp. 123-51. My article aims to expand on that discussion by contributing to an aspect of Irish sporting and medical history. In 1934 the National Athletic and Cycling Association suggested hosting a women's 100 yards sprint as part of their national championship. The response to this innovation reveals much about the position of women in Irish society at that time. The ensuing debate on women in sport provides a way of analysing the role of women in Ireland in the 1930s, '40s and '50s. Discussion frequently centred on the attire to be worn by sportswomen. Given the restrictions on women's movements, it is easy today to underestimate the sporting spaces which women could inhabit. This article will discuss both the restrictions upon and opportunities for sportswomen in Ireland during the 1930s, '40s and '50s.

Voices had been raised against the spectre of women indulging in vigorous physical exercise in public in 1928. The conservative and unionist *Irish Times* was intent on supporting Pope Pius XI in his desire to avert robust forms of female sporting activity. An *Irish Times* editorial was provoked by an athletics competition for women in Italy. Women had been holding their own in competitions with men in lawn tennis and golf. Girls' schools included gyms and hockey pitches and these had provided 'immense boons' to 'women's health'. However, the editorial claimed that in France, Germany, Italy and 'even in England many girls are devoting themselves to public sports which demand violent exercise and sometimes, it would seem, a notable scantiness of clothing'. Even more frightening, for the editor, was the fact that these 'performances are done before crowds of male spectators'. 'His Holiness', he intoned, 'is surely in the right when he says that they are "irreconcilable with woman's reserve"' and that 'in this matter Christian Europe ought not to be less modest than pagan Rome.' The conclusion drawn was that the 'extreme exertion' associated with 'running and rowing' must be fatal 'for even the most robust women; already, no doubt, it had shortened many lives.' Finally, the editor hoped that the Fascist government in Italy would 'pay due heed to the Pope's warning and that the Irish people never will give the slightest encouragement to the practices which it deplores'.[2] Just three years earlier, the pious Catholic *Boston Pilot* announced that Pope Pius XI extolled modesty of dress.[3] This concern was part of an international phenomenon, with modesty crusades in Italy and France, in order to counteract the advance of the 'modern woman'. This crusade interacted with sporting opportunities, in particular, the events women were permitted to participate in once a mixed-gender audience was present. Ironically, it was the Fascist regime in Germany which sought to highlight the abilities of the female physique through performance at a high level in the Olympic Games in Berlin in 1936. However, that was closely linked to the propaganda needs of the Nazis.

Athletics for women had been introduced at the Olympic Games in 1928 after the retirement of the founder of the modern Olympic movement, Baron Pierre de Courbetin. He had very clear views on the place of women in sport. He declared: 'women have but one task, that of the role of crowning the winner with garlands, as was their role in ancient Greece'.[4] Even when women competed at the Olympic Games, several competitors were subjected to the 'full weight of male condescension'. Furthermore in 1928, 'ill-informed physiological and psychological assumptions were immediately used to deduce that women were incapable of running more than a couple of hundred yards without succumbing to a fit of the vapours.'[5] By 1956 the longest women's race on the programme was 200 metres. The 3,000 metres and marathon were introduced only in 1984. The 3,000 metres steeplechase was introduced in 2008.

In Ireland, leading the resistance to mixed athletics in 1934 was Revd John Charles McQuaid, then President of Blackrock College, an all-male, Catholic institution under the management of the Holy Ghost Fathers. In a letter to The *Irish Press*, on 24 February 1934, which was also published in *The Irish Times* the same day, he made it clear that 'the issue is not: in what forms of athletic sport may women or girls indulge, with safety to their well-being. That question should be duly determined by medical science, rightly so called.' Neither, he argued, was it a question of female activity within their own colleges and associations, that 'question should be duly solved by the principles both of Christian modesty and of true medical science.' He made it abundantly clear that 'mixed athletics and all cognate immodesties are abuses that right-minded people reprobate, wherever and whenever they exist.' To clinch his argument he declared, 'God is not modern; nor is his Law'. Women competing in the same sporting arena with men were 'un-Irish and un-Catholic' and mixed athletics were a 'social abuse' and a 'moral abuse'. He then went on to quote the encyclical letter of Pope Pius XI, *Divini Illius Magistri*, which he helpfully translated: 'in athletic sports and exercises, wherein the Christian modesty of girls must be, in a special way, safeguarded, for it is supremely unbecoming that they flaunt themselves and display themselves before the eyes of all.'[6] Paul Rouse has suggested that mixed doubles in tennis were seen as a mating ritual. These opportunities would not be tolerated by McQuaid.[7]

In private correspondence, Fr John Roe, of the Marist College in Dundalk, congratulated Dr McQuaid on his 'splendid protest in the recent athletic proposition. Please God your timely action will prevent the carrying out of the monstrous suggestion.'[8] To introduce mixed athletics was an 'unchristian imposition on a Catholic people', according to Revd Dr Conway, the chaplain at St Mary's Training College for Catholic females in Belfast.[9]

Writing in The *Irish Press*, J.P. Noonan of St Mary's College, Marino, the Christian Brothers Training College, congratulated McQuaid and expressed the hope that the protests would 'kill the pagan proposal of the athletic association'.[10] Thus a newspaper debate was initiated on women's opportunities in sport. The *Daily Mail* suggested that there were plans to establish a women's athletic association, though these came to nought.[11] This was not an entirely original idea as the Women's Amateur Athletic Association was established in Britain in 1923 by, amongst others, Sophie Elliot-Lynn, a world record holder in the high jump and a native of Knockaderry, near Newcastle West in County Limerick.[12]

The GAA also waded in. Dr Magnier (Cork) supported the views of McQuaid, since, 'people of influence', unnamed, of course, asked that women not be allowed to play at Croke Park. Dr Magnier pointed out that from the 'moral point of view it was absolutely wrong to be running young men and women in the same field in the same grab now effected for these events'. Echoing McQuaid, Mr O'Brien of Clare said that the Pope, in a recent encyclical, objected to women taking part in tug-o-war, 'wrestling and boxing competitions, but he did not object to them taking part in the lighter forms of athletics, such as running and jumping.' Revealingly, he believed that 'freer mingling of the sexes on an athletic field would do good.' An Ulster man, Mr O'Reilly, said that in Northern Ireland, women had been 'competing in athletic contests for a long time. Public opinion was so much against it, however, that the GAA in Antrim had to prevent women athletes from appearing in Corrigan Park in anything but gym dresses.'[13] Agnes O'Farrelly, president of the Camogie Association and a founder of the Ashbourne Cup, the intervarsity camogie competition, reminisced about the early years of the association; it was the 'time of the hobble skirts, when the girls went down like nine pins when they tried to run.'[14]

By March 1934, such was the impact of the discussion which McQuaid had provoked that the National Athletic and Cycling Association had decided not to implement mixed athletics, but officially they were in favour of the idea.[15] James McGilton, the Honorary Secretary of the NACA, assured McQuaid that his letter to them would be discussed at the next meeting. McGilton also placated McQuaid's ego by suggesting that the headmaster's 'protest was made in the best interests of the Association.'[16] Furthermore, McQuaid wrote to the *Daily Herald* and declared that 'no boy from the college would be permitted to compete at any meeting at which women were to take part.'[17]

The thirty-year-old, all-female Camogie Association supported McQuaid's proposal.[18] Sean O'Duffy, the organising secretary, reassured the readers of the *Sunday Independent* that the association 'would do all in its power to ensure that no girl would appear on any sports ground in a costume to which any acception [*sic*] of the world they could not go wrong.'[19] Not everyone shared this view, however. Mr McManus thought that 'something should be done to support women in this. They are taking part in different kinds of sport all over the world.'[20] When the NACA decided not to permit mixed athletics, McManus complained about the decision and pointed out that the 'largest clubs in the city have events for ladies-cycling and all.'[21] However, this seemed to be a minority view. The impact of McQuaid's complaints spread to the west. The *East Galway Democrat* explained that 'on the grounds of delicacy and modesty there is grave on objection to women taking part in athletics with men, and women should not be blind to this.'[22]

So far, only the male views expressed in this controversy have been discussed. What, then, did the women think? Miss Dockrell, the women's 100 yards swimming champion, thought it was 'hard to understand the ban, since there was no question of 'mixed athletics'.[23] Eileen Bulger, was according to the *Irish Press*, a well-known Irish runner. She did not see what objection could be taken to girls competing in reserved events. The 100 yards championship for girls were held annually at the Civil Service Sports and a competition for girls was included in the Garda Sports. J.J. McGilton, Secretary of the NACA, supported this development. He told an *Irish Press* reporter, that until the 1930s, women had competed in reserved events at men's meetings and no objection was taken. The 100 yards championship for women had been in existence for years.[24] However, after McQuaid's campaign, mixed athletics was not countenanced.

A decade later McQuaid was still concerned about the movements of Irish women. In April 1944 he wrote to Dr Conn Ward, Parliamentary Secretary to the Minister for Local Government and Public Health, regarding a recent meeting with his fellow bishops.[25] McQuaid had been appointed Roman Catholic Archbishop of Dublin in 1940 and he informed Ward that the 'Low Week Meetings of the Bishops, I explained very fully the evidence concerning the use of internal sanitary tampons, in particular, that called Tampax. On the medical evidence made available, the bishops very strongly disapproved of the use of these appliances, more particularly in the case of unmarried persons.' 'Married persons' was a euphemism for women. Did men actually use tampax? Were they seen as a contraceptive device, perhaps for petite males! It requires a remarkable gynaecological imagination to see tampax as a contraceptive. However, the more pertinent fear was that women might derive sexual stimulation from tampax. This reflects the cultural anxieties of the era.

Revealingly, McQuaid's medical advisor was Dr Stafford Johnson, who had studied in Clongrowes Wood College and graduated in medicine from UCD in 1914.[26] He took a particular interest in medico-moral issues and was an enthusiastic advocate of Catholic ethics in medicine. Early in 1934, Stafford Johnson wrote to McQuaid requesting the return of the *Catholic Medical Guardian* 'in which there was given the pronouncement of the English Hierarchy on Internal Tamponage.'[27] With an ill-disguised sinister tone, Stafford Johnson explained that an 'interesting development has occurred. Tampax has been off the market here for over a year & a half. One of our Knight Chemists [Stafford Johnson was a Supreme Knight[28]] has just rung me up to say it is about to be in stock once more but has not been delivered from the Agent.' The 'moral dangers' of Tampax were pointed out to the chemist and the crisis was averted. It was 1944 after all! The obsession with female fertility so concerned the Archbishop that certain middle-class, Catholic, all-girls schools were discouraged from playing hockey since the twisting movements were alleged to have caused hockey parturition, that is infertility. Hence, lacrosse was favoured.[29] The latter activity did not necessitate as much midriff movement. Given these restrictions on women's movements, it is clear that the sporting spaces which women could inhabit without diluting their modesty were grossly diminished.

Maryann Valiulis has made much of the Mary Immaculate College of Education Modest Dress and Deportment Crusade. This sought to eliminate immodest dress amongst prospective primary teachers. She links this with the restrictions on mixed-athletics, and its ban by John Charles McQuaid.[30] O'Connor, the official historian of Mary Immaculate Training College, points out that the crusade 'attracted thousands of members from all walks of life.' Their fashion guidelines were as follows:' dresses to be worn not less than four inches below the knee' and 'sleeves to be not more than one inch above the elbow for day wear, not more than two inches above the elbow for evening wear and sleeves to the wrist for Church wear.' Furthermore, members of the deportment crusade were to abstain from 'loud talking and boisterous laughter in public.'[31]

However, these same students indulged in physical activities. Therefore, the traditional picture of female restrictions in the sporting arena may have to be modified, when one looks at all-female educational institutions. Many students in Limerick played basketball (hardly a sport noted for its sedate pace), baseball and tennis. This may in part, be due to the enthusiasm of Sr Veronica Cullinan, who became principal of the college in 1923.[32] She was a great believer in outdoor activities, and loved fresh air. Such was the interest in games that the students were allowed to forgo their Sunday walk. This walk was normally a ritual in all-female boarding establishments. The students played basketball matches instead. These activities may be seen as part of the European gymnastic movement which contributed, in part, to the revival of the Olympic Games in 1896 and organised games in the early twentieth century. However, this was usually associated with Swedish Drill. Hence, it comes as a surprise to see demure Mary Immaculate students racing around a court.

The much-maligned elastics were the subject of an article by M.B. (1928) a senior student in Limerick during the late 1920s. She pondered: 'surely the elastics remind you of the Games. Don't you remember the Base-Ball and the Basket-Ball, and don't you remember how awkward you felt the first few days and how hard you found it to be frisky, when encased in a brand new pair of elastics?[33] It is clear that although these students were physically active, this was within the confines of an all-female environment. Schools under the management of the Loreto sisters participated in the Loreto Sports from 1905. The Loreto Shield was introduced specifically for athletics, twenty-three years before women were allowed to compete at the Olympic Games. Students at various Sr Louis schools played a variety of games from basketball to camogie.[34] Significantly, these sports took place within an all-female environment.

Once women were not flaunting themselves in front of males, it was possible to pursue sporting activities. The WAAA (a women's only athletics organisation) was to have particular impact on the development of athletics for women in Northern Ireland. Furthermore, when the Northern Ireland Amateur Athletic Association appointed Franz Stampfh as coach in the 1950s, he worked with Thelma Hopkins, who went on to break the world record (in May 1956) as well as win an Olympic silver medal (the following December) in the high jump. Hopkins remembered that when she first played hockey for Ireland 'we had to wear long black stockings and tunics down to our knees. Really, it was extremely difficult to play. But in the North, we had a lot of support from the men, mainly because Stampfl was there and his athletes were taken seriously.'[35] It may be no accident that Maeve Kyle (*née* Shankey) who was born in Kilkenny and played hockey for Trinity College and Ireland, did not become involved in athletics until she married an athletics coach, Sean Kyle, and moved to Ballymena in County Antrim. In 1956, she became the first Irish woman in athletics to compete for the Republic of Ireland at the Olympic Games.[36]

As late as the 1960s McQuaid was still concerned with 'unnatural pleasures' associated with female gymnastics, especially the pommel horse.[37] He was unaware of the unnatural pain associated with the event. Both McQuaid and later commentators' obsession with female activity, have blinded many to the varieties of activities which women could indulge in, but the sensual sight of mixed athletics did not become a reality in Ireland until the 1960s.[38]

Chapter 20

Councillor Tully's views on women and paid work[1]

In 1925, a Kells councillor, Mr Tully, complained that the 'modern young woman cannot be easy unless she has a man's job, and a man's trouser's on'. He lamented: 'it's very unfair, in ten years' time we'll have nothing in this unfortunate country but old maids and cats. It is the greatest curse in Ireland to be having women in everything. Because they're cheeky and cheap they are succeeding in ousting the young men out of positions in every department of the public service, in the banks and in commercial undertakings. The government offices are crammed with women. Hence, the young men are flying from the country as fast as they can go. If young men had these jobs, they would, in time, be in a position to marry, but women in these positions seldom marry, and besides, men are afraid to marry that type of woman ... are we going to be bossed by petticoats ... woman was made for one job by God Almighty, and she is a fool in her interests if she does not stick to it.'[2]

This paper will dissect the views of Mr Tully, as a prelude to a fuller consideration of professional women in Ireland between 1880 and 1930. He was articulating concerns regarding the rise in female employment. Throughout the early twentieth century this was a major issue. In particular, after the First World War and the disruption of the War of Independence and the Civil War, employment opportunities in Ireland were diminishing. Hence, his comments should not be seen in isolation. However, how accurate was he? I will examine each of his statements in turn.

Old maids and cats

Unfortunately, the census statistics for 1926 do not include the number of feline creatures in the Irish Free State and Northern Ireland. However, we do have details on the number of single females. The social connotations of certain words are fascinating. 'Old maid' conjures up the image of a wizened woman complete with feline friends. One never hears of an 'eligible spinster', but 'eligible bachelor' has completely different connotations.

In 1926, there were 343,894 women in employment in the Irish Free State. Only 23,895 were married, 55,334 were widowed and 264,665 were single. But how many could be defined as old maids? Let us assume that anyone who is fifty-five years and over is an 'old maid', than there were 19,750 single women in that category who were 'gainfully employed'. However, there were over a million females in the state; hence, the country was not being overwhelmed by old maids and cats.

Women in everything

Well, not quite. Women, if they were in paid employment, worked in female-dominated occupations. The biggest category of female employment was domestic service. If women enjoyed professional careers, they tended to be teachers or nurses. These professionals were not distinguished by high salaries or impressive status. While women did dominate, numerically speaking in health and education, the management of these occupations was primarily in male hands.

Cheeky and cheap

Mr Tully may have been slightly accurate here. It is virtually impossible to assess the cheekiness of women in the 1930s. If anything, women were valued for their willingness to work for long hours for very little pay. Hence, it suited the State to employ the cheaper sex. Perhaps Mr Tully is suggesting that cheap does not refer to their low rates of pay. Nonetheless, pay differentials were widespread. Women, on average, earned 60 per cent of male salaries. Not surprisingly, females dominated in poorly-paid occupations.

Ousting the young men out of positions in every department of the public service, the banks and commercial undertakings

It is incontestable that women were moving into new areas of employment. For example, as Mary E. Daly has noted, the 'number of women civil servants increased from 940 in April 1922 to 2,260 in April 1932'.[3] However, it will not surprise anybody that women dominated in the lower ranks of the public service. By 1926, there were 8,368 males working as civil service officials and clerks. In Northern Ireland, there were 2,897 males and 1,124 females working as civil service officials and clerks, so this was hardly a female takeover. Furthermore, men were strongly represented in the commercial sector, with 34,350 men and 13,366 women in commercial finance and insurance occupations in Northern Ireland. Predictably, these figures are duplicated in the Irish Free State, with single women constituting the largest female component in commerce, and, finance.

Young men flying from the country

This is where Mr Tully's arguments become completely unstuck. Throughout the 1920s, female emigration exceeded male. As Pauric Travers has observed, in the 'century from 1871 to 1971, net female emigration outnumbered male overall', and there was a 'female predominance between 1901-11, 1926-36, 1946-51 and 1961-71'.[4] Were women voting with their feet? More revealingly, the majority of women who emigrated in the early twentieth century worked as domestic servants. It was the young women who were flying from the country. Why? Few jobs were created for females, and male unemployment was seen as a serious problem. Conversely, female unemployment was not seen as a serious issue.

Made for one job by God Almighty

This was an area where there is a lot of anecdotal, if not statistical, information. The 1937 Constitution makes its philosophy of gender-segregated employment clear: 'citizens shall not be forced by economic necessity to enter avocations unsuited to their sex'.[5] It was perceived that women were unfit for certain occupations. Females were educated in a culture of compliance. Both men and women inculcated a particular view of women's role in society. Modesty was emphasised. If one looks, for instance, at the cultural formation of students at second-level in the 1920s, it is clear that obedience, rather than ambition,

was fostered. In her history of Loreto Convent in Navan, Margaret
Gibbons suggested that examinations were 'unsuitable for the respectable, middle-class female youth of Ireland who will be the wives
and mothers of the farmers.' She cited the Roman Catholic Bishop
of Meath, who reinforced this view. He deplored 'the advent of the
new woman who demanded equal rights with her brother in admission to a study of the exact sciences and to the Pagan literature of
Greece and Rome'.[6] Apparently, it was acceptable for males, especially
those studying for the priesthood, to imbibe this paganism. 'Experts'
suggested that females who sat examinations were characterised by
'rounded shoulders' and a 'peculiar gait', as well as 'impaired eyesight'
and 'epilepsy'. One school principal suggested that her students 'try to
cultivate the calm repose which stamps the case of Vere de Vere'.[7] The
politician Frank Hugh O'Donnell believed that schools were manufacturing 'young feminine failures and non-values for the decline, the
depression and the destruction of the Irish nation'. Furthermore, he
argued that female students were 'fit for nothing under heaven except
casting flowers before the Banner of the Sodality'.[8] However, despite
greater educational opportunities in the early twentieth century,
woman chose, or were encouraged to opt for, traditional occupations.

In 1935, Dr J.C. Flood, a surgeon and demonstrator at the
Department of Physiology and Biochemistry, at University College,
Dublin, suggested that 'woman, as woman, had not and never had
any need of emancipation; in all ages she has almost invariably
obtained whatever she wanted, and sometimes what she deserved'.[9]
It is deeply reassuring to note that Dr Flood was secretary of the
National University of Ireland Appointment Bureau.

Thus far, this paper has looked generally at women and work.
Perhaps it might be worth considering in general terms the opportunities available to women who were fortunate enough to receive an
education in the late-nineteenth and early twentieth century. Given
the ideology of female subordination, it is very easy to underestimate
the public spaces where females were welcome. Welfare-type work
was one public space where females were welcomed. Olwen Hufton
has suggested that, 'at the practical level, the social conscience of the
nineteenth century is largely in female hands'.[10] Though she was
referring to all of western Europe, the same observation could be
made of Ireland. The professions to which women flocked were
those which gave precedence to nurturing activities. Hence, through
their work, professional women became more aware and made

others alert to, the social needs of society. In some ways, they paved the path towards the welfare State. As ever, economic factors were to retard their work. Additionally, while many may have been motivated by the opportunity to improve the lives of others, this was not their only reason for choosing a particular career.

To what extent were professional women responding to increased opportunities? Undoubtedly, the educational improvements of the late-nineteenth century opened up avenues for the advancement of women. Ironically, the Royal University of Ireland was established in 1879 to facilitate middle-class, catholic males. This did not prevent females availing of the chance to pursue a university degree. While professional women were faced with a greater range of career choices, they were also subjected to more intense competition for jobs. More males, with higher qualifications, ensured that when demand exceeded supply for professional positions, women were frequently the losers. Their best hope for a professional occupation lay in the public sphere, in health or education. Even in these occupations, professionals were segregated by sex, with women working as nurses and females teaching girls. Though professional women may have been serving the public, they worked in private institutions. These institutions were subject primarily to their own rules. Only when we examine women in the higher professions do we see a certain level of independence. In general, they would have had greater control over their own careers, and were fortunate enough to be able to afford the long training associated with a high-status profession. The vast majority of women examined in this period grasped the opportunity to pursue at least a semi-professional career. Nonetheless, they were denied the security of a high-status profession. The female doctors, dentists and accountants were less likely to resign on marriage, and could pursue their career until retirement.

Despite the greater availability of jobs in the areas where women predominated, social barriers remained in the higher professions. While future female accountants and lawyers benefited for the Sex Disqualification (Removal) Act of 1919, it was a far greater challenge to be accepted by others in the profession. This was less of an issue for female teachers and nurses. Yet, the female face of these professions ensured that they would be less able to press for greater autonomy and increased pay. Given that so many jobs were not advertised, and with localism still prevalent for some, it was the triumph of proximity over performance. If one was in the right place at the right time, then employment by osmosis was possible. For those not so geographically favoured, unemployment or emigration loomed. It is not difficult to understand why so many women decided to take their talents elsewhere. In the 1920s and 1930s, as noted earlier, most emigrants were female.[11] Many of these were unskilled, however, and tended to work as domestic servants. While emigration was a concern of government, little seemed to have been done to stem the tide of female emigration. Political power remained in male hands, though women were making their mark in local government.

Despite the challenges faced by those who were pioneers in their occupational fields, they could be considered the fortunate ones, in socio-economic terms. One is struck by the sheer waste of human capital when assessing the careers of many women. Ultimately, women's involvement in the professions, while relatively high, was in a limited number of areas. Though opportunities increased for most women in Ireland, between 1880 and 1920, this was to change over the next two decades. With the establishment of Northern Ireland and the Irish Free State, many avenues became cul-de-sacs. The parsimonious 1920s, when social welfare was not a priority for new governments, ensured that there were fewer jobs in health and education. In the longer term, the worldwide recession in the 1930s ensured that the more vulnerable members of the labour force (women and poorly-paid men) were often the losers. For those who opted for careers which depended on State support, the 1930s were not fruitful. It is not surprising that the Irish Free State introduced a marriage ban for primary teachers in the 1930s. In a depressed era, female employment was seen as a luxury. Salaried women were perceived as denying a male his right to work. That many unemployed males did not have the necessary qualifications for professional work was not considered. Economics triumphed over equality. This was a worldwide phenomenon, with openings for women also declining in the United States and western Europe. The fascist states in Italy, Spain and Germany were noted for their traditional views of women. A cult of female domesticity dominated. Hence, careers for women, particularly professional careers were becoming less politically acceptable by the 1930s.

For many professional women in Ireland, between 1880 and 1930, work was a vital part of their lives. Despite their elevated status, economic survival often propelled them into the workplace. In this, as in many other elements of their lives, they were no different from their brothers and sisters in the wider world.

Notes

Introduction
1. Laurel Thatcher Ulrich, *Well-behaved Women Seldom Make History* (Alfred Knorf: New York, 2007)

Chapter 1
1. Central Association of Irish Schoolmistresses, Minutes of February 1889 (first meeting) TCD Ms. 9722/1.
2. See Susan Parkes, *Kildare Place: The History of the Church of Ireland Training College 1811-1969* (Dublin, 1984) for the archival sources of this institution.
3. I am grateful to the matron, Miss Mary Kelly, for her help with the Rotunda archives.
4. I am grateful to Dr Frances Carruthers for introducing me to the Peamonut Archives.
5. Gerry McAllister, 'The WNHA 1907-1911' (MA minor, St Patrick's College, Drumcondra, 1999) has made excellent use of these archives.
6. I am grateful to Robert Millis, librarian at the Royal College of Physicians, for his help.
7. For further details on Dr Dorothy Price and the elimination of childhood Tuberculosis see Joost Augustjein (ed.) *Ireland in the 1930s: New Perspectives* (Dublin, 1999).
8. Helen Bradley of the King's Inn is familiar with these records.
9 I am grateful to Tara McCafferty for alerting me to various sources in the headquarters of the Pharmaceutical Society of Ireland, Dublin.

Chapter 2

1. D. Fleischman, *An Outline of Careers for Women: A Practial Guide to Achievement* (London, 1929), p. xi.
2. David Fitzpatrick, 'The Modernisation of the Irish Female' in Patrick O'Flanagan, Ferguson and Whelan (eds) *Rural Ireland: Modernisation and Change, 1600-1900* (1987), p. 164.
3. *ibid.*, p. 165.
4. Anne O'Connor, 'Influence Affecting Girls' Secondary Education in Ireland 1860-1910' (MA thesis, University College Dublin, 1981).
5. Síle Chuinneagáin 'Women Teachers and INTO Policy 1905-16 (MEd minor thesis, Trinity College Dublin, 1993), p. 10.
6. 1911 Census.
7. Harold Perkin, *The Rise of Professional Society: England Since 1800* (London, 1989), p. 4.
8. Women entered the medical profession in 1877, the legal profession in 1919 and the chartered accountancy in 1925. However, female representation was quite low in these professions.
9. Mary Carberry, *The Farm by Lough Gur* (London, 1937); O'Connor (1981).
10. Olwen Hufton, *The Prospect Before Her: A History of Women in Western Europe. Vol. 1 1500-1800* (London 1995), p. 65.
11. Rose O'Neill, *A Rich Inheritance: Galway Dominican Nuns 1644-1994* (Galway: School Publication, 1994), p. 117.
12. Cited in O'Connor (1981).
13. Parliamentary Paper: 'Annual Report of the Commissioners of Education in Ireland for the year 1918', p. 524.
14. *ibid.*, pp. iii-xix.
15. National Archives ED 11, file 1/54, 499-18c. Miss Phelan was applying for a position as female/junior (the words were interchangeable!) inspector. The application forms had to be returned by 22 January 1918.
16. Royal College of Science Register of Associate Students and their Successes B63 and B64. Register of Occasional and Non-Associate Students 1867-1906 B65 in UCDA.
17. Patricia Philips, *The Scientific Lady: A Social History of Women's Scientific Interests 1520-1918* (London, 1990), p. 214.
18. Obituary 23 April 1946 in National University Women Graduates' Association (hereafter NUWGA) Papers 1/2, in UCD Archives.
19. Jordan (1994), pp. 20-1.
20. 1911 Census.
21. *ibid.*
22. Anne O'Connor, and Susan Parkes, *Gladly Teach and Gladly Learn: Alexandra College and School 1866-1966* (Dublin: Blackwater Press, 1984), pp. 35-52.
23. Meeting 22 May 1906 in NUWGA 1/3.
24. *ibid.*
25. Eibhlin Breathnach, 'A History of the Movement for Women's Higher Education in Dublin (MA thesis, UCD, 1981), p. 10.

26. Minutes of Central Association of Irish Mistresses (hereafter CAISM) 1889-1981; TCD Ms. 9722.

27. CAISM Minutes Ms. 9722/1, 5 December 1905.

28. CAISM Minutes Ms. 9722/1, 5 December 1905.

29. Eighty exhibitioners out of 106 did not take Greek or maths in *ibid.*

30. Cited in Jordan (1994), p. 21.

31. *Lyceum*, August 1893.

32. Alexandra College Archives memorial to the Board of TCD 10 December 1902.

33. O'Connor (1981), p. 168.

34. F.H. O'Donnell, *The Ruin of Education in Ireland* (London, 1902), p. 152.

35. Quoted in *ibid.*, p. 152.

36. *New Ireland Review*, December 1901 quoted in *ibid.*, p. 153. How representative were the views of O'Donnell who went on to be a TD and his anonymous friend, the barrister? They were not lone voices as the views of William Starkie, a resident commissioner of education, quoted later make clear.

37. Jordan (1995), p. 48.

38. *Lyceum*, August 1893.

39. Summer Matriculation Examination, 1918 in National University of Ireland college calendar 1919, pp. 537-46.

40. Belinda Finnegan, 'The Democratisation of Higher Education and the Participation of University Women in the Labour Force, 1920-50' (MA thesis, UCD, 1985), p. 50.

41. Parkes and O'Connor (1984), pp. 53-86.

42. Frances Sheehy-Skeffington Papers in the National Library of Ireland (hereafter NLI) Ms. 22,256/1. See Loze (1994). I am grateful to the author for the permission to use her thesis.

43. Finnegan (1985), p. 101.

44. Lara Loze, 'The Robertson Commission: Its Achievements in Contributing to the Admittance of Women to University Education in Ireland' (MA, minor thesis, UCD, 1994), p. 21.

45. *St Stephen's* (1905), cited in Finnegan (1985), p. 73.

46. Mary Hogan, *UCD Women's Graduates' Association 1902-83* (Dublin, 1982), p. 33.

47. *Ibid.*, p. 34.

48. William Starkie, 'The History of Irish Primary and Secondary Education During the Last Decade' (1911). See also Starkie (London, 1941) for reminiscences about her father.

49. Cahill (1924) quoted in Valiulis (1995).

50. Phillips (1990), p. 255.

51. Valiulis (1995), p. 175.

Chapter 3

1. O'Donnell (1902), pp. 151-53. This article is dedicated to Dr Ciara Breathnach and Professor Gearoid Ó Tuaithaigh, *fíor stairai*, I am also deeply grateful to the always perceptive Dr Lindsey Earner-Byrne.

2. 1881 Census.

3. See chapter 4; and Judith Harford, *The Opening of University Education to Women in Ireland* (Dublin: Irish Academic Press, 2007).

4. See especially O'Connor (1981); also Deirdre Raftery and Susan Parkes, *Female Education in Ireland 1700-1900: Minerva or Madonna?* (Dublin: Irish Academic Press, 2007), especially chapter 3 by Susan Parkes. For a learned vista on the Dominicans, see Máire Kealy, *Dominican Education in Ireland, 1820-1930* (Dublin: Irish Academic Press, 2007), pp. 60-121.

5. Linda Colley, *Britons: Forging the Nation, 1707-1837* (New Haven: Yale University Press, 1992), p. 239.

6. Cited in Hanna Donovan, 'History of Women's Higher Education' (MA thesis, History, University College Cork, 1919), p. 26.

7. Judith Harford 'The Education of Girls within the National System', in Rafferty and Parkes, p.33.

8. Caitriona Clear, *Nuns in Nineteenth-Century Ireland* (Dublin: Gill and Macmillan, 1987), p. 19.

9. Matha Vicinus, *Independent Women: Work and Community for Single Women, 1850-1920* (London: Virago Press, 1985), p. 177.

10 Mary Colum, *Life and the Dream* (Oxford: Oxford University Press, 1966), p. 23. For the perspective of both students and teachers at the St Louis Schools in Carrickmacross, and Monaghan town, County Monaghan, see chapter 7 and Margaret Ó hÓgartaigh, 'The St Louis Contribution to Education in County Monaghan, 1859-1966' in Terence Dooley, P.J. Duffy, and Eamonn Ó Ciardha (eds), *Monaghan: History and Society* (Dublin: Geography Publications, forthcoming).

11. See the National University of Ireland Calendars.

12. Henrietta White, 'The Position of Women at Universities' (1912) *Speeches on Women and Education*, Alexandra College Archives.

13. Ninth Annual Report of the Queen's Institute (of Female Professional Schools) (Dublin: Queen's Institute, 1871), p. 7.

14. Linda Clark, *Schooling the Daughters of Marianne: Textbooks and the Socialization of Girls in Modern French Primary Schools* (New York: State University of New York Press, 1984), p. 16.

15. *ibid.*, p. 72.

16. Felicity Hunt, *Lessons for Life: The Schooling of Girls and Women 1850-1980* (Oxford: Oxford University Press, 1987), pp. 11, 13.

17. Cited in Hunt, p.18. Regardless of gender, some teachers inculcated particular views of Ireland and its history. See, for instance, Margaret Ó hÓgartaigh, 'Mother Columba Gibbons of Loreto Convent in Navan and author of the ballad "Who Fears to Speak of Easter Week"', *Ríocht na Midhe, Records of the Meath Archaeological and Historical Society*, Vol. 16, 2005, pp. 189-93.

18. 1911 Census.

19. Kathleen Lynch, 'The Universal and Particular: Gender, Class and Reproduction in Second-Level Schools', *UCD Women's Studies Forum Working Paper No. 3* (1987), p. 7.

20. O'Connor (1981), p. 188.

21. 1911 Census.

22. John McIvor, *Popular Education in the Irish Presbyterian Church* (Dublin: Gill and Macmillan, 1969), p. 134.

23. *ibid.*, p. 140.

24. Tom Garvin, *Nationalist Revolutionaries in Ireland 1858-1928* (Oxford: Oxford University Press, 1987), p. 24.

25. 1919 National University of Ireland Calendar; interview with Dr Finola Kennedy, daughter of Dr Nora Stack, July 1996.

26. Starkie (1911), p. 16. For attitudes regarding the training of first-level teachers, see chapter 5.

27. Report of the Department of Education for the School Year 1924-5 p. 43; hereafter cited as Deptartment of Education Annual Report 1924-5.

28. Deptartment of Education Annual Report 1924-5, p.106. On the role of teachers in the underdeveloped west of Ireland, see chapter 8.

29. Margaret Ó hÓgartaigh, 'Intermediate Education (Ireland) Act, 1878,' in Brian Lalor (ed.), *Encyclopaedia of Ireland* (Dublin: Gill and Macmillan, 2003), p. 524.

30. Isabella Mulvany, 'The Intermediate Act and the Education of Girls,' *Irish Educational Review*, 1 (1907), pp. 15, 19.

31. O'Connor (1981), p. 146.

32. Alison Jordan, *Margaret Byers: Pioneers of Women's Education and Founder of Victoria College Belfast* (Belfast: Institute of Irish Studies, 1991), p. 26.

33. O'Connor (1981), p. 152.

34. O'Connor and Parkes (1984); Margaret Ó hÓgartaigh, *Kathleen Lynch, Irish Woman, Patriot, Doctor* (Dublin Irish Academic Press, 2006), especially chapter 1.

35. Maria Luddy, 'Isabella Tod,' in Mary Cullen and Maria Luddy (eds) *Women, Power and Consciousness in Nineteenth-Century Ireland: Eight Biographical Studies* (Dublin: Wolfhound, 1997), pp. 197-230.

36. Report of Dale and Stephens on Intermediate Education in Ireland xxviii, 1905, NLI Cd 2546, p. 77.

37. *Irish Catholic and Nation*, 21 July 1894.

38. Margaret Gibbons, *Loreto Navan: One Hundred Years of Catholic Progress 1833-1933* (Navan: School Publication, 1933), p.111. Ironically, Mary White, a student at this school, finished first in Ireland in the Senior Grade of the Intermediate exam in the 1889s. After a brilliant university career where she regularly beat Eoin MacNeill for first place in history exams, she became a Loreto nun (Mother Josephine).

39. 1926 Census.

40. *Lyceum*, April 1893, p. 144.

41. O'Neill (1994), pp. 117, 130.

42. Intermediate Education Board for Ireland. Rules and Programme of Examinations for 1906. Parliamentary Paper Vol. 40, Cd. 249, p. 437.

43. Gráinne Ó Flynn, 'Some Aspects of the Education of Irish Women Through the Years,' *The Capuchin Annual* (1977), p. 175.

44. Anne O'Connor, 'The Revolution in Girls' Secondary Education

in Ireland 1860- 1910,' in Mary Cullen (ed.) *Girls Don't Do Honours: Irish Women in Education in the Nineteenth and Twentieth Centuries* (Dublin: Women's Education Bureau, 1987), p. 49.

45. *ibid.*, p.121.

46. W.E. Ellis, *The Irish Education Directory 1882* (Dublin: THOM), pp. 111, 113, 114, 115.

47. Harford (2007), p. 110.

48. CAISM minutes of February 1889 meeting (first meeting). TCD Ms. 9722/1.

49. CAISM minutes TCD Ms. 9722/1, 5 December 1905. Eighty exhibitioners out of 106 did not take Greek or mathematics. For sporting participation, see chapter 19.

50. CAISM Minutes, 15 October 1907, TCD Ms. 9722/1.

51. Department of Education Annual Report 1928-9, pp. 88, 168. Inspectors argued that high failure rates were due to 'defective' training and cramming of subjects at the end of the year.

52. CAISM Annual Reports 1921-30, pp. 1-2 TCD Ms. 9722/5.

53. Timothy Kelly, 'Education' in Michael Hurley (ed.) *Irish Anglicanism*, (Dublin: Gill and Macmillan, 1970), p. 56.

54. CAISM Annual Report 1924, p. 3 TCD Ms. 9722/8/1; CAISM Annual Report 1926-7, p. 3 TCD Ms. 9722/10

55. CAISM Annual Report 1929 TCD. Ms. 9722/12 p. 1.

56. 1918 Summer Examinations, Matriculation, *NUI College Calendar*, 1919.

57. J.W. Henderson, *Methodist College, Belfast 1868-1938: A Survey and Retrospect* (Belfast: School Publication, 1939).

58. Report of the Royal Commission on University Education in Ireland (Robertson) 1902 xxxi, Cd. 826. Evidence of Henry McIntosh Headmaster of Methodist College Belfast September 1901, p. 180.

59. O'Connor (1987), p.37.

60. Dale and Stephens Report 1905, Vol. xxvii, Cd. 2546 Appendix vi, p. 98.

61. Maria Reynolds De Sousa and Dina Canco, *Portugal: Status of Women 1991* (Lisbon: Commission for Equality and Women's Rights, Prime Minister's Office, 1991), p. 25.

62. Nessa Agnew, 'Typical Day in the Life of a St Louis Boarder,' in *Louis Lines: 1988 Centenary Edition*, p. 48.

63. Thomas O'Donoghue, 'The Irish Secondary School. Curriculum and Curricular Policy in Ireland 1921-1962' (PhD dissertation (Education) University College Dublin, 1988), pp. 213-34.

64. Testimonial of Francis Gray MA (Dublin) Mistress at St Paul's Girls' School, Hammersmith, 25 April 1911. Dorothy Stopford-Price Papers NLI. Ms. 15,343 (1) and (2).

65. Máire Brugha, 'Mary MacSwiney' (1988). The author, who is Mary MacSwiney's niece, graciously provided me with a copy of her radio address. See also Máire Brugha, *History's Daughter* (Dublin: O'Brien Press, 2005).

66. Personal communication from Máire Brugha, May 1998. *History's Daughter* (see previous note) provides further information on her educational experiences in Ireland and Germany.
67. *Our Schools* (Dublin: School Publication, 1915), pp. 9, 17, 39.
68. Testimonial of Francis Gray, 25 April 1911. Dorothy Stopford-Price Papers NLI. Ms. 15,343 (1); chapter 10.
69. O'Connor and Parkes, *Alexandra*, p.69. Dr Katherine Maguire file in Kirkpatrick Archive Royal College of Physicians Archive, Dublin. See also Jordan (1991), p. 61.
70. Papers of Dr Nan Watson, Public Record Office of Northern Ireland (hereafter PRONI) D/3270/J.
71. Papers of Dr Nan Watson, PRONI D/3720/J.
72. *Report of the International Board for Ireland 1918 Parliamentary Paper*, Vol. 39. See also Mary E. Daly, 'Women in the Irish Free State, 1922-39; The Interaction between Politics and Ideology,' in Joan Hoff and Maureen Coulter, *Irish Women's Voices, Past and Present: Special Issue of the Journal of Women's History*, 6, 4/7, 1 (Winter-Spring 2005) (Bloomington: Indiana University Press, 1995), p. 106-7.
73. O'Donnell, pp. 151-53. O'Donnell was not unique in holding such opinions: see chapter 20.
74. See: Mairéad Ní Ghachain (ed.) *Comóradh 75, Bliain Bhríde Raghnallach; Laoise Gabhánach Ní Dhufaigh agus Scoil Bhríde*, (Dublin: School Publications, 1992). Both publications mark the seventy-fifth anniversary of Scoil Bhríde.
75. Jordan (1991), p. 21.
76. Department of Education Annual Report 1924-5, p. 100.
77. Seamus Ó Buachalla, *Education Policy in Twentieth-Century Ireland* (Dublin: Institute of Public Administration), p. 78.
78. Donovan, 'History of Women's Higher Education During the Nineteenth Century' (MA thesis, UCC, 1983), p. 60. The author, joined a French religious order and, as Sr Augustine, taught Irish and Latin for decades at a school in Drishane in Millstreet, County Cork. For the growth of professional opportunities, see chapters 1 and 2 and Margaret Ó hOgartaigh, 'Educational Influences on the Growth of Professional Women,' *History Review*, 10 (1996), pp. 28-36.

Chapter 4

1. *St Stephen's*, February 1904, p. 44.
2. *ibid.*, June 1903, p. 258.
3. *ibid.*, p.266; *St Stephen's*, November 1905, p. 179. Agnes Perry was the sister of Alice Perry BE, who became the first female engineer in Ireland in 1906.
4. *St Stephen's*, February 1904, p.44. One of the reports from *St Stephen's* indicates the manner in which nationalism and suffragism became interwined, particularly in the Catholic University. One female student threw a heavy volume of Byron at the Union Jack

flag above the lecturer, and shouted *'Vivient les femmes!'*, *St Stephen's*, June 1904, p. 89.

5. *Alexandra College Magazine* (hereafter *ACM*), December 1899, pp. 427-33, 440-44.

6. *ibid.*, June 1908, pp. 39, 59.

7. *ibid.*, June 1917, p. 64.

8. Mary Macken, 'Women in the University and College: A Struggle Within a Struggle' in Michael Tierney (ed.), *Struggle With Fortune: A Miscellany for the Centenary of the Catholic University of Ireland* (Dublin, 1954), pp. 142-65. Joyce Padbury is currenly completing a major biography of Professor Mary Hayden.

9. Macken, 'Women in the University and the College', pp. 153-54.

10. Colum (1966), p. 82.

11. Olive Purser, *Women in Dublin University 1904-1954* (Dublin, 1954), pp. 8, 14.

12. Barbara Miller Solomon, *In the Company of Educated Women: A History of Women and Higher Education in America* (New Haven, 1985), p. 64.

13. O'Connor and Parkes (1983), p. 44.

14. Oliver Rafferty, *Catholicism in Ulster 1603-1983: An Interpretative History* (Dublin, 1944), p. 175.

15. R.F.G. Holmes, *Magee 1865-1965: The Evolution of the Magee Colleges* (Belfast, 1965), pp. 46, 70, 75.

16. RCS Students Registers UCDA B64 1905-25.

17. RCS Students Registers UCDA b65 Register of Occasional and Non-Associate Students 1867-1906; 1879 Nos. 50-61; 1887 No. 1, 1889 No. 22.

18. RCS Student registers UCDA B65 Register of Occasional and non-Associate Students 1886-87 No. 32.

19. Hogan (1982), p. 10.

20. UCG Calender 1930; interview with Christy Townley (who worked in UCG between 1936 and 1982; he was librarian from 1960 to 1982), July 1995.

21. Thomas O'Donoughue, 'The Irish Secondary School: Curriculum and Curricular Policy in Ireland 1921-1962' (PhD, UCD, 1988), p. 250.

22. Christy Townley 'UCG: A Short History - The Early Years' in *Cois Coiribe* 1993, p.26.

23. John A. Murphy, *The College: A History of Queen's University College Cork, 1845-1995* (Cork, 1995), p. 130

24. Peter Flora, *State, Economy and Society in Western Europe 1815-1975. A Data Handbook. Vol. 1 The Growth of Mass Democracies and Welfare States* (Frankfurt, 1983), pp. 574, 575, 589, 596, 601.

25. Quoted in Bhreathnach (1981), p. 146.

26. Sport scholarship statistics courtesy of Dr Tony O'Neill. One female athlete was consistently refused a scholarship she competed in the Olympic Games in Atlanta. She graduated with an Honours degree.

Chapter 5

1. Garvin (1987), pp. 24, 27.
2. T. Garvin, 'Great hatred, little room: social background and political sentiment among revolutionary activists in Ireland, 1890-1922', in D. G. Boyce (ed.), *The Revolution in Ireland, 1879-1923* (Dublin: Gill and Macmillan, 1988), p. 102.
3. Quoted in S. Farren, *The Politics of Irish Education, 1920-65* (Belfast: Institute of Irish Studies, 1994), p. 110.
4. J. Coolahan *Irish Education: History and Structure* (Dublin: institute of public Administration, 1981), p. 125.
5. N. Johnson, 'Nation-building, Language and Education: The Geography of Teacher Recruitment in Ireland, 1925-55, *Political Geography*, Vol. 11, No. 2 (1992), p. 172.
6. *ibid.*, p. 178.
7. Chuinneagáin (1993), p. 8.
8. J. Sheehan, 'Irish Primary Education, *Irish Monthly*, January 1917, p. 50.
9. *ibid.*, pp. 50-1, 58.
10. R. Marshall, *Stranmillis College Belfast* (Belfast: Blackstaff Press, 1972), p. 2.
11. Dale (1905), p. 17.
12. *ibid.*, p. 211.
13. Coolahan (1977), p. 27.
14. *ibid.*, p. 28.
15. Quoted in *ibid.*, pp. 32-3
16. Morley, quoted in C. O'Keefe, *Colaiste Bhantiarna na Trocaire Our Lady of Mercy College Centenary 1877/ 1977* (Dublin: Carysfort, 1977), p. 5.
17. Quoted in M. Sturrock, *Women of Strength, Women of Gentleness: The Brigidines in Victoria* (Melbourne: Melbourne University Press, 1995), p. 24.
18. I. Finn, 'Women in the Medical Profession in Ireland, 1876-1919,' in Whelan, B. (ed.) *Women and Paid Work in Ireland, 1500-1930* (Dublin: Four Courts press, 2000), p. 118 and Ó hÓgartaigh (2004), pp. 162-4.
19. J. Mokyr, 'Why "More Work for Mother?" Knowledge and Household Behaviour, 1870-1945', *The Journal of Economic History*, Vol. 60, No. 1, (2000), p. 9.
20. C. Coady *Memories of a Carysfort Student, Education Files*, Mercy Archives, Booterstown (undated), pp. 2-3.
21. Quoted in O'Keefe (1977), p. 32.
22. E. Calwell, The letter of 1906, Past Students' Association of the Church of Ireland College of Education Newsletter, April 1996, pp. 20-1.
23. *ibid.*, p. 21.
24. M. Valiulis, 'Neither Feminist nor Flapper: The Ecclesiastical Construction of the Ideal Irish Woman', in M. O'Dowd and S. Wichert (eds), *Chattel, Servant or Citizen: Women's Status in Church, State and Society* (Historical Studies XIX, Belfast: Institute of Irish Studies 1995), p. 174.
25. Loreto O'Connor, *Passing on the Torch: A History of Mary Immaculate College, 1898-1998* (Limerick, 1998), p. 40. I am grateful to Sr Loreto

who gave me a copy of this book and facilitated my access to the
voluminous mary Immaculate College Archives.
26. 'B.L.' Mary Immaculate Training College Annual 1927, Limerick
    (1927), pp. 26-7.
27. 'M.B.' ary Immaculate Training College Annual 1928, Limerick:
    Mary Immaculate Training College (1928), p. 9.
28. Fynne, cited in Parkes (1984), p. 137.

Chapter 6

1. *Irish School Weekly* (hereafter *ISW*), 2 April 1904.
2. *ibid.*, 11 February 1905.
3. *ibid.*, Vol. 1, No. 1, appeared in 1904.
4. Viceragal Committee of Enquiry into Primary Education (Ireland)
   1918, Vol. xxi), cmd. 178, (hereafter Killanin Report).
5. Killanin Report, evidence of T.J. O'Connell, pp. 13-14.
6. *ibid.*, p. 17.
7. *ibid.*, pp. 18-19.
8. T.J. O'Connell, *History of the INTO* (Dublin, 1968), pp. 274-87.
9. Sile Chuinneagáin, 'Women teachers and INTO policy, 1905-1916'
   (unpublished MEd, Trintiy College Dublin, 1994) and 'The Politics
   of Equality: Catherine Mahon and the Irish National Teachers'
   Organisation, 1905-1916,' *Women's History Review*, Vol. 6, No. 4 (1997),
   pp. 527-49.
10. Teachers sought salary increases, in line with other public servants, as
    wartime inflation reduced the value of their salaries.
11. Chuinneagáin (1994), pp. 93, 166, 232, 264, 296.
12. *Sláinte* (journal of the Women's National Health Asssociation), sup-
    plement, May 1912.
13. *Irish Independent* 10 April 1912. I am grateful to Dr Maureen Keane
    for this reference.
14. Irish Protestant National Teachers' Union (hereafter IPNTU),
    Minute Book 20 June 1914, PRONI. D/517.
15. IPNTU Minute Book 24 October 1914, 31 May 1915, PRONI
    D/517.
16. IPNTU Minute Book 13 October 1917, PRONI D/517.
17. UNTU executive meetings 25 September 1920, 29 January 1921
    (there were four women on the executive for 1920-21 Mrs Mary E.
    Ross, Miss Hagin, Miss Sarah Butler, Miss McColgan), 25 June 1921,
    29 April 1922. Throughout 1921-22, links with Queen's University,
    Belfast, and training college at Stranmills were discussed. UNTU
    executive meetings in PRONI D/3944/A/1.
18. Executive Meeting UNTU 14 June 1924 in PRONI D/3944/A/1.
19. Executive Meeting UNTU, 27 September 1924, in PRONI
    D/3944/A1.
20. Mary Kinnear, *In Subordination: Professional Women, 1870-1970*
    (Montreal and Kingston, 1995), p. 123; Clark (1984), p. 73.
21. *Thom's Directory* 1900, p. 656, 1920 p. 795 and 1930 p. 512.

22. Report of the Vice-Regal Committee on the Condition of Service and Remuneration of Teachers in Intermediate Schools, and on the Distribution of Grants from Public Funds for Intermediate Education in Ireland, 1919, Vol. xxi, (Cmd. 66), hereafter Molony Commission.

23. Augustine Birrell was the Chief Secretary. His energy ensured the successful passage of the 1914 Intermediate Education Act.

24. Molony Commission, p. 18.

25. *ibid.*, p. 28.

26. *ibid.*, p. 35.

27 *ibid.*, p. 41-2, 46. Significantly, Corcoran represented convent schools on the registration council.

28. Intermediate Education Board for Ireland Rules and Schedule containing the Programme of Examinations for 1920, Parliamentary Paper Vol. xi, Cmd 1507, p. 20.

29. 1918 Report of the Intermediate Education Board for Ireland Parliamentary Paper, Vol. xxi, Cmd 179, p. 3.

30. 1918 Report of the Intermediate Education Board for Ireland, list of schools with figures relating to salaries grant, numbers of qualified teachers etc, pp. 6-39; Wesley College figures on p. 33.

31. Mary E. Daly, *Women and Work in Ireland* (Dundalk, 1997), p. 48.

32. John Coolahan (1984), p. 45.

33. Patrick Riordan, 'The Association of Secondary Teachers, Ireland, 1909-1968; some aspects of its growth and development' (MEd minor thesis, University College Cork, 1975), p.130.

34. Coolahan (1984), p. 81.

35. Cited in Coolahan.

36. Coolahan (1984), pp. 56, 90.

37. ASTI, *Security of Tenure* (1934), pp. 29-30.

38. *ibid.*, pp. 32-3.

39. ASTI Convention, 7 April 1926 p. 99 in ASTI/47 Minute Book of Conventions in ASTI Archive, ASTI Headquarters, Dublin.

40. ASTI Convention, 19/20 April 1927, in ASTI/47 Minute Book of Convention in ASTI Archives.

41. If there were fewer lay female teachers working in the 1920s then, logically, many would have become unemployed. There is a file catalogued in the ASTI Archives (ASTI/117) which is a list of unemployed teachers but I was unable to locate it. It seems likely that female teachers were more likely to be unemployed than male teachers.

42 Patrick Riordain 'The Association of Secondary Teachers, Ireland, 1909-1968. Some Aspects of its Growth and Development' (MEd, minor thesis, UCC, 1975), pp. 134, 224.

43 ASTI/33 Dublin Branch Minutes in ASTI Archives, Dublin. Doyle signed herself as Eibhlín Ní Dhubhgháil.

44 ASTI, *Security of Tenure*, pp. 34-5.

45 'The regulations of the Ministry provide that a teacher must possess definite qualifications, to the satisfaction of the profession are

gradually improving', in *Northern Ireland Ministry of Education Report*,
1925-6 in PRONI ED25/1/4. Ulster Headmistresses' Association
[UHMA] Papers PRONI D3820/2/1.
46. Northern Ireland Ministry of Education, 'Preparatory, Intermediate
and Secondary Schools, 1925-26 Rules and Regulations', p. 11 in
PRONI ED26/6/14.
47. Jordan (1991), pp. 43-4.
48. *ibid.*, p. 45.
49. *Belfast Newsletter*, 15 November 1924.
50. Meetings of UHMA, 1922-30, in PRONI D/3820/2/1.

Chapter 7

1 'Memoirs of Susan Stephens,' courtesy of the Stephens family. I am
very grateful to her late son, Donal Stephens, and her daughter
Sr Colmcille Stephens for additional details regarding her life.
Personal communication, Donal Stephens, 24 November 1999,
telephone communications, Sr Colmcille Stephens, 2006. This
memoir was written for Susan Stephens' eldest grandchild, Deirdre,
in 1969.

Chapter 8

1. This article is dedicated to the memory of Lawrence McBride, who
made an enormous contribution to Irish history. My thanks to Ciara
Breathnach for all her advice and encouragement.
2. See, for example, the various essays in Bernadette Whelan (ed.),
Women and Paid Work in Ireland, 1500-1930 (Dublin and Portland: Four
Courts Press, 2000); chapters 1, 5, 6, 15, 16, 17 and 20; Margaret Ó
hÓgartaigh, 'I am Lady or Engineer?' Early Irish Female Engineers'
in the *Irish Engineers' Journal*, December 2002, 48-9; 85-6. The work
of workhouse nurses is discussed by Siobhan Horgan-Ryan in
Margaret Preston and Margaret Ó hÓgartaigh (eds) *Gender and
Medicine Ireland 1700-1950* (New York, Syracuse University Press,
2011).
3. Martha Vicinus, *Independent Women: Work and Community for Single
Women 1850-1920* (London, Virago press, 1985), p. 120.
4. See the first report of the Jubilee Institute, 1898, Dublin; Lady
Dudley's husband, Lord Dudley, the Lord Lieutenant, headed the
commission on the Congested Districts; for the history of the
Congested Districts Board see, Ciara Breathnach, *The Congested
Districts Board of Ireland, 1891-1923* (Dublin, 2005).
5. *WNHA Golden Jubilee 1907-1957*, p. 5. The 1909 WNHA report
referred to the link between the WNHA and the Jubilee Institute, in
relation to the employment of district nurses, p. 20. On the WNHA,
see chapter 12 and Greta Jones, '*Captain of All these Men of Death':
The History of Tuberculosis in Nineteenth and Twentieth Century Ireland*
(Amsterdam and New York, 2001), pp. 101-26.

6. Queen Victoria Jubilee Institute Irish Branch, Fourth Report, 1927, pp. 4, 18, 21 and 22.

7. *Irish Nursing News* (hereafter *INN*), November 1928, p. 15.

8. *INN*, January 1929 p. 46.

9. *Irish Nursing Union Gazette* (hereafter, *INUG*), May 1925, p. 7.

10. For example, Nurse Richardson was appointed in 1923, at £150 per annum as a health visitor and school nurse, Department of Health files, NAI SM28/41.

11. One midwife was struck off the roll for failing to keep a record of the pulse of a patiet and not notifying the 'local supervising authority that medical aid was required', *INN*, March 1928, p. 71.

12. *INUG*, May 1925, p. 2. Later that year, the *INUG* reported on a deputation to the Coombe Hospital 'whereby the students from the hospital would discourage the presence of 'handy women'. The difficulties facing midwives, given that many people could only afford a handy women, were made clear. The Board of the hospital pointed out that, 'in the case of poor people', they accepted help wherever they could obtain it, *INUG*, October 1925, p. 5.

13. Joseph Robbins, 'Public Policy and the Maternity Services', in Alan Browne (ed.) *Master's Midwives and Ladies in Waiting: The Rotunda Hospital 1745-1995* (Dublin: A & SA Farmar, 1995), p. 238.

14. *Irish Nursing and Hospital World* (hereafter *INHW*), September 1931, p. 20.

15. Lady Dudley's Scheme. Second Report, 1905, p. 15.

16. Lady Dudley's Scheme. Seventh Report, 1910, p. 10.

17. Lady Dudley's Scheme. First Annual Report, 1904, pp. 5, 10.

18. N.M. Falkiner, 'The Nurse and the State' in *Journal of the Statistical and Social Inquiry Society of Ireland*, October 1920, pp. 29-60. My thanks to Mary. E. Daly, who alerted me to this revealing article.

19. Enid Fox, 'Universal Health Care and Self-help: Paying for District Nursing before the National Health Service', in *Twentieth-Century British History*, Vol. 7, No. 1, 1996, pp. 83-109.

20. Lady Dudley's Scheme for the Establishment of District Nurses in the Poorest Parts of Ireland. Eighth Annual Report, 1910, p. 13.

21. Nellie Ó Clerigh, *Hardship & High Living, Irish Women's Lives 1808-1923* (Dublin, 2003), pp. 125, 127, 128, 129, 131, 136, 138, 141, 144, 146.

22. Lady Dudley's Scheme for the Establishment of District Nurses in the Poorest Parts of Ireland. Eighth Annual Report, 1910, p. 9.

23. *Ibid.*, p. 15. This is almost certainly Myrrha Bradshaw who edited, in 1907, *Open Doors for Irish Women*: Irish Central Bureau for the Employment of Women. This book was published in Dublin. The bureau was first opened in 1904, when there were 3,160 requests for information. It was an advice centre with correspondents from all over the country. The bureau was still inexistence in 1930. See *Thom's Directory*, 1930, p. 935.

24. Mary E. Daly 'Essay in Review. Women and Labour: Margins to Mainstream?' in *Saothar* No. 19, 1994, pp. 70-4.

25. *INUG*, October 1925, p.3.

26. Lady Dudley's Scheme. Eighth Annual Report, 1910, p. 21.

27. Daly (1997), p. 39.

28. Ronald Marshall, *Stranmillis College Belfast* (Belfast, 1972), p. 2. I am grateful to the librarian of Stranmillis College, Wesley McCann, for alerting me to this work.

29. James Healy, 'Teacher Education Policy in Ireland 1920-1975 with Comparative Reference to International Trends' (MEd, UCC, 1981), p. 70.

30. Indenture of Sarah Potts Public Record Office of Northern Ireland, T. 1848/2.

31. See, for example, *Student Registers* for Baggot Street/Carysfort College in Mercy Archives, Booterstown, Dublin. This material has now been transferred to Mercy Archives, Baggot Street, Dublin. These list: 'Registration number, College number, Date of Entry, Name of Candidate, Address, Age on January next, Married or not, Roll number (of school they attended), District number, Diocese of birth, Diocese of present residence, Parish of birth, Parish of residence, Position in school (whether Principal, Assistant Monitress or Pupil), If monitress date of appointment, Date and Result of last examinations, If teachers when appointed to present school, When appointed under Board to present school, When appointed under board, Class and Division and when obtained, Name and address of manager, Examination results during training, first year, final year, Date of leaving, Classification when leaving, Special subjects (French, Drawing, Vocal Music, Instrumental Music, Hygiene, Botany, Physics, Domestic Economy, Practical Cookery), Doctrine and Scripture History, Training Diploma, and Remarks. The latter were usually of a financial nature, for example, 'Diploma awarded and grant of bonus awarded'. This grant of £7 was not given to the college until the student had passed her two years of probationary teaching. Students who had been monitors were the most numerous candidates in the Carysfort registers

32. Clear (1987), p. 27.

33. Marshall (1972), p. 2.

34. See ED8/4 in NAI for inspectors' reports.

35. Information courtesy of Jim Whelan, a student in a one-teacher rural school in East Clare in the 1940s.

36. Lawrence W. McBride, 'Young Readers and the Learning and Teaching of Irish History, 1870-1922', in Lawrence W. McBride (ed.) *Reading Irish Histories, Texts, Contexts and Memory in Modern Ireland* (Dublin and Portland, 2003).

37. Camilus O'Keefe, *Our Lady of Mercy College* (Dublin, 1977), p. 24. I am grateful to Sr Frances Lowe of the NLI for giving me a copy of this booklet.

38. Papers Regarding Education Box xxvii in Mercy Archives, Booterstown.

39. Walsh to 'My Dear Lord', 4 July 1885, also enclosed is Forde's letter of 28 June 1885 to Walsh, P/L/11 in Mercy Archives, Booterstown.

Forde's letter is yet another example of locals gaining preference in the allocation of jobs which were supposed to be allocated on the basis of professional merit.

40. Quoted in Susan Parkes, *Church of Ireland Training College* (Dublin, 1983), p. 93.
41. *ibid.*, p. 93.
42. *ibid.*, p. 92.
43. *ibid.*, p. 112.
44. Quoted in *ibid.*, p. 120.
45. For an excellent discussion of the impact of JAMs (junior assistant mistresses) on the teaching profession, see Úna Ní Bhroiméil' "Sending gossoons to be made oul' mollies of": Rule 127 (b) and the Femininsation of Teaching in Ireland', in *Irish Educational Studies*, Vol. 25, No. 1, pp. 35-51.
46. John Coolahan, 'The Origins of the Payment by Results Policy in Education and the Experience of it in the National and Intermediate schools of Ireland' (TCD, MEd, Minor thesis, 1975), pp. 4, 8.
47. I am grateful to Sr Magdalena Frisby, archivist at Booterstown, for pointing out the connection between Mother Ligouri Keenan and Patrick Keenan, Mother Ligouri Keenan was an important figure in the training college. She was principal of the college from 1877 to 1892, from 1888 to 1894 and from 1900 to 1908. See Angela Bolster, 'Catherine McAuley, Her Educational Thought and Its Influence on the Origin and Development of an Irish Training College', in Educational Box xxvii, Mercy Archives, Booterstown. Keenan was described as 'queenly'. Her initiative and energy during the early years of the training college helped to sustain it. However, the many petty regulations at the training colleges were attributed to the 'semi-aristocratic' views of Mother Ligouri. See Education files Pres/H/6-9 (miscellaneous, untitled documents) in Mercy Archives, Booterstown.
48. Quoted in Coolahan (1975), p. 136.
49. See ED8/4, NAI for inspectors' reports.
50. Coolahan (1975), p. 136.
51. Janet Nolan, *Servants of the Poor: Teachers and Mobility in Ireland and Irish America* (South Bend, 2004), pp. 25-42
52. John Musson, 'The Training of Teachers in Ireland, from 1811 to the Present Day' (QUB, 1955, PhD), p. 208.
53. For a selection of some of these activities see Virginia Davis, 'Curious Goings-On in the National Schools 1870-95', in *Retrospect, Journal of the Irish History Students' Association*, 1980, pp. 24-32; see also the inspectors' reports, ED8/4 NAI.
54. The major report, on a professional dominated by women, had only one female on its committee, Margaret Doyle, MA, Women Assistants' Representative, Irish National Teachers' Organisation. The Committee was to 'inquire and report as to possible improvements in the position, conditions of service, promotion and remuneration of the teachers in Irish National Schools, and the distribution of grants

from public funds for Primary Education in Ireland with a view to recommending suitable scales of salaries and pensions for different classes of teachers, having regard to the character and length of training necessary, special qualifications obtained, the nature of the duties which have to be performed, and other relevant considerations.'

55. Killanin general report, p. 4.
56. *ibid.*, p.7.
57. *ibid.*, p. 8.
58. *ibid.*, p. 9.
59. *ibid.*, p. 11.
60. *ibid.*, p. 12.
61. *ibid.*, p. 12.
62. *ibid.*, p. 14.
63. *INUG*, May 1925, p. 7.

Chapter 9

1. I am grateful to Dr Finola Kennedy for a copy of her mother's reference.
2. See, for example, William Lawson, 'Infant Mortality and the Notification of Birth Acts, 1907, 1915' in *Journal of the Statistical and Social Inquiry Society of Ireland* part xcvii, Vol. xii, October 1919, pp. 479-97.
3. Greta Jones, *Social Hygiene in Twentieth-Century Britain* (London, 1986), p. 10.
4. Countess of Aberdeen 'The Sphere of Women in Relation to Public Health' in *The Dublin Journal of Medical Science* September 1911, pp. 161-70.
5. Isabel Magill, 'A Social History of T.B. in Belfast' (DPhil, University of Ulster at Jordanstown, 1992), p. 79.
6. Molly Ladd-Taylor, *Raising the Baby the Government Way: Mother's Letters to the Children's Bureau 1915-1932* (London, 1986), p.12.
7. *ibid.*, p. 19.
8. *INHW*, 15 October 1931, p. 12.
9. Maria Maguire, 'The Development of the Welfare State in Ireland in the Postwar Period' (PhD, European University Institute, 1985), p. 2.
10. Susanne Day, *The Amazing Philanthropists* (London, 1916), p. 35.
11. Patricia Harkin, 'La Famille, Fruit du Passe, Germe de L'Avenir. Family Policy in Ireland and Vichy France' (MA minor, UCD, 1992), p. 37.
12. Golden Jubilee 1907-1957. The Women's National Health Association of Ireland (Incorporated), p. 6.
13. Golden Jubilee 1907-1957. The Women's National Health Association of Ireland pp. 1-12. The WNHA was not dissolved until the 1960s.
14. Lawson (1919), p. 487.
15. Janet Dunwoody 'Child Welfare' in David Fitzpatrick (ed.) *Ireland and the First World War, Trinity History Workshop* (Dublin, 1986), pp. 69-75.

16. Council Meetings of the WNHA 1908-13 in Peamount Archives, Newcastle, Co. Dublin.
17. Kirkpatrick Biographical Archive, Royal College of Physicians, Dublin; *British Medical Journal* (hereafter *BMJ*), 12 February 1927.
18. Quoted in Anna Day, *Turn of the Tide: The Story of Peamount* (Dublin, 1987), p. 20.
19. 1929-30 Peamount Sanatorium Annual Report p. 5.
20. Day (1987), pp. 58, 66, 71, *passim*.
21. *INN*, December 1928, p. 66.
22. Report of the Irish Public Health Council on the Public Health and Medical Services in Ireland, Vol. xvii, 1920, Cmd. 761. There were two other females on the council; Mrs M.L. Dickie, Commissioner, National Health Insurance Commission, Ireland and Mrs McMordie, CBE, Member of the Belfast Corporation: Chairman of the Tuberculosis Committee of the Belfast Corporation.
23. I would like to thank Mr Robert Mills, librarian at the Royal College of Physicians, where the St Ultan's Archives are located, for his help.
24. Information on Dr Lynn is available in the following: Kirkpatrick Archive; *Evening Mail*, 10 June 1916, 31 October 1918; Kathleen Murphy obituary in *Journal of the Irish Medical Association*, Vol. 37, 1955, p. 321; J.B. Lyons, *Brief Lives of Irish Doctors*, pp. 159-60; Medb Ruane, 'Ten Stories' Kathleen Lynn' in the Women's Commemoration and Celebration Committee *Ten Dublin Women* (Dublin, 1991), pp. 61-7; Hazel Smyth 'Kathleen Lynn M.D., F.R.C.S.I. (1874- 1955)' in *Dublin Historical Record*, Vol. xxx, No. 2, March 1977, pp. 51-57; Pearl Dunlevy, 'Patriot Doctor – Kathleen Lynn FRCSI' in *Irish Medical Times*, 4 December 1981 (courtesy of Mary O'Doherty, RCSI archivist); Medb Ruane, 'Lecture on Life and Times of Remarkable Mayo Woman' *The Western People*, January 1996 (courtesy of Canon Wynne); Interview with Medb Ruane, October 1995; Interview with Canon William Wynne, a relation of Kathleen Lynn, May 1996; Kathleen Lynn Diaries (courtesy of Daphne and Stephen Wynne. These diaries are now in the Royal College of Physicians and have been carefully tran-scribed by Margaret Connolly); Andre Sheehy Skeffington, 'A Coterie of Lively Suffragists', pp. 45-7; W.W. (William Wynne) 'Kathleen Lynn', *The Irish Times*, 9 April 1994. The St Ultan's Papers in the Royal College of Physicians Archive have also considerable material on Dr Lynn.
25. Dr Lynn was aware of this link, as one of her diaries has a newspaper clipping on Hazelwood, which was threatened with destruction. In a further medical connection, Hazelwood House was used as an 'annex of Sligo Mental Hospital', in the early 1900s, until bought by the Nazereth Sisters in 1910. It was a home for the aged and orphaned children. By 1956, there were 150 children and 100 adults at Hazelwood. Patrick Henry, *Sligo: Medical Care in the Past 1800-1965* (Manorhamilton, 1995), pp. 73, 90.

26. Kirkpatrick Biographical Archive, Royal College of Physicians; *Lancet*, 24 January 1931.

27. David Mitchell, *A 'Peculiar' Place, The Adelaide Hospital, Dublin: Its Time, Place and Personalities, 1839-1989* (Dublin, 1989), p. 148.

28. *Sunday Express* 28 September 1952 in Photographs/Press Cuttings Album in St Ultan's Archives, Royal College of Physicians (hereafter SUA).

29. Gearoid Crookes, *Dublin's Eye and Ear: The Making of a Monument* (Dublin, 1993), p. 105.

30. *ibid.*, p. 88.

31. Insert from Kilmainham Jail 25 April and 17 May in Lynn Diary, Royal College of Physicians.

32. Kirkpatrick Biographical Archives; *Evening Mail*, 31 October 1918.

33. Letter from Berne, Switzerland 19 January 1923 to Minister of External Affairs in Department of An Taoiseach, S. 3147 in N/A. Dr Lynn was in Lausanne with Kathleen O'Brennan. They presented a petition on behalf of the Irregulars (anti-treaty group) to the International Red Cross Committee. I am grateful to Dr Gerard McKeown for this reference.

34. Lynn Diaires, 18 May 1925.

35. W.W. (William Wynne) 'Kathleen Lynn' in *The Irish Times*, 9 April 1994.

36. *The Irish Times*, 1 June 1956 in Photographs/Press Cuttings Album in SUA.

37. Maire O' Neill, *From Parnell to De Valera: A Biography of Jennie Wyse Power 1858-1941* (Dublin, 1991).

38. First Minute Book of St Ultan's 19 March 1918 in SUA.

39. Edmond McWeeney, 'On the Recent Action of the State with Regard to Venereal Disease' in *The Journal of the Statistical and Social Inquiry Society of Ireland*, part xcvii, Vol. xiii, October 1919, pp. 498-517. He refers to the Royal commission on Venereal Disease (Cd. 8189).

40. See, for example, T.P.C. Kirkpatrick, 'Treatment of Syphilis' paper read to Royal Academy of Medicine, *Irish Journal of Medical Science* March 1918, pp. 339-57.

41. Kirkpatrick 'Syphilis' p. 351.

42. First Minute Book of St Ultan's, 2 May 1918 SUA.

43. *ibid.*, 9 April 1918 in SUA.

44. *ibid.*, 7 November, 30 November, 30 December 1918 in SUA

45. St Ultan's Annual Report 1926

46. St Ultan's Annual Report 1920s; Dr John Cowell, who was to succeed Dr Dorothy Stopford-Price as Chair of the National BCG Committee, recalled that prior to naming the hospital Dr Kathleen Lynn toured Co. Meath with a copy of William Wilde's *The Beauties of the Boyne and Blackwater* (1849). Dr William Wilde was also a famous doctor.

47. Second Minute Book but First Official Minute Book of St Ultan's (hereafter Official Minute Book) 15 September 1921.

48. *ibid.*, 18 November 1920 in SUA.

49. *ibid.*, 17 November 1921 in SUA.

50. Typescript entitled 'Teach History Notes' in SUA.

51. St Ultan's Annual Report, 1923.

52. Cited in Jane Lewis, *The Politics of Motherhood: Child and Maternal Welfare in England,* 1900-1939 (London, 1980), pp. 89, 92.

53. Kirkpatrick Biographical Archive; *Irish Independent,* 10 February 1938; *The Irish Times,* 10 February 1938.

54. A brief summary of Dr Webb's career is available in Mitchell (1989), pp. 260-2. However, it contains several errors, for example, he notes she was awarded her MD in 1925 (the RUI Calendar indicates it was 1906) and he also suggests she only became involved in St Ultan's after her husband's death in 1929, The St Ultan's minutes have several references to the Webbs working in the hospital in the early 1920s. Kirkpatrick Biographical Archive; *The Irish Times,* 26 August 1946; *The Irish Times,* 27 August 1946; *Irish Press* 26 August 1946; *Lancet* 4 June 1916; *BMJ,* 7 September 1946.

55. *St Stephen's,* November 1904, p. 111.

56. *ACM,* June 1924, p. 33.

57. Letitia Overend was an expert mechanic and drove a Rolls Royce 'Twenty' around Dublin for nearly fifty years. O'Connor (1983), pp. 57, 100.

58. Interview with Dr Barbara Stokes, November 1995; Mitchell (1989) p. 262.

59. Kirkpatrick Biographical Archive; *BMJ,* 22 August 1931; *The Irish Times,* 3 December 1931.

60. Mitchell (1989), pp. 80-1.

61. *ACM,* June 1894, p. 221.

62. *ACM,* June 1898, pp. 258-61; Maryann Gialanella Valiulis, 'Toward "The Moral and Material Improvement of the Working Classes": The Founding of the Alexandra College Guild Tenement Company, Dublin, 1898' in *Journal of Urban History,* Vol. 63 No. 3, March 1997, pp. 295-314; Mitchell (1989), p. 111.

63. Liam Price (ed.), *Dr Dorothy Price: An Account of Twenty Years' Fight Against Tuberculosis in Ireland* (Oxford, for private circulation only, 1957), pp. 4-5. I am very grateful to Pauric Dempsey for locating this book for me in the Royal Irish Academy.

64. *ACM,* January 1893, p. 38.

65. Kirkpatrick Biographical Archive; *BMJ,* 22 August 1931; *The Irish Times,* 3 December 1931.

66. Material on Dr Price is available in the following: Liam Price, *Dorothy Price,* Dorothy Stopford-Price Papers NLI Ms. 15, 343 ; Correspondence of the Crowley family of Kilbrittain, Co. Cork NLI Accession 4767; St Ultan's Papers SUA Royal College of Physicians Archives; Prichard, Sarah 'Dorothy Stopford-Price and the Control of Tuberculosis in Dublin' in Alexandra College Archives (I am grateful to the author for permission to cite this excellent essay and Anne O'Connor for alerting me to it); T.G.M. (T.G. Moorhead) 'In Memoriam. Dorothy Price M.D.' in *Irish Journal of Medical Science,* March 1954, p. 95 (courtesy of Mary O'Doherty, RCSI

Archivist); H.E. Counihan, 'In Memoriam for Dr Price' *Journal of the Irish Medical Association* March 1954 pp. 84, 72; *BMJ*, 6 March 1954; *Lancet*, 13 March 1954; Kirkpatrick Biographical Archive; *The Irish Times* 8 January 1925, 5 October 1951; Lyons (1978), pp. 160-1; Leon O'Broin, *Protestant Nationalists in Revolutionary Ireland. The Stopford Connection* (Dublin, 1985) *passim. A Short History of the Royal City of Dublin Hospital* (Dublin, 1995).

67. This is tuberculosis which spreads all over the body. I am grateful to Dr Barbara Stokes for this clarification

68. L. Price (1957), p. 13.

69. Quoted in O'Broin (1985), p. 169.

70. Dorothy Price to Bridie and Cissie Crowley 27 Dec no year in NLI Accession 4767.

71. *ibid.*

72. L. Price (1957), pp. v-vi, 3.

73. Dr Boxwell 27 Mar 1921? In Dorothy Stopford-Price Papers NLI 15,343 (1).

74. Quoted in O'Broin (1985), pp. 138-9.

75. L. Price (1957), pp. xi, 6, 26.

76. *ibid.*, p. 7.

77. *ibid.*, pp. 23-4.

78. *ibid.*, pp. 12, 13, 18, 41.

79. T.G.M (T.G. Moorhead) (1954), p. 95.

80. Dorothy Stopford-Price, 'The Need for BCG Vaccination in Infants' in *Tubercule* Vol. xxx, No. 1, January 1949, pp. 11-13. Paper read at the conference of the British Tuberculosis Association on 1 July 1948. I am very grateful to Dr Barbara Stokes for giving me a copy of this paper.

81. Quoted in Lyons (1978), p. 161.

82. Typescript entitled 'Teach History Notes' in SUA.

83. Cited in Lewis (1980), pp. 89, 92.

84. Newspaper Scrapbook at SUA; Smyth (1977), p. 55.

85. Timothy Corcoran, 'Is the Montessori Method to be Introduced into Irish Schools?' in *Irish Monthly*, March 1924, pp. 118-24.

86. Official Minute Book, 4 January 1923 in SUA.

87. Interview with Dr Barbara Stokes (a colleague of Drs Lynn and Price at St Ultan's) November 1995.

88. St Ultan's Annual Report 1924.

89. St Ultan's Annual Report 1935.

90. *St Stephen's*, March 1902, p. 93.

91. The following is based on the scrapbooks of Dr Angela Russell and an interview with her son, Mr Matthew Russell, May 1997.

Chapter 10

1. My thanks to the following for their help in the preparation of this paper: Dr Joost Augusteijn, Dr John Cowell, Dr H.E. Counihan,

Professor Mary E. Daly, Dr Pearl Dunleavy, Professor J.B. Lyons, Robert Mills (librarian, Royal College of Physicians), Mary O'Doherty (archivist, Royal College of Surgeons) and Dr Barbara Stokes.

2. F.S.L. Lyons, *Ireland Since the Famine* (London, 1973), p. 550.

3. Dr Noel Browne's controversial time in office and his efforts to combat tuberculosis in Ireland in the face of resistance and apathy are recounted in his autobiography *Against the Tide* (Dublin, 1987). His description of events has been criticised since; cf. James Deeny, 'Towards Balancing a Distorted View', *Irish Medical Journal*, Vol. 80, viii (August 1987).

4. Davis Coakley, *Irish Masters of Medicine* (Dublin, 1992); Lyons (1978).

5. James Deeny, *To Cure and to Care* (Dublin, 1994). See also James Deeny, *The End of an Epidemic: Essays in Irish Public Health 1935-65* (Dublin, 1995).

6. For material on Dr Price (1890-1954) see note 66, chapter 9.

7. Interview with Dr Barbara Stokes, November 1995.

8. Testimonial of Dorothy Stopford-Price by Frances Gray, St Paul's, 25 April 1911, NLI, ms 15,343 (I).

9. Dorothy Stopford-Price Letters 1916, NLI, ms. 21,205(4).

10. General Meeting 15 February 1912, minutes of the Dublin University Biological Association, Mun. Soc. Biol. 1909-55, TCD, Manuscripts Department.

11. Dr Euphran Maxwell worked in the Royal Victoria Eye and Ear and Adelaide Hospitals and she was the first ophthamologist, male or female, to be appointed to the Meath Hospital in 1918, Peter Gatenby, *Dublin's Meath Hospital* (Dublin, 1996), p. 94. In 1915 TCD appointed her to the 'recently established Montgomery lectureship in ophthalmology' Kirkpatrick Biographical Archive, Royal College of Physicians, *Lancet* 12, June 1915; *BMJ* 12, June 1915.

12. Dorothy Stopford-Price Papers, NLI, ms. 15,343 (I); John Fleetwood, *The History of Medicine in Ireland* (Dublin, 1983), p. 290.

13. Dr Boxwell 27 March about 1921, Dorothy Stopford-Price Papers, NLI, ms. 15,343 (I)

14. When Dr Price used the BCG vaccine initially on two infants at St. Ultan's Hospital one of them died. After a post-mortem examination it was revealed that the infant died from a stomach infection, which was unrelated to the vaccine.

15. Quoted in Ó Broin (1985), p. 173.

16. Dr Alice Barry qualified in 1904 and was closely associated with the Babies' Clubs in Dublin which were organised by the Women's National Health Association (WNHA). Lawson (1919), p. 479-97. Between 1912 and 1929 Dr Barry was in charge of the nine Dublin Babies' Clubs and she became Resident Medical Officer at Peamount which had been established by the WNHA to cater for TB patients, *1929-30 Peamount Sanatorium Annual Report*, 5. Peamount Archives. I am grateful to Frances Carruthers for introducing me to the extensive of Peamount Hospital archives.

17. Quoted in Ó Broin (1985), p. 141.

18. Dorothy Stopford-Price to Bandon Rural District Council 28 November 1921, NA, DELG 6/2.

19. L. Price (1957), p. 13.

20. George Bancroft, *The Conquest of Tuberculosis* (London, 1946), p. 120.

21. Quoted in Ó Broin (1985), p. 169.

22. *ACM*, June 1926, p. 53.

23. Dorothy Stopford-Price to Bridie and Cissie Crowley, 27 Dec. no year, NLI, Accession 4767.

24. I am grateful to Andrew O'Brien for a copy of his unpublished bibliography of Liam Price's articles.

25 J.P. Shanley, 'The State and Medicine', *Irish Journal of Medical Science* (May 1929), p. 191-6

26. L. Price (1957), v.

27. Dorothy Stopford-Price to Bridie and Cissie Crowley, 27 December no year, NLI, Accession 4767.

28. Free State Census 1926-1946.

29. See for example Lawson (1919).

30 Dr Kathleen Lynn had graduated from the Cecilia Street Medical School in 1899. After working in Sir Patrick Dun's, the Rotunda and Royal Victoria Eye and Ear Hospitals she devoted the rest of her career to St Ultan's and her private practice at Belgrave Road, Rathmines. During the 1916 Rising she was a captain in the Irish Citizen Army (ICA). See Smyth (1977), p. 51-7; St Ultan's Papers and Kathleen Lynn Diaries in Royal College of Physicians Archives. Madeleine ffrench-Mullen shared the political outlook of Dr Lynn and was a sergeant in the ICA. She acted as the administrator of St Ultan's R.M. Fox, *The History of the Irish Citizen Army* (Dublin, 1944), p. 231.

31. Official Minute Book of St Ultan's Hospital, 17 August 1922, SUA, Royal College of Physicians.

32. L. Price (1957), p. 3

33. Emmett Gill, 'Tuberculosis and the Northern Ireland Tuberculosis Authority' (MA thesis, The Queen's University of Belfast, 1999). See also, H.G. Calwell, and D.H. Craig, *The White Plague in Ulster: A Short History of Tuberculosis in Northern Ireland* (Belfast 1989), p. 44.

34. F.B. Smith, *The Retreat of Tuberculosis 1850-1950* (London, New York and Sydney, 1988), p. 194-5.

35. *ibid.*, 194-195, 198, and 209 (note 151)

36. L. Price (1957), p. 3.

37. Smith (1988), p. 200.

38. L. Price (1957), p. xi, 6, 26.

39. *Ibid.*, 15

40. Annual Report of the Department of Local Government and Public Health 1933-4, p. 67.

41. J.B. McDoughall, 'The Incidence of Tuberculosis in Different Countries', Dennt Papers, Tuberculosis box, Royal College of Surgeons Archives.

42. Jean and Rene Dubos, *The White Plague, Op. cit.*, 165. Dr Price's notes
   are in the Royal College of Surgeons' (RCS) copy of the book.

43. *ibid.*, p. 165, 167.

44. L. Price (1957), p. v–vi, 3.

45. Information courtesy of Professor J.B. Lyons.

46. Dr Katherine Maguire graduated in first place in her final medical
   examinations at Royal University of Ireland in 1891 and was one
   of the first female students admitted to Adelaide. She had a private
   practice in Mount Street and later in Merrion Square in Dublin.
   Noted for her involvement in social work; her paper in 1898 to the
   Alexandra College Guild on 'Social Conditions of the Dublin poor'
   motivated the guild to establish model tenement houses, Kirkpatrick
   Biographical Archive in Royal College of Physicians Archives; *BMJ*
   22, August 1931; *The Irish Times*, 3 December 1931; *ACM*, June 1898,
   p. 258–61; Valiulis (1997), p. 295–314.

47. L. Price (1957), p. 4–5.

48. *ACM*, January 1893, p. 38.

49. *BMJ*, August 1931.

50. *ACM*, June 1926, p. 53.

51. Dr Ella Webb, like Dr Maguire, graduated with first place in her medical degree from the Royal University of Ireland, much to the delight
   of 'Speranza' of *St Stephen's* (the student magazine of the Catholic
   University) who declared: 'it was a record to gain it over the heads of so
   many competitors of the sterner sex, which, until recent years, regarded
   medicine as exclusively its own ground'. She graduated with her MD
   in 1906. Her work commitments included the Adelaide, the Stillorgan
   Children's Sunshine Home (which she helped found) as well as St
   Ultan's. In 1924 Dr Webb wrote a paper on 'Sunshine and Health' for
   the Alexandra Guild Conference and this interest coincided with her
   research on rickets, Kirkpatrick Biographical Archive; *The Irish Times*, 26
   and 27 August 1946; *Irish Press*, 26 August 1946; *BMJ* 7, September 1946;
   St Stephen's, November 1904, III; *ACM*, June 1924, p. 3.

52. Quoted in Ó Broin (1985), p. 138–9.

53. L. Price (1957), p. 6.

54. *ibid.*, p. 3, 5.

55. *ibid.*, p. II.

56. *ibid.*, p. 6.

57. Coakley (1992), p. 325–6. Coakley believes that Dr Price 'was largely
   responsible for the for the elimination of childhood tuberculosis in
   Ireland', p. 326.

58. Annual Reports of the Local Government and Public Health; see
   also James Deeny 'Development of Irish Tuberculosis Services', Talk
   given to the Royal Academy of Medicine in Ireland 26 March 1982,
   Deeny Papers, Royal College of Surgeons, Tuberculosis box. There is
   no reference to Dr Price in his talk.

59. Smith (1988), p. 220–1.

60. Department of Local Government and Public Health Annual
   Report 1938–9, p. 32.

61. L. Price (1957), p. 6.

62. *ibid.*, p. 8-9

63. Dorothy Price, 'The Prevention of Tuberculosis in Infancy', *Irish Journal of Medical Science*, July 1942, p. 252-5.

64. L. Price (1957), p. 27.

65. *ibid.*, p. 12.

66. *ibid.*, p. 10.

67. St Ultan's Annual Reports 1930s in SUA.

68. L. Price (1957), p. 7.

69. *ibid.*, p. 17, 22 and 25.

70. *ibid.*, p. 13.

71. *St Ultan's 50th Annual Report 1968*, 12-13 in SUA.

72. L. Price (1957), p. 23-4

73. 30 May 1946, Minute Book of the Medical Board of St Ultan's Hospital in SUA.

74. L. Price (1957), p. 12, 13, 18, 41.

75. Price (1942), p. 252-5.

76. *ibid*, 254.

77. L. Price (1957), p. 12-13, 20.

78. *ibid.*, p. 19; St Ultan's Annual Reports, SUA.

79. Archbishop Byrne to St Ultan's, 20 December 1935, Joint Committee Report SUA.

80. Ffrench-Mullen to Price, 8 January 1936, Joint Committee Report SUA.

81. L. Price (1957), pp. 28-31.

82. *ibid.*, pp. 31-2.

83. T.G.M, 'In Memoriam. Dorothy Price M.D.', *Irish Journal of Medical Science* (1954), p. 95.

84. Annual General Meeting of St Ultan's 30 May 1946, Minute Book of the Medical Board of St Ultan's Hospital in, SUA.

85. Alan Browne, 'Mastership in Action at the Rotunda 1945-95', in Alan Browne, E.W. Lillie, Ian Dalrymple, George Henry and Michael Darling (eds), *Mastes, Midwives and Ladies-in-Waiting* (Dublin, 1995), pp. 21-65.

86. Dorothy Stopford-Price to Bridie Crowley, 27 December 1948, NLI, Accession 4767.

87. The National BCG Committee St Ultan's Hospital, Dublin, July 1949-50, 2, in Royal College of Physician's Archives.

88. *Ibid.* BCG meetings were held at Dr Price's home in Fitzwilliam Square and her old friend Dr Wassen of Sweden gave free supplies of BCG between July 1949 and August 1950: cf. *Ibid.*, p. 20.

89. Dorothy Stopford-Price (1949), p. 11-13. Paper read at the conference of the British Tuberculosis Association Association on 1 July 1948. I am very grateful to Dr Barbara Stokes for giving me a copy of this paper.

90. James Deeny, *Tuberculosis in Ireland: Report of the National Tuberculosis Survey* (Dublin, 1954), pp. 240, 254.

91. Smith (1988), p. 203.

92. WHO Monograph series, BCG vaccination. Studies by the WHO TB, Research Office, Copenhagen (Geneva, 1953), pp. 13, 14, 29.

93. Interview with Dr John Cowell, Medical Director of BCG Committee in the 1950s, December 1997.

94. In 1952 Dr Price noted that Czechoslavakia introduced mass BCG vaccination in 1950, though in Ireland she thought this would 'take time'. More optimistically, she noted that 'the increasing number of vaccinations performed adds to our efficiency and experience: in December 1950, over 18,000 persons had been vaccinated by the committee's vaccination'. In her paper Dr Price also acknowledged the help of 'Dr Noel Browne, who, as Minister for Health, established the National BCG Committee under the auspices of St Ultan's Hospital' and 'Dr Cowell, Medical Director of the Committee, who placed at my disposal his great knowledge of tuberculin tests I Ireland, gained whilst putting through BCG programmes in nearly every county.' Dorothy Stopford-Price, 'A Tuberculin Survey in Ireland', *Irish Journal of Medical Science* (February 1952), pp. 85-91.

Chapter 11

1. *INN*, June 1928, p. 114. The *INN* was first published in 1922, by the Irish Guild of Catholic Nurses. It can be described as a combination of the *Readers' Digest*, the *Irish Messenger* and a medical journal.

2. Maria Luddy, *Women and Philanthropy in Nineteenth-century Ireland* (Cambridge, 1995).

3. *ibid.*, pp. 48-9.

4. *ibid.*, p. 53

5. N.M. Falkiner (1920), pp. 29-43.

6. *ibid.*, pp. 45, 54-9, 60.

7. Canon P.A. Sheehan, 'Irish Primary Education', *Irish Monthly* (January 1917), p.63.

8. Dr Ryan 'Suggestions as to Workhouse Hospitals', *Irish Monthly* (March 1904), p. 147.

9. *INN*, June 1929, p. 138.

10. Sr Stephanie De Jesus, 'Religious Sisterhoods and Professional Nursing' reprinted in *INN*, September 1929, pp. 174-6.

11. *ibid.*, pp. 176-9.

12. Katrin Schultheiss, '"La Veritable Médecines des Femmes": Anna Hamilton and the Politics of Nursing Reform in Bordeaux, 1900-1914', *French Historical Studies*, 19 (1995), pp. 202-5.

13. Anna Hamilton, 'Report for the International Council of Nurses on Nursing in France', *International Council of Nurses Report*, 1929, p. 132. The author is grateful to Professor Mary E. Daly for this reference.

14. *INHW*, 1 February 1932, p. 9. The establishment of such institutions received papal support in the sixteenth century in that Council of Trent 'did not specify the need for welfare systems but remained committed to the notion of voluntary charity as the means whereby the rich had

a chance of salvation.' Olwen Hufton, 'Introduction' in Olwen Hufton (ed.), *Women in the Religious Life* (Florence, 1996), pp. 11-26.

15. Alice Kelkian, 'Nuns, Entrepeneurs, and Church Welfare in Italy', in Huftun, *Women in the Religious Life*, pp. 119-37.

16. Patricia Kelly, 'From Workhouse to Hospital: The Role of the Irish Workhouse in Medical Relief to 1921' (MA thesis, National University of Ireland, Galway, 1972), pp. 227, 239, 242.

17. Black, *King's Nurse-beggar's Nurse: The Autobiography of 'Blackie' (Sister Catherine Black)* (London, 1939), p. 44. The author is grateful to Brendáin MacSuibhne for alerting her to this reference.

18. *INHW*, 15 January 1932, pp. 33-5.

19. *INN*, September 1927, p. 621.

20. National Archives of Ireland (hereafter NAI), Department of Health (herafter D/H), SM28/41, Tipperary North, Public Health Nurses 1930-50, Vol. 1. These files include material which predate the establishment of the department in 1946.

21. NAI, D/H, SL7/24, Seán O'Grady, Ennis to Local Government and Public Health, 7 March 1928 in Mental Nurses, Attendents (*sic*) 1928-40, part I. The pay scale for female nurses in 1922 started at 27*s* a week while males were paid 34*s*. In 1928, the maximum rate for females was 39*s* and 46*s* for males.

22. Margaret Huxley, 'The Requirements of Nursing as a Vocation: Its Rewards as a Profession', *ACM*, June 1901, pp. 140-3.

23. Seamus Cowman, 'Understanding Student Nursing Learning' (PhD thesis, Dublin City University, 1993), pp. 14-15.

24. PRONI, Papers of Belfast Maternity Hospital D/1326/11 Bundle 7.

25. Schultheiss (1995), pp. 183-214, 195-6, 200.

26. Royal College of Physicians Archives, *Freeman's Journal*, 1 June 1922 in Kathleen Lynn's diary.

27. See, for example, Edward Cahill's graphic description of the death of Christ for the monthly day of recollection for nurses. *INN*, May 1928, p. 103.

28. *ibid.*, March 1919, pp. 81-2.

29. *ibid.*, October 1929, pp. 14-4.

30. *ibid.*, November 1927, p. 24.

31. *ibid.*, August 1927, p. 619.

32. *ibid.*, February 1928, p. 57.

33. *INHW*, 1 September 1931, pp. 23-4. Margaret Ó hÓgartaigh, 'Irische Krankenschwestern in England nach dem Zweiten Weltkrieg' in Klaus J. Blade, Pieter C. Emmer, Leo Lucassen and Jochen Oltmer (eds) *Enzyklopädie Migration in Europa vom 17. Jahrhundert bis zur Gegenwart* (Wilhelm Fink Verlag/Ferdinand, Schöningh Verlag, Paderborn/München, 2007), pp. 655-7 and soon to be published in English as 'Irish Nurses in Post World War II England', in Klaus J. Blade, Pieter C. Emmer, Leo Lucassen and Jochen Oltmer (eds) *Encyclopedia: Migration in Europe Since the 17th Century* (Cambridge University Press, New York, 2011).

34. *ibid.*, 31 October 1931, p. 6

35. *INN*, September 1927, p. 632.

36. *ibid.*, May 1929, p. 119.

37. *ibid.*, May 1930, p. 114

38. *ibid.*, November 1928, p. 13, May 1929, p. 112. These nurses were seen as servants of the State who contributed to 'national efficiency'. See Anne Summers, *Angels and Citizens British Women as Military Nurses 1854-1914* (London, 1988), p. 220.

39. *INN*, February 1928, p. 59. Article III of the Guild's constitution declared their aim was to 'unite Catholic nurses in their spiritual activities and to promote a spirit of fraternal charity between members of all branches of the profession.' They also sought to 'develop and stimulate the initiative and right ambition of Irish nurses to achieve leadership in their professions.' This was no insular group. They had four annual triduums between 1923 and 1926 which attracted 1,023 nurses *INN* (September 1927), pp. 7-8. Their journal can be regarded as a popular voice of Irish nurses.

40. *INN*, February 1928, p. 63.

41. Peggy Donaldson, *Yes Matron – A History of Nurses and Nursing at the Royal Victoria Hospital, Belfast* (Belfast, 1989), p. 90.

42. *INN*, August 1928, p. 129.

43. *ibid.*, January 1929, p. 46.

44. *INUG*, May 1925, p. 4.

45. *INHW*, 1 January 1932, p. 23.

46. One individual wrote to Annie Smithson at the *INHW* inquiring about male training facilities. There was no such facility. *INHW*, 1 January 1932, p. 26.

47. *INHW*, 1 January 1932, pp. 34-5.

48. *INUG*, October 1925, p. 4.

49. See Mary Kenny, Tess Power (Hughes) and Grace Power 'Nursing in the Richmond' in Eoin O'Brien, Lorna Browne, Kevin O'Malley (eds.), *The House of Industry Hospital 1772-1987* (Dublin 1988), pp. 201-8.

50. *INHW*, 15 September 1931, p. 31

51. 'John Brennan', 'The Irish Hospital Nurse: Slave and Lady' in *Bean na hÉireann*, April 1909, p. 14. Margaret Ward, *Unmanageable Revolutionaries: Women and Irish Nationalism* (London, 1989).

52. F.O.C. Meenan, *St Vincent's Hospital 1834-1994: An Historical and Social Portrait* (Dublin, 1995), p. 145. Meenan thought these stories may have been exaggerated.

53. Elizabeth Malcolm, 'Health Services' in S.J. Connolly (ed.), *The Oxford Companion to Irish History* (Oxford, 1998), pp. 236-7.

54. During the Crimean War, there were internal hospital battles between lay and religious nurses, of no less intensity than those taking place outside the hospitals. Associations of proselytising and personality clashes characterised relations between nurses. Mary Ellen Doona, 'Sister Mary Joseph Croke: Another Voice from the Crimean War, 1854-1856', *Nursing History Review*, 3 (1995), pp. 3-41. The author is grateful to Dr Doona for giving her a copy of this article. See also Cecil Woodham-Smith, *Florence Nightingale 1820-1919* (London, 1950), pp. 229-32. The perspective of the Mercy nuns

is detailed in Evelyn Bolster, *The Sisters of Mercy in the Crimean War* (Cork, 1964). She argues that the sisters' presence ensured 'permanency as against the matrimonial deluge which was sweeping away so many of the secular staff'. Bolster (1964), p. 91. This idea of 'permanency' emerges as a decisive factor for local government officials involved in the selection of nursing staff in Ireland during the 1920s.

55. NAI, Department of Local Government (hereafter D/ELG) 16/9, Leitrim county council, 30 March 1922.
56. Anna Hamilton (1929), pp. 133-4.
57. NAI, D/ELG, 21/19, Mayo county council, 1921-23.
58. NAI, D/ELG, 17/15, Limerick county council, 1921.
59. *INHW*, 1 December 1931, p. 18.
60. James Murray, *Galway: A Medico-socio History* (Galway, 1994), pp. 67-8, 164.
61. Dublin Diocesan Archives (hereafter DDA), Byrne Papers (hereafter BP), Irish Nurses' Union file, box 4, Smithson to Byrne, 6 June, 1933. The author is grateful to Professor Maria Luddy for alerting her to this file.
62. DDA, BP, box 4, Irish Nurses' Union file, Smithson to Byrne, undated but probably after 6 June 1933.
63. *INN*, January 1929, p. 45.
64. *INUG*, May 1925, p. 6.
65. Kinnear (1995), p. 99.
66. See Roisin Ingle, 'Florence Nightingale? Goodbye to All That', *The Irish Times*, 8 February 1997.

Chapter 12

1. Magill (1992) p. 47.
2. Margaret Rossiter, *Women Scientists in America: Struggles and Strategies to 1940* (Baltimore, 1982), pp. 73-99.
3. Morantz-Sanchez Markell, Regina *Sympathy and Science: Women Physicians in American Medicine* (Oxford, 1985), p. 145.
4. Charles Cameron *History of the Royal College of Surgeons* (Dublin, 1912), p. 143.
5. F.O.C. Meenan, *The Catholic University School of Medicine 1855-1931* (Dublin, 1987), pp. 80-5.
6. Dublin University Calendar 1929-30, p. 250.
7. Quoted in J.D.H. Widdess, *A History of the Royal College of Physicians in Ireland 1654-1963* (Edinburgh, 1963), p. 211.
8. Kirkpatrick Biographical Archive in Royal College of Physicians in Ireland Archive; A.H. Bennet, *English Medical Women: Glimpses of their Work in Peace and War* (London, 1915) p. 21. My thanks to Dr John Fleetwood (Snr) for lending this book to me.
9. Sophia Jex-Blake in Groag Bell and Offen (eds) *Women, the Family and Freedom: The Debate in the Document. Vol. 1 1750-1880* (Stanford, 1983), p. 477.

10. *ACM*, June 1927, p. 33.

11. Katherine Maguire. 'Social Conditions of the Dublin Poor' in *ACM*, June 1898, pp. 258-61. *ACM*, June 1898, p. 260; Valiulis (1997), pp. 295-315.

12. *ACM*, December 1908, p. 54.

13. WHNA Booklet frontpiece, cited in Thomas G. McAllister, 'The Anti-Tuberculosis Campaign of the Women's National Health Association, 1907-191' (MA St Patrick's College Drumcondra, 1999), p. 22. My thanks to the author for giving me a copy of his thesis.

14. First Annual Report of the WNHA, p. 37.

15. McAllister (1999), pp. 20, 24, see also Third Annual Council meeting of ythe WNHA 19 April 1910.

16. McAllister (1999), pp. 25-6

17. WNHA 1909 Report p. 3,4.

18. Quoted in Day (1987), p. 20.

19. 1929-30 Peamount Sanatorium Annual Report, p. 5.

20. Day (1987), pp. 58, 66, 71, *passim.*

21. Report of the Irish Public Health Council on the Public Health and Medical Services in Ireland Parliamentary Paper, Vol. xvii, 1920, Cmd. 761. There were two other females on the council, Mrs Dickie, Commissioner, National Health Insurance Commission, Ireland, and Mrs McMordie, CBE, Member of the Belfast Corporation and chair of the Tuberculosis Committee of the Belfast Corporation

22. Ladd-Taylor (1986), p. 5

23. *ibid.*, pp. 6, 11, 13, 26.

24. *ibid.*, pp. 19-20

25. *ibid.*, p. 12.

26. *ibid.*, p. 19.

27. Commision on Vocational Organisation NLI Ms. 94 1, Vol. 20, pp. 1-15.

28. *St Stephen's* March 1902 p. 93.

29. Louisa Martindale *The Woman Doctor and Her Future* (London, 1922), pp. 85, 89, 101. My thanks to Rebecca Bartlett for introducing me to the Martindales.

30. Kinnear (1984), pp. 56-57.

31. Pepi Summer, 'The Career Pattern of Women Graduates of the University of Buffalo Medical, Dental and Law Schools between 1895 and 1915' (PhD, 1980, SUNY, Buffalo), p. 192.

Chapter 13

1. Mac Aodh, 'Ode to the Lady Medicals', *St Stephen's*, March 1902, p. 93.

2. John Rickard, *Australia: A Cultural History*, 2nd edition. (London and New York, 1969), p. 169.

3. Joel Mokyr, 'Why "More Work for Mother?" Knowledge and Household Behaviour, 1870-1945', *The Journal of Economic History*,

Vol. 60, No. 1 (March 2000), p. 9. I am grateful to Cormac Ó Gráda for alerting me to this important article.

4. Lawson (1919), p. 485.

5. Ida Bloom, 'Equality and the Threat of War in Scandinavia, 1884-1905' in T.G. Fraser and Keith Jeffrey (eds), *Men, Women and War* (Dublin, 1993), p. 108.

6. *ACM*, June 1908, p. 60.

7. Countess of Aberdeen, 'The Sphere of Women in Relation to Public Health', *The Dublin Journal of Medical Science*, September 1911, pp. 161-70.

8. Edward Coey Bigger, *The Carnegie United Kingdom Trust Report on the Physical Welfare of Mothers and Children* (Dublin, 1917), Vol. iv, p. 9. Coey Bigger was the Medical Commissioner of the Local Government Board for Ireland.

9. Jan Bassett, *The Oxford Illustrated Dictionary of Australian History* (Melbourne, 1933), p. 66.

10. Markell Morantz-Sanchez (1985), p.145.

11. Cameron (1916), p. 143. *QUB College Calendar*, 1923, p. 218.

12. Meenan (1987), p. 82.

13. Dublin University Calendar, 1929-30, p. 250.

14. Quoted in Widdess (1963), p. 211.

15. Kirkpatrick Biographical Archive in Royal College of Physicians Archives; Bennett (1915), p. 21.

16. Jex-Blake in Groag Bell and Offen (1983), I, p. 477.

17. Rotunda Lying-In Hospital 250th Exhibition included a picture dated 1900 of A. MacDiarmuid, Aberdeen University, who was a medical student.

18. Meenan (1987), pp. 82-3.

19. NUI College Calendar 1931.

20. Robertson Commission Appendix to 3rd Report, Vol. xxxii, cd. 1229 (1902), p. 333.

21. Information on women medical graduates from University College Cork Archives. My thanks to Virginia Teehan, University College Cork archivist, for alerting me to this information.

22. Carlos McDowell, Presentation to the Royal College of Physicians on 'Leading Ladies in Irish Medicine', 1994. My thanks to Carlos McDowell for giving me a copy of her paper.

23. Marshall Cummins, *Some Chapters of Cork Medical History* (Cork, 1957), p. 38. His sister, Mary Elice Cummins Hearn, was the first female fellow of the Royal College of Physicians in Ireland and another sister, Iris Asley Cummins, was the second female to qualify as an engineer in Ireland: see Margaret Ó hÓgartaigh, 'Women Engineers in Early Twentieth Century Ireland', *The Engineer's Journal*, December 2002, pp. 48-9.

24. Central Midwives Board of Ireland Minutes 19 October 1920, *An Bord Altranais* Archives, Dublin. They are now in the UCD Archives.

25. Brian Walker and Alf McCreary, *Degrees of Excellence: The Story of Queen's Belfast 1845-1995* (Belfast, 1994), p. 33; however, see

Kirkpatrick Biographical Archive in Royal College of Physicians for
more details on Dr Elizabeth Gould-Bell's career.

26. John B. Bridges, *Belfast Medical Students* (Belfast, 1986), p. 35

27. Murray (1994), p. 198.

28. J.B. Lyons, 'History of Early Irish Women Doctors' in *Irish Medical
Times* (January 1992), pp. 38-40; courtesy of Mary O'Doherty, Royal
College of Surgeons Archivist.

29. Majorie Perrin Behringer, 'Women's Role and Status in the
Sciences: An Historical Perspective' in June Butler Kahle (ed.),
Women in Science: A Report from the Field (Philadelphia, 1985), p. 17.

30. Corkonian Lucy Boole, daughter of the famous mathematician
George Boole, studied chemistry and became a demonstrator,
lecturer, and, ultimately, head of the chemical laboratories at the
London School of Medicine for Women. She was also the first professor of chemistry at the Royal Free Hospital, London and a Fellow
of the Institute of Chemistry; see Desmond MacHale, *George Boole:
His Life and Work* (Dublin, 1985), p. 265.

31. Ellen More, 'The Blackwell Medical Society and the
Professionalisation of Women Physicians', *Bulletin of the History of
Medicine*, Vol. 61, part 4 (1987), p. 603.

32. Emma Russell, 'The Queen Victoria Hospital', *Australian Historical
Studies*, No. 106 (April 1996), pp. 170-5.

33. *ibid.*, p. 173.

34. Fleetwood (1983), p. 181; H.G. Calwell, 'The History of the Royal
Belfast Hospital for Sick Children 1873-1948' (MA thesis, Queen's
University, Belfast, 1972), p. 103; Robert Marshall, *The Story of the
Ulster Hospital Part 1 1873-1952*, Kathleen Kelly, *The Story of the Ulster
Hospital, Part 2 1952-73* (Belfast, 1975), pp. 20, 98.

35. See minutes of the Belfast Eugenics Society, Ms. 66/1 in Special
Collections Library, Queen's University, Belfast.

36. First Minute Book of St Ultan's 18 July 1918, in SUA.

37. *ibid.*, 19 March 1918.

38. *ibid.*, 2 May and 9 April 1918.

39. Dr Kathleen Lynn, 'The Milk and the Mother of Babies', *Old Ireland*,
21 August 1920, pp. 449-50.

40. Charles Webster, 'Healthy or Hungry Thirties', *History Workshop*, Vol.
13 (Spring 1982), p. 120. My thanks to Catherine Conway for alerting me to this article.

41. 'Breastfeeding and Infant Mortality', in *BMJ*, August 2001, abstract in
The International Journal of Clinical Medicine, Modern Medicine of Ireland,
Vol. 31, No. 10 (October 2001), p. 66.

42. Bigger (1917), pp. 45-6.

43. Typescript entitled 'Teach History Notes' in SUA; St Ultan's Annual
Report, 1923.

44. Cited in Lewis (1980), pp. 89, 92.

45. Magill (1992), p. 67.

46. William Thompson, 'A Few Outstanding Points in Connection
with the Vital Statistics of the Irish Free State', *Irish Journal of Medical*

Science, April 1925, p. 151. Terminology specific to the period in question is used in order to avoid ahistorical terms, hence the use of the word 'illegitimate'.

47. Medical Committee, 15 October 1922, SUA. The Medical Committee of St Ultan's usually met once a month. Drs Maguire, Lynn, Tennant, and Barry, with Webb in the chair, constituted the medical committee.

48. Medical Committee, 17 January 1923, SUA.

49. Medical Committee, 10 February 1926, SUA; Judith Raferty, 'Professional Advice-giving and Infant Welfare', in *Journal of Australian Studies* (June 1995), p. 78. The successful efforts of St Ultan's physician, Dr Dorothy Stopford-Price, to eliminate childhood tuberculosis are analysed in Margaret Ó hÓgartaigh, 'Dr Dorothy Price and the Elimination of Childhood Tuberculosis', in Joost Augustejin (ed.), *Ireland in the 1930s* (Dublin, 1999), pp. 67-82.

50. Erik Olssen, 'Towards a New Society', in Geoffrey W. Rice (ed.), *The Oxford History of New Zealand*, 2nd edition (Auckland, 1992), p. 26.

Chapter 14

1. Joan Jacobs Brumbery and Nancy Tomes 'Women in the Professions: A Research Agenda for American Historians' in *Reviews in American History*, June 1982, pp. 275-296.

2. Mary E. Daly, *The Buffer State: The Historic Roots of the Department of Environment* (Dublin, 1997), p. 109.

3. Interview with Charles Lysaght, October 1996; Charles Lysaght, personal communication, May 1997.

4. I am grateful to Laura, Gerry and Nuala McGinley, for information on the career of Dr Kathleen Moran.

5. Padraic Ó Máille TD to Minister for Local Government, 26 March 1922; Minister for Local Government to Ó Máille, 30 March 1922 in Leitrim DELG 16/9, National Archives. I am grateful to Professor Mary E. Daly for the DELG (Department of the Environment, formely the Department of Local Government and Public Health) references.

6. Daly, *The Buffer State*, p. 113.

7. Longford DELG 19/13, National Archives.

8. J.J. Lee, *Ireland 1912-1985* (Cambridge, 1989), pp. 161-2.

9. *Catholic Bulletin*, Vol. 21, No. 2, p. 143, quoted in Dermot Keogh, *The Vatican, the Bishops and Irish politics 1919-39* (Cambridge, 1986), p. 169

10. Dr Gilmartin statement in Letitia Dunbarr Harrison file, Department of An Taoiseach S2547A in National Archives; the case is discussed in a witty manner by Lee in his *Ireland 1912-1985* pp. 161-8. Mary E. Daly has made clear the local dimension in the selection of candidates for local authority positions, see 'Local Appointments' in Mary E. Daly (ed.) *County & Town: One Hundred Years of Local Government in Ireland* (Dublin, 2001), pp. 45-55.

11. Denis Boyle, *A History of Meath County Council, 1889-1999: A Century of Democracy in Meath* (Navan, 1999), pp. 151, 143, 144, 145.
12. *Meath Chronicle*, cited in Boyle (1999), p. 145.
13. *ibid.*, pp. 146, 151.

Chapter 15

1. Susan Parkes (ed.), *A Danger to the Men? A History of Women in Trinity College Dublin, 1904-2004* (Dublin, 2004).
2. John Lee, *The Evolution of a Profession and of its Dental School in Dublin* (Dublin, 1993), pp. 8, 21, 22, 24, 30, 36, 37.
3. Henderson (1939) Vol. II, p. 329.
4. Lee (1972), p. 9.
5. *Woman's Life*, 1 May 1937 p.1 6. I am grateful to Catherine Conway for this reference.
6. Nancy Milwid, 'Women in Male-Dominated Professions' (PhD thesis, University of Wisconsin, 1983), p. 127.
7. I am very grateful to Dr Peter Doherty, of Ratoath Dental Centre, for his gentle professionalism.
8. A Meath Chronicle Centenary Publication. *One Hundred Years of Life and Times in North Leinster* (Meath, 1997), p. 113; chapter 20.
9. Ivana Bacik, Cathryn Costello and Eileen Drew (eds) *Gender Injustice: Feminising the Legal Professions?* (Dublin, 2003), pp. 51-64. I am grateful to the TCD law school for giving me a copy of this book; Margaret Ó hÓgartaigh '"Am I a Lady or an Engineer?" Early Irish Female Engineers' in the *Irish Engineers' Journal*, December 2002, pp. 48-9; Ciarán and Margaret Ó hÓgartaigh 'Old Maids and Cats: The First Female Members of the Irish Institute of Chartered Accountants' in Accountancy Ireland, October 1999, pp. 22-3.
10. Commision on Vocational Organisation (hereafter CVO) National Library of Ireland, Manuscripts Department (hereafter NLI) Ms. 922, Vol. 1, p. 249. This commision, chaired by Dr Michael Brown, Roman Catholic Bishop of Galway, sat between 1939 and 1943.
11. Caitriona Clear, 'The Women Can Not be Blamed: The Commision on Vocational Organisation, Feminism and Home-makers in Independent Ireland in the 1930s and '40s' in Mary O' Dowd and Sabine Wichert (eds) *Chattel, Servant or Citizen* (Belfast, 1995) pp. 179-86.
12. The CVO Papers in NLI Ms. 941, Vol. 20, pp. 10-15.
13. 1927 Minutes, Eccles Street Past Pupils' Union, 1914-1930; the minute book is courtesy of Loreto Diskin, Rostrevor, Wynnsward Drive, Dublin 4.
14. Dental Register of Saorstát Éireann, 1930; figures courtesy of the Dental Council Ireland, 57 Merrion Square, Dublin 2. I am grateful for their help and hospitality.
15. 1926 Irish Free State Census and Northern Ireland Census.
16. See chapter 19.

17. Based on an interview with Dr Rosemary Daly who graduated from the National University of Ireland, Cork, Dental School, in 2003. I am very grateful for her Help.
18. Figures courtesy of the Dental Council of Ireland.

Chapter 16

1. Statistics of the Pharmaceutical Society of Ireland, 1930. These were taken from the Calendars of the Pharmaceutical Society of Ireland.
2. Dorothy Jones, 'Progress of Women in Pharmacy.' *The Chemist & Druggist*, 10 November 1959, pp. 185-7.
3. *The Chemist & Druggist*, 20 July 1935.
4. W. Gorman, 'The Silver Jubilee of the Pharmaceutical Society of Northern Ireland', *The Chemist & Druggist*, 24 June 1950, pp. 801-4.
5. She qualified in 1900, the second female to qualify as a pharmacist in Ireland.
6. Pharmaceutical Society of Ireland Calendar, 1904, p. 171.
7. Although his sister also qualified as a pharmacist, she became a nun. Interview with Sr Vincent Wilson, daughter of Christina Wilson. Personal communication, September 1997
8. Hannah and Frances Mcgrath, personal papers.
9. Interview with Gemma Hussey, daughter of Patricia Rogan, March 1997.
10. Henderson (1939), p. 427.

Chapter 19

1. I am grateful to Lindsey Earner-Byrne, Finola Kennedy, David Sheehy and Margaret MacCurtain for their advice and encouragement. The award of a Fulbright Fellowship enabled me to do research in Boston. This article is dedicated to Kerry Wardick with whom I have spent many pleasant sporting moments.
2. *The Irish Times*, 4 May 1928.
3. *Boston Pilot*, 28 November 1925. I am grateful to Mary Moriarity of St John's Seminary Library, Boston for her help. This library is now part of Boston College.
4. Pierre de Coubertin cited in Tom McNabb, *Olympic Games 1984* (London, 1984), p. 63.
5. Sebastian Coe with Nicholas Mason, *The Olympians. A Quest for Gold: Triumphs, Heroes and Legends* (London, 1988), p. 63.
6. *Irish Press*, 24 February 1934. (DDA McQuaid Papers, AB8/A/II26).
7. Paper on women in sport delivered by Dr Paul Rouse at the Women's History Association of Ireland, Annual Conference, Dublin, November, 2004.
8. Roe to McQuaid 12 February 1934. (DDA, McQuaid Papers, AB8/A/II/26).

9. P.J. Conway to McQuaid 8 February 1934. (DDA, McQuaid Papers, AB8/A?ii?26).

10. *Irish Press*, 9 February 1934.

11. *Daily Mail*, 11 March 1934.

12. Lindie Naughton, *Lady Icarus: The Life of Irish Aviator Lady Mary Heath* (Dublin, 2004), pp. 67 and 247. Eliot-Lynn was also the author of a book *Athletics for Women and Girls* which was published by Robert Scott in London, in 1925.

13. Undated newspaper article on the GAA. (DAA, McQuaid Papers, AB8/A/II/26).

14. Eoghan Corry, *God and the Referee: Unforgettable GAA Quotations* (Dublin, 2005), p. 122.

15. *Irish Independent*, 12 March 1934.

16. *Irish Independent*, 22 February 1934.

17. *Daily Herald*, 11 March 1934.

18. For a brief history of Camogie, see chapter 18.

19. *Sunday Independent*, 26 February 1934.

20. Undated newspaper article. (DDA, McQuaid Papers, AB8/A/II/26).

21. *Irish Press*, 12 March 1934. The popularity of cycling for both men and women in counties Louth and Meath is discussed in Brian Griffing, 'The Early History of Cycling in Meath and Drogheda', *Ríocht na Midhe*, Vol. XV, 2004, pp. 123–51.

22. *East Galway Democrat*, 10 February 1934.

23. *The Irish Times*, undated (DDA, McQuaid Papers, AB8/A/II/26).

24. *Irish Press*, 9 February 1934.

25. McQuaid to Conn Ward 24 April 1944. (DDA, McQuaid Papers, Department of Local Government and Public Health files, AB8/B-Box 4).

26. The Royal University of Ireland and the National University of Ireland, Calendars, give details of Stafford Johnson's academic career. He was a student at University College, Dublin with McQuaid.

27. Stafford Johnson to McQuaid 25 January 1944. (DDA, McQuaid Papers, Department of Local Government and Public Health files, AB8/B- Box 4).

28. Evelyn Bolster, *Knights of Columbanus* (Dublin, 1974), p. 84.

29. I am very grateful to Dr Finola Kennedy for this observation. Ironically, because Our Lady's School in south Dublin was the only Catholic school playing lacrosse, their matches were against Protestant schools such as Masonic and Glengara. This ecumenical result was not anticipated by McQuaid. Email correspondence from Finola Kennedy, 8 August, 2005.

30. Maryann Valiulis, 'Neither Feminist nor Flapper: The Ecclesiastical Construction of the Ideal Irish Woman' in Mary O'Dowd and Sabine Wichert, (eds), *Chattel Servant or Citizen: Women's Status in Church, State and Society. Historical Studies XIX* (Belfast, 1995), pp. 168-178.

31. L. O'Connor (1998), p. 40.

32. Interview with Sr Loreto O'Connor, 29 July, 1999.

33. *Mary Immaculate Training College Annual 1927*, pp. 26-7; 1928 pp. 34-7; chapter 5.
34. Kilkenny Loreto website www.loretokk.ie (see under sport); Marie des Victiores Fitzsimmons, *Reflections, 1859-1977: Clochar Lughaidh Muineachán*, (Dublin, 1977), p. 86. I am grateful to Dr Eithne McGee (née Conway) for giving me a copy of this valuable book.
35. Lindie Naughton and Jihnny Watterson, *Irish Olympians* (Dublin, 1992), pp. 82-3.
36. Noel Henry, *From Sophie to Sonia: A History of Woman's Athletics* (Dublin, 1998), pp. 24-6.
37. I am grateful to Professor Maureen Murphy, a student at UCD in the 1960s, for this observation.
38. See the mixed gender photograph of Dublin University Harriers and Athletic Club, 1964/5, in Parkes (2004), facing p. 113.

Chapter 20

1. This paper was originally delivered at the Irish Council for Civil Liberties Conference on Equality in October 1999. My thanks to the director of the ICCL, Donncha O'Connell, for his invitation to speak at this conference.
2. *Meath Chronicle* 1925; in 1997 the *Meath Chronicle* published a selection of its articles and photographs in book form as part of its centenary. This book is an excellent sample of the issues concerning people in Meath and the wider world between 1897 and 1997. The book was freely available with a copy of the *Meath Chronicle*. See p. 113 for the Tully quotation. It would be excellent if the other provincial newspapers decided to celebrate anniversaries in a similar manner.
3. M.E. Daly, 'Women and Trade Unions' in Donal Nevin (ed.), *Trade Union Century* (Dublin, 1994), pp. 106-16.
4. Pauric Travers, 'Emigration and Gender: The case of Ireland, 1922-60' in O'Dowd and Wichert (eds) (1995), pp. 187-99.
5. *Bunreacht na hEireann* (Constitution of Ireland) 1937, p. 152.
6. Margaret Gibbons, *Loreto Navan: One Hundred Years of Catholic Progress* (Navan, 1933), p. 111. This Margaret Gibbons should not be confused with the Margaret Gibbons who wrote novels and magazine articles in the 1930s and was married to fellow writer Patrick McGill. My thanks to Nadia Smith of Boston College for clarifying this to me.
7. Prospects of the Lodge, Fortwilliam Park, Belfast, PRONI, D3114/1.
8. O'Donnell, *The Ruin of Education in Ireland* (1902), pp. 151-3.
9. *Modern Girl and Ladies Home Journal*, March 1935, p. 22.
10. Olwen Hufton, *The Prospect Before Her: A history of women in western Europe 1500-1800* (London, 1995), p. 491.
11. Travers (1995), pp. 187-99.

Bibliography

Primary Sources

Manuscript Material

Alexandra College Archives, Dublin
Alexandra Guild file
Central Association of Irish School Mistresses file
Conference of Women's Workers (newspaper reports)
Letters to Henrietta White (Principal 1890-1932)
Memorial to Dr Katherine Maguire
Memoirs of Alexandra College Students
Reports of the Lady Principal to the Council of Alexandra College
    1880-1920
Survey on 'The Position of Women in Universities'
Universities of the Empire file
White, Henrietta 'The Position of Women at Universities', 'Women in
    Public Life' and 'Federation of University Women'
An Bord Altranais, Dublin
Minutes of Central Midwives Board 1918-1930
Minutes of General Nursing Council 1919-1930
Association of Secondary Teachers in Ireland (ASTI), Dublin
Dublin branch minutes 1924-1930 ASTI/33
Official Programme of 1930 Convention ASTI/40
Minutes of Conventions 1923-1930 ASTI/47
Register of Intermediate School Teachers 1936 ASTI/118
Dental Council, Dublin
Register of the Dental Council 1930
Dublin Diocesan Archives, Dublin
William Walsh Papers
Edward Byrne Papers

John Charles McQuaid Papers
Holles Street, Dublin
Matron's Register of Midwives 1918-1930
Irish National Teachers' Organisation (INTO), Dublin
Central Executive Committee Minutes 1917-1922
Congress Minutes 1921-1930
County Louth National Teachers' Association Minutes 1917-1926
Programme for Students in Training 1923-1924
Military Archives, Dublin
Dr Bridget Lyons-Thornton box PC519
National Archives, Dublin
Bodkin Papers 1155
Commission of Inquiry into the Civil Service 1932-1934. (Brennan
   Cimmission) BC/2 and BC/3
County Council Minutes DELG Leitrim 16/9, Limerick 17/15, Mayo
   21/19 and Longford 19/13. 1919-1922 (these relate to the first and
   second Dail)
Commissioners of National Education: ED8 (reports of inspectors on
   National education), ED 11 (letters to Commissioners of National
   Education) and ED15083 Box 304, admission of nuns to training
Department of Health files LA9/65/35 (Conditions of Employment in
   Kilkenny Co. Sanatorium, no date), SL7/24 (Mental Nurses part 1,
   1928-1940) and SM28/4 (Tipperary North Public Health Nurses
   1930-1950)
Department of An Taoiseach S files 3147; 4460; 8278; 8298 and 10540

National Library of Ireland (Manuscripts Deptartment), Dublin

Crowley Family Correspondence Acc.4767
Commission on Vocational Organisation Evidence Ms.922-941
Larcom Papers Ms. 7779
Newspapers Cuttings on Irish Hospitals Ms.11662
Dorothy Stopford-Price Papers Ms.15341, 15343, 16063 and 21205
Mary Hayden Papers Ms.16628, 16641, 16683, 23403 and 240009
Hanna Sheehy-Skeffington Papers Ms.22256 and 22262
National University of Ireland, Dublin
Matriculation Certificates 1880-1910
Peamount Hospital, Dublin
Peamount Sanatorium Annual Reports 1915-1930
Sláinte (Journal of the Women's National Health Association) 1910-1930
WNHA Dublin Baby and Health Week Programme 1925
Pharmaceutical Society of Ireland, Dublin
Calendar of the Pharmaceutical Society of Ireland 1931
Public Record Office, Northern Ireland (PRONI), Belfast
Irish Protestant National Teachers' Union Minute Book 1911-1926
   D/517
Lady Hermione Blackwood's Nursing Career D/1071

Belfast Maternity Hospital Papers D/1326
Queen Charlotte's Lying-In Hospital D/1326
Bangor School Papers D/1341
Women's National Health Association (Omagh) D/1884
Ellen Ferguson Papers D/2990
Prospectus of The Lodge D/3114/1
Dr Nan Watson Papers D/3270
Dr Florence Stewart Memoirs D/3612
Reminscences of The Lodge D/3712
Ulster Headmistresses' Association Papers 1921-1930 D/3820
Ulster Teachers' Union Minutes 1919-1930 D/3944
Ministry of Education Reports 1924-1930 ED/25
Ministry of Education Rules and Regulations 1923-1930 ED/26
Royal Victoria Hospital. Medical Staff Minute Book MIC/514/1/2/3
Inspectors' Reports 1900-1930 Sch/1/5/3
Prospectus of Ladies Collegiate School T/1389/3
Indenture of Sarah Potts T/1848/2
Non-recognition policy of teachers T/2886
Queen's University, Belfast
Queen's University Belfast, Women Graduates' Association Annual
    Reports 1925-1930
Rotunda Lying Hospital, Dublin
Statistics on midwives regarding pre-training, length of training, national-
    ity, age profile and marital status, courtesy of the matron, Mary Kelly.
Royal College of Physicians, Dublin
Kirkpatrick Biographical Archive
St Ultan's Papers 1918-1956
Diaries of Dr Kathleen Lynn
Royal College of Veterinary Surgeons, Wellcome Library London
Biographical information on Irish female veterinary surgeons
Registers of Veterinary Surgeons 1900-1930
Trinity College Dublin (Manuscripts Deptartment), Dublin
Central Association of Irish Schoolmistresses Ms.9722
Biological Association Papers (Mun. Soc. Biol)
Ulster Museum, Belfast
Material on nurses' badges, careers and registration, courtesy of Tom
    Wylie
University College, Cork
Admittance of females to UCC 1885-1900
File on Hanna Donovan, MA
University College, Dublin
Mary MacSwiney Papers P.48a
National University Women Graduates' Association Papers
Prospectus for Scoil Ide
Royal College of Science Registers B63, 64 and 65
Scoil Bhrighde Papers P.86
Material in Private Hands
Boran, Marie (material on her two aunts, a teacher and a nurse)

Cummins Family History, courtesy of Nicholas Cummins
Eccles Street Past Pupils' Union Minutes 1914-1930, courtesy of Loreto
    Diskin
Immaculata Past Pupils' Union Minutes, St Mary's Convent, Cabra
    1925-1930, courtesy of Sr Terence O'Keefe
Dr Angela Russell Scrapbooks, courtesy of Mathew Russell
Memoirs of Susan Stephens, courtesy of the Stephens family

Periodicals

A Record of College Life. Queen's College, Galway – the City of the Tribes
Alexandra College Magazine (ACM)
An Leabharlann
Bean na h-Eireann
Belfast Newsletter
Blas Aniar
British Medical Journal
Catholic Bulletin
Chemist and Druggist
Cork Examiner
Dublin Journal of Medial Science
Englishwoman's Journal
Galway Advertiser
Graduate News
Hall-Marked
Irish and Industrial Review
Irish Builder
Irish Catholic and Nation
Irish Chemist and Druggist
Irish Citizen
Irish Journal of Medical Science
Irish Medical Association Journal
Irish Monthly
Irish Nursing and Hospital World
Irish Nurses' Union Gazette
Irish Nursing News
Irish Nursing and Hospital World
Irish School Weekly
Irishman
Journal of the Irish Free State Medical Union
Journal of the Irish Medical Association
Lancet
Leader
Lyceum
Model Housekeeping
Modern Girl
National Student
New Statesman

Studies
St Stephen's
The Irish Times
The Lady of the House and Domestic Economist
Veterinary Record
Woman's Life

British and Irish Government Publications

Census Reports 1881, 1891, 1901, 1911 and 1926
Dale and Stephens Report on Intermediate Education Parliamentary
    Paper (hereafter PP) 1905,Vol. xxviii
Local Government and Local Taxation (Irl) PP 1906,Vol. cciv.
Medical Register of Saorstat Eireann (Dublin) 1930
Ministry of Health. Annual Report of the Chief Medical Officer, 1919-
    1920 Vol. xvii
Regulations for the Registration of Intermediate Teachers PP 1919,Vol.
    xix
Report of Mr Dale, His Majesty's Inspector of Schools, Board of
    Education, on Primary Education in Ireland 1904 PP Vol. xx
Commission on Emigration and other Population Problems, 1948-54.
    Reports (Dublin, 1954)
Report of the Conference Between the Department of Local
    Government and Public Health and Representatives of Local Public
    Health and Public Assistance Authorities 1930
Report of the Irish Public Health Council on the Public Health and
    Medical Services in Ireland PP 1920,Vol. xvii
Report of the Second National Programme Conference (1925-26
Report of the Vice-Regal Commmittee of Enquiry into Primary
    Education (Ireland) PP 1918-1919,Vol. xxi (Killanin Committee)
Report of the Vice Regal Committee on Primary Education in Ireland
    PP 1914,Vol. xxviii (Dill Report)
Returns from the National Training Colleges PP 1892,Vol. lxi.i.
Saorstat Eireann Irish Free State Official Handbook (Dublin, 1932)

Books and Pamphlets

Aberdeen, Lady *The International Congress of Women of 1899: Women in the
    Professions Vols III and IV* (London, 1900)
Aberdeen, Lady *Ireland's Crusade against T.B. being a series of lectures deliv-
    ered at the Tuberculosis Exhibition, 1907, under the auspices of the WNHA
    of Ireland Vols I and II* (Dublin, 1908)
Association of Intermediate and University Teachers, *Ireland Secondary
    Education in Ireland: A Plea for Reform by the Association of Intermediate
    and University Teachers, Ireland* (Dublin, 1904)
Bean-riaghalta (Mhuineachain) (Nuns, St Louis, Monaghan) *Cuirp-eolas*
    [Biology] (Monaghan, no date)
Bennett, A.H. *English Medical Women: Glimpses of their Work in Peace and
    War* (London, 1915)

Blackburn, Helen (ed.) *A Handy Book of Reference for Irishwomen* (London, 1888)

Bradshaw, Myrrha (ed.) *Open Doors for Irish Women. Irish Central Bureau for the Employment of Women* (Dublin, 1907)

Butler, Eleanor *Cruinne eolas: For the Teaching of Geography through the Medium of Irish* (Dublin, 1923)

Day, Susanne *The Amazing Philanthropists* (London, 1916)

Martindale, Louisa *The Woman Doctor and her Future* (London, 1922)

Morley, Edith (ed.) *Women Workers in Seven Professions: A Survey of their Economic Conditions and Prospects* (London, 1914)

O'Donnell, F.H. *The Ruin of Education in Ireland* (London, 1902)

Our Schools (Dublin, 1915)

Smithson, A.P. *Her Irish Heritage* (Dublin, 1917)

The Fingerpost *A Guide to the Professions and Occupations of Educated Women* (Holburn, 1906)

Tierney-Downes, Margaret *The Case of the Catholic Lady Students of the Royal University Stated* (Dublin, 1888)

University of Dublin *A Catalogue of Graduates of the University of Dublin Vol. IV*, 1905-17

Articles

Brennan, John 'The Irish Hospital Nurse. Slave and Lady' in *Bean na hEireann*, April 1909, p. 14

Calwell, Elizabeth 'The Letter of 1906' in *Past Students' Association of the Church of Ireland College of Education Newsletter*, April 1996.

Corcoran, Timothy 'Current Notes on Educational Topics' in *Irish Monthly*, October 1924, pp. 219-25

Corcoran, Timothy 'Is the Montessori Method to be Introduced into Irish Schools?' in *Irish Monthly*, March 1924, pp. 118-24

Cummins, Iris 'The Woman Engineer' in *The Englishwoman's Journal* April 1920, pp. 37-44

Dickson, Emily 'The Need for Women as Poor Law Guardians' in *Dublin Journal of Medical Science* 1 April 1895, pp. 309-14

Cahill, Edward 'Notes on Christian Sociology' *Irish Monthly*, January 1925, pp. 33-4

Falkiner, N.M. 'The Nurse and the State' in *Journal of the Statistical and Social Inquiry Society of Ireland*, October 1920, pp. 29-43

Houston 'The Extension of the Field for the Employment of Women' in *Journal of the Statistical and Social Inquiry Society of Ireland*, November 1866, pp. 345-53

Huxley, Margaret 'The Requirements of Nursing as a Vocation: Its Rewards as a Profession', pp. 140-3 in *ACM*, June 1901

Kirkpatrick, T.P.C. 'Treatment of Syphilis' Paper read to Royal Academy of Medicine in *Irish Journal of Medical Science*, March 1918, pp. 339-57

Lady Aberdeen 'The Sphere of Women in Relation to Public Health' in *The Dublin Journal of Medical Science*, September 1911, pp. 161-70

Lawson, William 'Infant Mortality and the Notification of Births Acts, 1907, 1915' in *Journal of the Statistical and Social Inquiry Society of Ireland*, part xcvii, Vol. xii, October 1919, pp. 479-97

Lyons Thornton, Brigid 'The Warp and Woof of History' in *Longford News* (no date)

McWeeney, Edmond 'On the Recent Action of the State with Regard to Venereal Disease' in *The Journal of the Statistical and Social Inquiry Society of Ireland*, part xcvii, Vol. xiii, October 1919, pp. 498-517

Mulvany, Isabella 'The Intermediate Act and the Education of Girls' in *Irish Educational Review*, Vol. 1, 1907, pp. 14-20

Roche, Katherine 'The Training of Teachers' in *The New Ireland Review*, January 1903, pp. 292-9

Shanley, J.P. 'The State and Medicine' in *Irish Journal of Medical Science* May 1929, pp. 191-6

Sheehan, Canon 'Irish Primary Education' in *Irish Monthly*, January 1917, pp. 49-64.

Sheehy Skeffington, Hanna 'Irish Secondary Teachers' in *The Irish Review*, October 1912, pp. 393-8

Starkie, William 'The History of Irish Primary and Secondary Education During the Last Decade' *Address at Queen's University Belfast*, 3 July 1911

Williams, W.J. 'Education' in *Saorstat Eireann: Irish Free State Official Handbook* (Dublin, 1932), pp. 179-95

Serial Publications

Annual Reports of Lady Dudley's Scheme for the Establishment of District Nurses in the Poorest Parts of Ireland (Dublin) 1904-1930

Annual Reports of Queen Victoria's Jubilee Institute (Irish Branch) (Dublin) 1925-1930

Annual Reports of the Board of Superintendents of the Dublin Hospitals (Dublin) 1920-1930

Annual Reports of the Bureau for the Employment of Women (Dublin) 1907-1915

Annual Reports of the Commissioners of Education (Dublin) 1880-1920

Annual Reports of the Department of Education (Dublin) 1925-1930

Annual Reports of the Intermediate Board for Ireland (Dublin) 1880-1920

Catholic Directories (Dublin) 1890-1930

College Calendars: Royal University of Ireland (1885-1905); Royal College of Surgeons, Ireland (1885-1930); Queen's College, Galway (1885-1905); Queen's College, Cork (1885-1905); Queen's College, Belfast (1885-1905); University College, Cork (1910-1930); University College, Dublin (1910-1930); University College, Galway (1910-1930); Queen's University, Belfast (1910-1920); DU (Dublin University, Trinity College Dublin) (1880-1930)

Ellis, W.E. *The Irish Education Directory* 1882–1888 (Dublin)

Irish Educational Yearbook. (Dublin) 1910–1930

Irish Free State Hospital Yearbook and Medical Directory 1st Edition
    1937

Mary Immaculate Training College Annuals (Limerick) 1925–1930

Medical Directories (London) 1890–1930

Ninth Annual Report of the Queen's Institute (of Female Professional
    Schools) (Dublin, 1871)

Pharmaceutical Society of Ireland Calendars. (Dublin) 1895–1930

Prospectus of Municipal Technical Institute Belfast 1914–15

The Hospitals' Commission. First General Report 1933–34

Thom's Directory (Dublin) 1880–1930

Memoirs

Agnew, Nessa 'A Typical Day in the Life of a St Louis Boarder' in *Louis
    Lines 1988 Centenary Edition* p. 48

A Lay Teacher 'The Stop-Gap Profession' in *Cork University Record*
    Easter 1949, pp. 21–3

Colum, Mary *Life and the Dream* (Dublin, 1966)

Kavanagh, Patrick *The Green Fool* (London, 1938)

Martindale Hilda *From One Generation to Another* (London, 1944)

Moffett, Frances 'UCG 70 Years Ago' Speech given to CCG (UCG
    Graduates' Association) 9 September 1989

Skinnider, Margaret *Doing My Bit for Ireland* (New York, 1917)

Smithson, Annie *Myself and Others: An Autobiography* (Dublin, 1944)

Starkie, Enid *A Lady's Child* (Dublin, 1944)

Secondary Material

Books and Pamphlets

*A Meath Chronicle Centenary Publication: One Hundred Years of Life and
    Times in North Leinster* (Meath, 1997)

Abel-Smith, Brian *History of the Nursing Profession in Great Britain*
    (New York, 1960)

Akenson, D.H. *A Mirror to Kathleen's Face: Education in Independent Ireland
    1922–1960* (Montreal and London, 1975)

Akenson, D.H. *Education and Enmity: The Control of Schooling in Northern
    Ireland 1920–50* (Newton Abbot, 1973)

AST! *'Security of Tenure 1909-1934': A Statement of the Association's Efforts*
    (1934)

Atkinson, Norman *Irish Education: A History of Educational Institutions*
    (Dublin, 1969)

Auchmuty, James *Irish Education: A Historical Survey* (Dublin, 1937)

Bailey, Kenneth *A History of Trinity College Dublin 1892-1945* (Dublin,
    1947)

Barrington, Ruth *Health, Medicine and Politics in Ireland 1900-70* (Dublin,
    1987)

Barry, Jim *The Victoria Hospital Cork: A History 1874-1986* (Dublin, 1992)

Beckett, J.C. and T.W. Moody *Queen's, Belfast 1845-1949: The History of a University. 2 Vols* (London, 1959)

Blum, Albert (ed.) *Teacher Unions and Association: A Comparative Study* (Chicago, 1969)

Bolster, Evelyn *The Sisters of Mercy in the Crimean War* (Cork, 1964)

Bourdieu, Pierre and Jean-Claude Passeron *Reproduction in Education, Society and Culture* (London, 1977)

Bourke, Joanna Women, Economic Change, and Housework in Ireland, 1890-1914 (Oxford, 1993)

Bowden, Brian 200 Years of a Future Through Education. A History of the Masonic Girls' Charity (Dublin, 1992)

Bradley, Anthony and Maryann Gialanella Valiulis (eds) *Gender and Sexuality in Modern Ireland* (Amherst, 1997)

Bridges, J.B. *Belfast Medical Students* (Belfast, 1986)

Browne, Alan (ed.) *Masters, Midwives and Ladies-in-Waiting: The Rotunda Hospital 1745-1995* (Dublin, 1995)

Butler-Kahle, Jane (ed.) *Women in Science: A Report from the Field* (Philadelphia, 1985)

Clark, Linda *Schooling the Daughters of Marianne* (New York, 1984)

Clear, Caitriona *Nuns in Nineteenth-Century Ireland* (Dublin, 1987)

Coakley, Davis *Baggot Street: A Short History of the Royal City of Dublin Hospital* (Dublin, 1995)

Coakley, Davis *Irish Masters of Medicine* (Dublin, 1992)

Colley, Linda *Britons: Forging the Nation 1707-1837* (Yale, 1992)

Collis, Robert *To be a Pilgrim* (London, 1975)

Comoradh 75 Bliain Scoil Bhride Raghnallach and Ni Ghachain, Mairead (ed.) *Luise Gabhanach Ni Dhufaigh agus Scoil Bhride.* (Dublin, 1992). Both publications mark the 75th anniversary of Scoil Bhride.

Coolahan, John *Irish Education: Its History and Structure* (Dublin, 1981)

Coolahan, John 'Education in the Training Colleges 1887-1977' in *Our Lady of Mercy College, Blackrock* (Dublin, 1981)

Coolahan, John *The A.S.T.I. and Post-Primary Education in Ireland in Ireland 1909-1984* (Dublin, 1984)

Cosgrove, Art and Donal McCartney (eds) *Studies in Irish History* (Dublin, 1979)

Crookes, Gearoid *Dublin's Eye and Ear: The Making of a Monument* (Dublin, 1993)

Crossman, Virginia *Local Government in Ireland* (Belfast, 1994)

Cullen, Mary (ed.) *Girls Don't Do Honours: Irish Women in Education in the Nineteenth and Twentieth Century* (Dublin, 1987)

Cullen, Mary and Maria Luddy (eds) *Women, Power and Consciousness in Nineteenth Century Ireland. Eight Biographical Studies* (Dublin, 1995)

Cummins, Marshal *Some Chapters of Cork Medical History* (Cork, 1957)

Curtin, Deirdre *Irish Employment Equality Law* (Dublin, 1989)

Daly, M.E. *Dublin. The Deposed Capital: A Social and Economic History 1860-1914* (Cork, 1984)

Daly, M.E. *The Buffer State: The Historic Roots of the Department of the Environment to 1973* (Dublin, 1997)

Daly, M.E. *Women and Work in Ireland. Studies in Irish Economic and Social History* 7 (Dundalk, 1997)

Day, Anna *Turn of the Tide: The Story of Peamount* (Dublin, 1987)

Deeny James *To Cure and To Care* (Dublin, 1994)

Deeny, James (edited by A.A. Farmar) *The End of an Epidemic: Essays in Irish Public Health* (Dublin, 1995)

Digby, Anne *Making a Medical Living* (Cambridge, 1994)

Dingwall, Robert and Philip Lewis (eds) *The Sociology of the Professions. Lawyers, Doctors and Others* (London, 1983)

Donaldson, Peggy *Yes Matron: A History of Nurses and Nursing at the Royal Victoria Hospital, Belfast* (Belfast, 1989)

Drake McFeely, Mary *Lady Inspectors: The Campaign for a Better Workplace 1893-1921* (Oxford and New York, 1988)

Duffy, Patrick *A Study of the Position of the Lay Teacher in an Irish* Catholic Environment (Dublin, 1967)

Etzioni, Amitai (ed.) *The Semi-Professions and their Organization. Teachers, Nurses, Social Workers* (New York, 1969)

Farmar, A.A. *A History of Craig Gardner and Company: The First One Hundred Years* (Dublin, 1988)

Farmar, A.A. *Holles Street 1894-1994: The National Maternity Hospital* (Dublin, 1994)

Farmar, A.A. *Ordinary Lives: Three Generations of Irish Middle Class Experience 1907, 1932, 1963* (Dublin, 1991)

Ferriter, Diarmuid *Mothers, Maidens and Myths: A History of the Irish Countrywomen's Association* (Dublin, 1995)

Fleetwood, John *The History of Medicine in Ireland* (Dublin, 1983)

Flora, Peter *State, Economy and Society in Western Europe 1815-1975: A Data Handbook. Vol. 1. The Growth of Mass Democracies and Welfare States* (Frankfurt, 1983)

Ford, Connie *Aleen Cust: Britain's First Woman Vet* (Bristol, 1990)

Fox, R.M. *The History of the Irish Citizen Army* (Dublin, 1944)

Fraser, T.G. and Keith Jeffery (eds) *Men, Women and War* (Dublin, 1993)

Gallagher, John *Courageous Irishwomen* (Castlebar, 1995)

Gallagher, Tom and James O'Connell (eds) *Contemporary Irish Studies* (Manchester, 1983)

Garvin, Tom *Nationalist Revolutionaries in Ireland 1858-1928* (Oxford, 1987)

Gibbons, Margaret Loreto Navan *One Hundred of Catholic Progress 1833-1933* (Navan, 1933)

Gourvish, T.R. and Alan O'Day (eds) *Later Victorian Britain* (Basingstoke, 1988)

Groag-Bell, Susan and Karen Offen (eds) *Women, the Family and Freedom: The Debate in the Documents. Vol. 1, 1750-1880* (Stanford, 1983)

Harkness, David *Northern Ireland since 1920* (Dublin, 1983)

Harris, Mary *The Catholic Church and the Foundation of the Northern Ireland State* (Cork, 1993)

Heaney, Seamus *The Government of the Tongue* (London, 1989)

Henderson, J.W. *Methodist College Belfast 1868-1938: A Survey and Retrospect 2 Vols* (Belfast, 1939)

Henry, Patrick Sligo *Medical Care in the Past 1800-1965* (Manorhamilton, 1995)

Hensey, Brendan *The Health Services in Ireland* 2nd edition (Dublin, 1972)

Hogan, Daire *The Legal Profession in Ireland 1789-1922* (Naas, 1986).

Hogan, Mary *U.C.D. Women's Graduates' Association 1902-82* (Dublin, 1982)

Holmes, Janice and Diane Urquhart (eds) *Coming into the Light: The Work, Politics and Religion of Women in Ulster in Ulster 1840-1940* (Belfast, 1994)

Holmes, R.F.G. *Magee 1865-1965: The Evolution of the Magee Colleges* (Belfast, 1965)

Howorth, Jolyon and Philip Cervy (eds) *Elites in France: Origins, Reproduction and Power* (London, 1981)

Hufton, Olwen *The Prospect Before Her: A History of Women in Western Europe. Volume One 1500-1800* (London, 1995)

Hufton, Olwen (ed.) *Women in the Religious Life* (Florence, 1996)

Huggett, Albert and T.M. Stinnett *Professional Problems of Teachers* (New York, 1956)

Hunt, Felicity *Lessons for Life: The Schooling of Girls and Women 1850-1980* (Oxford, 1987)

Hurley, Michael *Irish Anglicanism 1869-1969* (Dublin, 1970)

Irish Nurses' Organisation *The Irish Nurses' Organisation: Souvenir Book* (1947)

Jones, Greta *Social Hygiene in Twentieth-Century Britain* (London, 1986)

Jones, Mary *These Obstreperous Lassies: A History of the Irish Women Workers' Union* (Dublin, 1988)

Jordan, Alison *Margaret Byers: Pioneer of Women's Education and founder of Victoria College, Belfast* (Belfast, 1991)

Kelleher, Margaret and James Murphy (eds) *Gender Perspectives in Nineteenth Century Ireland* (Dublin, 1997)

Kelly, Kathleen T*he Story of the Ulster Hospital Part 2 1952-73* (Belfast, 1975)

Kennedy, K.W.S. *50 Years in Chota Nagpur. An Account of the Dublin University Mission to Chota Nagpur from its Beginnings* (Dublin, 1939)

Kinnear, Mary *In Subordination. Professional Women, 1870-1970* (Montreal and Kingston, 1995)

Kirkpatrick, T.P.C. and edited by Henry Jellett *The Book of the Rotunda Hospital* (London, 1913)

Kirkpatrick, T.P.C. *History of the Medical Teaching in Trinity College Dublin and the School of Physic in Ireland* (Dublin, 1912)

Kirkpatrick, T.P.C. *The History of Doctor Steevens' Hospital, Dublin 1720-1920* (Dublin, 1924)

Ladd-Taylor, Molly *Raising a Baby the Government Way: Mothers' Letters to the Children's Bureau 1915-1932* (London, 1986)

Lee, John *Ireland 1912-1985* (Cambridge, 1989)

Lee, John *The Evolution of a Profession and of its Dental School in Dublin* (Dublin, 1993)

Lee, John *The History of the Irish Dental Association 1922-1972* (Dublin, 1972)

Lee, Sidney and Leslie Stephen (eds) *Dictionary of National Biography* (Oxford, 1891)

Lewis, Jane *The Politics of Motherhood. Child and Maternal Welfare in England, 1900-1939* (London, 1980)

Lillis, Mercedes *200 Years a Growing 1787-1987: The Story of the Ursulines in Thurles* (Roscrea, 1987)

Luddy, Maria *Hanna Sheehy Skeffington* (Dundalk, 1995)

Luddy, Maria *Women and Philanthropy in Nineteenth Century Ireland* (Cambridge, 1995)

Lyons, J.B. and Mary O'Doherty *Accouching the Rotundaties. A Guide to the Rotunda 250th Anniversary* Exhibition (Dublin, 1995)

Lyons, J.B. *Brief Lives of Irish Doctors* (Dublin, 1978)

Lyons, J.B. *The Quality of Mercer's: The Story of Mercer's Hospital 1734-1991* (Dublin, 1991)

Mac Curtain, Margaret and Donncha O'Corrain (eds) *Women in Irish Society: The Historical Dimension* (Dublin, 1978)

MacHale, Desmond *George Boole: His Life and Work* (Dublin, 1985)

Malcolm, Elizabeth *A History of St Patrick's Dublin, 1746-1989* (Dublin, 1989)

Markell-Morantz-Sanchez, Regina *Sympathy and Science. Women Physicians in American Medicine* (Oxford, 1985)

Marshall, Robert *The Story of the Ulster Hospital Part 1 1873-1952* (Belfast, 1975)

Marshall, Ronald *Methodist College Belfast: The First One Hundred Years* (Belfast, 1968)

Marshall, Ronald *Stranmillis College Belfast* (Belfast, 1972)

Maume, Patrick *D.P. Moran* (Dundalk, 1995)

Mc Dowell, R.B. and D.A. Webb *Trinity College Dublin, 1592-1952: An Academic History* (Cambridge, 1982)

Mc Elligott, T.J. *Secondary Education in Ireland 1870-1921* (Naas, 1981)

Mc Ivor, John *Popular Education in the Irish Presbyterian Church* (Dublin, 1969)

Meenan, F.O.C. (ed.) *The Children's Hospital, Temple Street. Dublin Centenary Book 1872-1972* (Dublin, 1973)

Meenan, F.O.C. *Cecilia Street. The Catholic University School of Medicine 1855-1931* (Dublin, 1987)

Meenan, F.O.C. *St Vincent's Hospital 1834-1994, an Historical and Social Portrait* (Dublin, 1995)

Migdal-Glazer, Penina and Miriam Slater *Unequal Colleagues: The Entrance of Women into the Professions, 1890-1940* (London, 1987)

Miller-Solomon, Barbara *In the Company of Educated Women: A History of Women and Higher Education in America* (New Haven, 1985)

Mitchell, David *A 'Peculiar' Place. The Adelaide Hospital, Dublin. Its Time, Places and Personalities 1839-1989* (Dublin, 1989)

Moran, Gerard (ed.) and Raymond Gillespie (associate ed.) *Galway: History and Society* (Dublin, 1996)

Morrissey, Thomas *Towards a National University: William Delaney SJ (1835-1924): An Era of Initiative in Irish Education* (Dublin, 1983)

Murphy, Cliona *The Women's Suffrage Movement and Irish Society in the Early Twentieth Century* (Hempel Hempstead, 1989)

Murphy, John *The College: A History of Queen's/University College Cork, 1845-1995* (Cork, 1995)

Murray, James *Galway: A Medico-Social History* (Galway, 1994)

Newmann, Kate *Dictionary of Ulster Biography* (Belfast, 1993)

Nolan, Eugene *One Hundred Years. A History of the School of Nursing and of Developments at Mater Misercordiae Hospital 1891-1911* (Dublin, 1991)

O'Brien, Eoin (ed.) *Essays in Honour of J.D.H. Widdess* (Dublin, 1978)

O'Brien, Eoin *The Charitable Infirmary. Jervis Street 1718-1987: A Farewell Tribute* (Dublin, 1987)

O'Brien, Eoin, Lorna Browne and Kevin O'Malley (eds) *The House of Industry Hospitals 1772-1987, the Richmond, Whitworth and Hardwicke (St Lawrence's Hospital): A Closing Memoir* (Dublin, 1988)

O'Connell, T.J. *A History of the Irish National Teachers' Organisation 1868-1968* (Dublin, 1968)

O'Connor, Anne and Susan Parkes *'Gladly Learn and Gladly Teach': Alexandra College and School 1866-1966* (Dublin, 1983)

O'Donel-Browne, T.D. *The Rotunda Hospital 1745-1945* (Edinburgh, 1947)

O'Dowd, Mary and Wichert, Sabine (eds) *Chattel, Servant or Citizen. Women's Status in Church, State and Society* (Belfast, 1995)

O'Flanagan, Patrick, Paul Ferguson and Kevin Whelan (eds) *Rural Ireland: Modernisation and Change, 1600-1900* (Cork, 1987)

O'Halloran, Clare *Partition and the Limits of Irish Nationalism* (Dublin, 1987)

O'Keefe, Camillus *Colaiste Bhantiarna na Trocaire. Our Lady of Mercy College Centenary 1877/1977* (Dublin, 1977)

O'Neill, Marie *From Parnell to De Valera: A Biography of Jennie Wyse Power 1858-1941* (Dublin, 1991)

O'Neill, Rose *A Rich Inheritance. Galway Dominican Nuns 1644-1944* (Galway, 1944)

O Broin, Leon *Protestant Nationalists in Revolutionary Ireland. The Stopford Connection* (Dublin, 1985)

O Buachalla, Seamus *Education Policy in Twentieth Century Ireland* (Dublin, 1988)

O Ceirin, Kit and Cyril *Women of Ireland: A Biographical Dictionary* (Kinvara, 1996)

Parkes, Susan *Kildare Place: The History of the Church of Ireland Training College 1811-1969* (Dublin, 1984)

Perkin, Harold *The Rise of Professional Society. England Since 1800* (London, 1989)

Perkin, Harold *The Third Revolution: Professional Elites in the Modern World* (London and New York, 1996)

Phillips, Patricia *The Scientific Lady. A Social History of Women's Scientific Interests 1520-1918* (London, 1990)

Phoenix, Eamon (ed.) *A Century of Northern Life. The Irish News and 100 Years of Ulster History 1890-1990s* (Belfast, 1995)

Phoenix, Eamon *Northern Nationalism. Nationalist Politics, Partition and the Catholic Minority in Northern Ireland 1890-1940* (Belfast, 1994)

Price, Dorothy *Tuberculosis in Childhood* (Bristol, 1942)

Price, Liam (ed.) *Dr Dorothy Price: An Account of Twenty Years' Fight Against Tuberculosis in Ireland* (Oxford, for private circulation only, 1957)

Purser, Olive *Women in Dublin University: 1904-1954* (Dublin, 1954)

Rafferty, Oliver *Catholicism in Ulster 1603-1983: An Interpretative History* (Dublin, 1994)

Reader, W.J. *Professional Men: The Rise of the Profession Classes in Nineteenth Century England* (London, 1966)

Robins, Joseph *Custom House People* (Dublin, 1993)

Robins, Joseph *The Lost Children: A Study of Charity Children in Ireland, 1700-1900* (Dublin, 1980)

Robins, Joseph *The Miasma: Epidemic and Panic in Nineteenth Century Ireland* (Dublin, 1995)

Robinson, H.W. *A History of Accountants in Ireland* (Dublin, 1983)

Roche, Desmond *Local Government in Ireland* (Dublin, 1982)

Rossiter, Margaret *Women Scientists in America. Struggles and Strategies to 1940* (Baltimore, 1982)

Rowe, David (ed.) *The Irish Chartered Accountant: Centenary Essays 1888-1988* (Dublin, 1988)

Ruane, Medb *Ten Dublin Women: The Women's Commemoration and Celebration Committee* (Dublin, 1991)

Scanlan, Pauline *The Irish Nurse. A Study of Nursing in Ireland: History and Education 1718-1981* (Manorhamilton, 1991)

Sheehy Skeffington, Andree *A Coterie of Lively Suffragists* (Dublin, 1993)

Sills, David (ed.) *International Encyclopaedia of the Social Science Vol. 12* (1968)

St Vincent's Hospital. Anniversary Yearbook One Hundred and Fifty Years Service 1834-1984 (Dublin, 1984)

Stolte-Heiskanen, Veronica (ed.) *Women in Science: Token Women or Gender Equality* (Oxford, 1991)

Summers, Anne *Angels and Citizens. British Women as Military Nurses 1854-1914* (London, 1988)

Tierney, Michael (ed.) *Struggle with fortune, a miscellany for the centenary of the Catholic University of Ireland* (Dublin, 1954)

Titley, E.Brian *Church, State and the Control of Schooling 1900-1944* (Dublin, 1983)

Tomkin, David and Patrick Hannifin *Irish Medical Law* (Dublin, 1994)

Walker, Brian and Alf McCreary *Degrees of Excellence: The Story of Queen's, Belfast 1845-1995* (Belfast, 1994)

White, Jack *Minority Report: The Protestant Community in the Irish Republic* (Dublin, 1975)

Widdess, J.D.H. *A History of the Royal College of Physicians if Ireland 1654-1963* (Edinburgh, 1963)

Woodham-Smith Cecil *Florence Nightingale 1820-1910* (London, 1950)

Widdess, J.D.H. *An Account of the Schools of Surgery: Royal College of Surgeons Dublin 1789-1948* (Edinburgh, 1949)

WNHA *Golden Jubilee 1907-1957* (Dublin, 1957)

Articles

Barker, Patricia 'The True and Fair Sex' in Rowe, David (ed.) *The Irish Chartered Accountant: Centenary Essays 1888-1988*, pp. 207-25

Blom, Ida 'Equality and the threat of War in Scandinavia, 1884-1905' in Fraser, T.G. and Jeffery (eds) *Men, Women and War*, pp. 100-18

Brown, Ian 'Who were the Eugenicists? A Study of the Formation of an Early Twentieth-Century Pressure Group' in *History of Education* 1988, Vol. 17, No. 4, pp. 295-307

Chua, Wai Fong and Chris Poullaos 'Rethinking the Profession-State Dynamic: The Case of the Victoria Charter Attempt, 1885-1906' in *Accounting, Organisations and Society*, Vol. 18, Nos 7/8, 1993, pp. 691-728

Chua, Wai-Fong and Stewart Clegg 'Professional Closure. The Case of British Nursing' in *Theory and Society* 1990, No. 19, pp. 135-74

Clancy, Mary 'On the "Western Outpost": Local Government and Women's Suffrage in Co. Galway, 1898-1918' in Moran, Gerard (ed.) and Gillespie (associate ed.) *Galway: History and Society*, pp. 557-87

Clear, Caitriona '"The Women Can Not be Blamed": The Commission on Vocational Organisation, Feminism and "Home-makers in Independent Ireland in the 1930s and '40s"' in O'Dowd, Mary and Wichert (eds) *Chattel, Servant or Citizen,* pp. 179-86

Coolahan, John 'The Position of Lay Teachers Under the Act' (1878 Intermediate Education Act) in *The Secondary Teacher* Autumn/Winter 1978, Vol. 8, nos 1 and 2, pp. 11-17

Counihan, H.E. '"Trials and Tribulations." The House of Industry Hospitals in the Twentieth-Century' in O'Brien, Eoin, Browne and O'Malley (eds) *House of Industry Hospitals*, pp. 63-71

Counihan, H.E. 'In Memoriam for Dr Price' *Journal of the Irish Medical Association* March 1954, p. 84

Crawford, Margaret 'Health and Welfare in Ulster since 1891' in Phoenix, Eamon (ed.) *A Century of Northern Life: The Irish News and 100 Years of Ulster History 1890-1990s*

Cullen, Mary 'Anna Maria Haslam' in Cullen, Mary and Luddy (eds) *Women, Power and Consciousness*, pp. 161-96

Daly, M.E. 'Essay in Review. Women and Labour: Margins to Mainstream?' in *Saothar* No. 19, 1994, pp. 70-4

Daly, M.E. 'The Development of the National School System in Ireland 1831-1840' in Cosgrove, Art and McCartney (eds) *Studies in Irish History* (Dublin, 1979), pp. 150-63

Daly, M.E. 'Women in the Irish Workforce from Pre-industrial to Modern Times' in *Saothar* No. 7, 1981, pp. 74-82

Daly, M.E. 'Women, Work and Trade Unionism' in MacCurtain, Margaret and O'Corrain (eds) *Women in Irish Society*, pp. 71-81

Daly, M.E. '"Oh! Kathleen Ni Houlihan Your Way's a Thorny Way!" The Condition of Women in Twentieth-Century Ireland' in Bradley, Anthony and Valiulis (eds) *Gender and Sexuality in Modern Ireland*, pp. 102-126

Daly, M.E. 'Women in the Irish Free State, 1922-39: The Interaction Between Politics and Ideology' in Hoff, Joan and Maureen Coulter (eds) *Irish Women's Voices. Past and Present. Journal of Women's History* Vol.6, No.4/Vol. 7, No.1 (Winter/Spring) (Indiana, 1995), pp. 99-116

Davis, Virginia 'Curious Goings-On in the National Schools 1870-95' in *Retrospect: Journal of the Irish History Students' Association*, 1980, pp. 24-32

Donoghue, Denis 'University Professor' in 'Re-Organising Irish Education' in *Studies* Vol. lvii, No. 227, Autumn 1968, pp. 225-88, pp. 284-8

Doona, Mary-Ellen 'Sister Mary Joseph Croke. Another Voice from the Crimean War, 1854-1856' in *Nursing History Review* 3, 1995, pp. 3-41

Dunlevy, Pearl 'Patriot doctor -Kathleen Lynn FRCSI' in *Irish Medical Times* 4 December 1981

Dunwoody, Janet 'Child Welfare' in Fitzpatrick, David (ed.) *Ireland and the First World War. Trinity History Workshop* (Dublin, 1986), pp. 69-75

Fahey, Tony 'State, Family and Compulsory Schooling in Ireland' in *The Economic and Social Review*, Vol. 23, No. 4, July 1992, pp. 369-95

Fitzpatrick, David 'The Modernisation of the Irish Female' in O'Flanagan, Patrick, Ferguson and Whelan (eds) *Rural Ireland: Modernisation and Change, 1600-1900*, pp. 162-80

Fitzpatrick, David 'Review Article: Women, Gender and the Writing of Irish History.' in *Irish Historical Studies* xxvii, No. 107, May 1991, pp. 267-73

Fox, Enid 'Universal Helath Care and Self-help: Paying for District Nursing before the National Health Service' in *Twentieth-Century British History* Vol. 7, No. 1, 1996, pp. 83-109

Friedson, Eliot 'The Theory of Professions: State of the Art' in Dingwall, Robert and Lewis (eds) *The Sociology of the Professions. Lawyers, Doctors and Others*, pp. 19-37

Froggatt, Peter 'Academic Education and Vocational Training: The Role of the University' The Canon Rogers Memorial Lecture, 1 December 1977

Garvin, Tom 'Great Hatred, Little Room: Social Background and Political Sentiment Among Revolutionary Activists in Ireland, 1890-1922' in Boyce, D.G. (ed.) *The Revolution in Ireland, 1879-1923* (London, 1988), pp. 91-114

Geraghty, Sidney 'Alice Jacqueline Perry. Engineer, Poet, Christian Scientist'. Unpublished paper presented to U.C.G. Women's Studies Group

Gorman, W 'The Silver Jubilee of the Pharmaceutical Society of Northern Ireland' in *The Chemist and Druggist*, 24 June 1950, pp. 801-4

Gourvish, T.R. 'The Rise of the professions' in Gourvish, T.R. and O'Day (eds) *Later Victorian Britain, 1867-1900*, pp. 13-35

Greene, David 'The Irish Language Movement' in Hurley, Michael (ed.) *Irish Anglicanism*, pp. 110-19

Holland, D.J. 'The Department of Pathology' in O'Brien, Eoin, Browne
 and O'Malley (eds) *The Houses of Industry Hospitals*, pp. 129-35
Hufton, Olwen 'Introduction' in Hufton, Olwen (ed.) *Women in the
 Religious Life*, pp. 11-26
Ingle, Roisin 'Florence Nightingale? Goodbye to All That' in *The Irish
 Times* 8 February 1997
Jacobs-Brumbeg, Joan and Nancy Tomes 'Women in the Professions:
 A Research Agenda for American Historian' in *Reviews in American
 History* June 1982, pp. 275-96
Jones, Dorothy 'Progress of Women in Pharmacy' in *The Chemist and
 Druggist*, 10 November 1959, pp. 185-7
Jones, Greta 'Eugenics in Ireland: The Belfast Eugenics Society, 1911-15'
 in *Irish Historical Studies* xxxiii, No. 109, May 1992, pp. 81-95
Jordan, Alison 'Open the Gates of Learning: the Belfast Ladies Institute,
 1867-97' in Holmes, Janice and Urquhart (eds) *Coming into the Light*,
 pp. 33-59
Kearney, Noreen 'The Historical Background' in *Social Work and Social
 Work Training in Ireland: Yesterday and Tomorrow* (Dublin, 1987) pp.
 5-15
Kelikian, Alice 'Nuns, Entrepreneurs, and Church Welfare in Italy' in
 Hufton, Olwen (ed.) *Women in the Religious Life*, pp. 119-37
Kelly, Mary 'The Development of Midwifery at the Rotunda' in Brown,
 Alan (ed.) *Masters, Midwives and Ladies-in Waiting: The Rotunda
 Hospital 1745-1995* pp. 77-117
Kelly, Timothy 'Education' in Hurley (ed.) *Irish Anglicanism 1869-1969*,
 pp. 51-64
Kenny, Mary, Tess Power (Hughes) and Grace Power 'Nursing in the
 Richmond' in O'Brien (ed.) *Houses of Industries Hospitals*, pp. 201-8
Kirkham, Linda and Anne Loft 'Gender and the Construction of the
 Professional Accountant' in *Accounting, Organizations and Society* 1993,
 Vol. 18, No.6, pp. 507-58
Laffan, Joseph 'Lt Bridget Lyons-Thornton - Our first Female Lt.' in *An
 Cosantoir*, October 1987, p. 32
Logan, John 'The Dimensions of Gender in Nineteenth-Century
 Schooling' in Kelleher, Margaret and Murphy (eds) *Gender
 Perspectives in Nineteenth-Century Ireland*, pp. 36-49
Luddy, Maria 'Isabella Tod' in Cullen, Mary and Luddy (eds) *Women,
 Power and Consciousness*, pp. 197-230
Luddy, Maria 'Presentation Convents in County Tipperary 1806-1900'
 in *Tipperary Historical Journal*, 1992, pp. 84-95
Luddy, Maria 'Women and Work in Clonmel: Evidence from the 1881
 Census' in *Tipperary Historical Journal* 1993, pp. 95-101
Luddy, Maria, Mary O'Dowd and Margaret MacCurtain 'An Agenda
 for Women's in Ireland, 1500-1900' in *Irish Historical Studies* xxviii,
 No. 109, May 1992, pp. 1-37
Lynch, Kathleen 'The Universal and Particular: Gender, Class and
 Reproduction in Second-Level Schools' *U.C.D. Women's Studies
 Forum Working Paper No. 3* 1987

Lyons-Thornton, Brigid 'Women and the Army' in *An Cosantoir* November 1975, pp. 364-5

Lyons, J.B. 'History of Early Irish Women Doctors' in *Irish Medical Times* January 1992, pp. 38-40

MacCurtain, Margaret 'St Mary's University College' in *University Review*, Vol. II, No. 4, (1963), pp. 33-47

MacCurtain, Margaret 'Women, the Vote and Revolution' in MacCurtain, Margaret and O'Corrain (eds) *Women in Irish Society*, pp. 46-57

MacCurtain, Margaret 'Late in the Field: Catholic Sisters in Twentieth-Century Ireland and the New Religious History' in O'Dowd, Mary and Wichert (eds) *Chattel, Servant or Citizen*, pp. 34-44

Macken, Mary 'In Memoriam: Mary T. Hayden' in *Studies* September 1942, pp. 369-71

Macken, Mary 'Women in the University and the College. A Struggle Within a Struggle' in Tierney, Michael (ed.) *Struggle with Fortune: A Miscellany for the Centenary of the Catholic University of Ireland*, pp. 142-65

Mayeur, Francoise 'Women and elites from the nineteenth to the twentieth century' in Howorth, Jolyon and Cervy (eds) *Elites in France: Origins, Reproduction and Power*, pp. 57-65

Mc Dowell, Carlos Address to the Royal College of Physicians entitled 'Leading Ladies in Irish Medicine'

Mc Garry, Niamh 'The Doctor's Daughter' in *Your Health* Vol. I, No. I, Winter 1994, pp. 16-17

Mc Sweeney, Geraldine 'Nursing - St Vincent's Hospital 1834-1984' in *Anniversary Yearbook: St Vincent's Hospital 150 Years Service 1834-1984*, pp. 34-42

Meenan, F.O.C. 'The Catholic University School of Medicine 1860-1880' in *Studies* Summer/Autumn, 1977, pp. 135-44

Meenan, F.O.C. 'The Catholic University School of Medicine 1880-1909' in *Studies* Summer/Autumn, 1981, pp. 135-44

More, Ellen 'The American Medical Women's Association and the Role of the Woman Physician, 1915-1990' in *Journal of the American Medical Women's Association* Vol. 45, No. 5, September/October 1990, pp. 165-80

More, Ellen 'The Blackwell Medical Society and the Professionalization of Women Physicians' in *Bulletin of the History of Medicine* Vol. 61, part 4, 1987, pp. 603-28

Moorhead, T.G. 'In Memoriam. Dorothy Price M.D.' in *Irish Journal of Medical Science*, March 1954, p.95

Murphy, Kathleen Obituary of Kathleen Lynn in *Journal of the Irish Medical Association* Vol. 37, 1955, p. 321

O'Brien, Eoin 'The Medical Staff through the Years' in O'Brien, Eoin (ed.) *The Charitable Infirmary. Jervis Street*, pp. 49-60

O'Connell, Marie 'The Genesis of Convents and their Institutions in Ulster, 1840' in Holmes, Janice and Urquhart *Coming into the Light*, pp. 179-201

O'Connor, Anne 'Anne Jellicoe' in Cullen, Mary and Luddy (eds) *Women, Power and Consciousness*, pp. 125-59

O'Connor, Anne 'The Revolution in Girls' Secondary Education in
    Ireland 1860-1910' in Cullen, Mary (ed.) *Girls Don't Do Honours*, pp.
    31-54

O'Dea, Tom 'Lay Teachers in Irish Catholic Schools. A Statistical Survey
    of Employment Practices' in *The Secondary Teacher* Vol. 2, No. 10,
    December 1967, pp. 5-8

O'Donoghue, Brendan 'The Office of Co. Surveyor. Origins and Early
    Years' in *Transactions of Irish Institute of Civil Engineers* Vol. 117, 23
    November 1992, pp. 197-270

O'Donoghue, Thomas 'The Role of the Inspectorate in Irish Secondary
    School Education 1924-62' in *The Secondary Teacher* No. 1, 1989, pp.
    10-12

O'Donoghue, Thomas 'The Role of the Lay Teacher in Irish
    Secondary Schools 1922-62' in *The Secondary Teacher* Vol. 17, No. 4,
    1988, pp. 8-9

O'Donoghue, Thomas 'The Secondary-School Curricular Policy in
    Ireland 1924-62, Part 1,' in *The Secondary Teacher* Vol. 18, No. 3, 1989,
    pp. 27-31

O'Donoghue, Thomas 'The Secondary-School Curriculum and
    Curricular Policy in Ireland 1924-62, Part 2,' in *The Secondary Teacher*
    Vol. 18, No. 4, 1989, pp. 7-10

O'Driscoll, Finbarr 'St Dominic's. The Rise and Fall of a Training
    College 1907-1924' in *Irish Educational Studies* Vol. 4, No. 1, 1984, pp.
    98-114

O'Flaherty, K. 'Admission of Women Students to Q.C.C.' in *Cork
    University Record* No. 15, Easter 1949, pp. 16-21

O'Flaherty, Louis 'Trade Unionism or Professionalism: A Dilemma for
    Teachers' in *The Secondary Teacher* Vol. 17, No. 3, 1988, pp. 2-8

O'Flynn, Grainne 'Some Aspects of the Education of Irish Women
    through the Years' *The Capuchin Annual* 1977, pp. 164-79

O'Leary, Eoin 'The Irish National Teachers' Organisation and the
    Marriage Bar for Women National Teachers, 1933-1958' in *Saothar.
    Journal of the Irish Labour History Society* No. 12, pp. 47-52

O hEili, Seamus 'The Origins of Secondary Teacher Education' in *The
    Secondary Teacher* Vol. 13, No. 4, 1984, pp. 27-30

Outram, Alison 'Inequalities in the Teaching Profession: The Effect on
    Teachers and Pupils, 1910-39' Hunt, Felicity (ed.) *Lessons for Life*, pp.
    101-123

Perrin-Behringer, Majorie 'Women's Role and Status in the Sciences:
    An Historical Perspective' in Butler, Kahle (ed.) *Women in Science. A
    Report from the Field*, pp. 4-26

Prichard, Sarah 'Dorothy Stopford-Price and the Control of
    Tuberculosis in Dublin' in Alexandra College Archives, Dublin

Pursell, Carroll '"Am I a Lady or an engineer?" The Origins of the
    Women's Engineering Society in Britain, 1918-1940' in *Technology
    and Culture* Vol. 34, part 1, 1993, pp. 78-97

Radtke, Heidrun 'Women in Science Careers in the G.D.R.' in Stolte-
    Heiskanen, Veronica (ed.) *Women in Science*, pp. 63-73

Ruane, Medb 'Lecture on life and Times of Remarkable Mayo Woman' *The Western People* January 1996

Russell, Emma 'The Queen Victoria Hospital' in *Australian Historical Studies* No. 106, April 1996, pp. 170-5

Schultheiss, Katrin '"La Veritable Medecine des Femmes": Anna Hamilton and the politics of Nursing Reform in Bordeaux, 1900-1914' in *French Historical Studies* 19(1) 1995, pp. 183-214

Simpson, Richard and Ida Harper Simpson 'Women and Bureaucracy in the Semi-Professions' in Etzioni, Amitai (ed.) *The Semi-Professions and their Organization. Teachers, Nurses, Social Workers*, pp. 196-265

Smyth, Hazel 'Kathleen Lynn M.D., F.R.C.S.I. (1874-1955)' in *Dublin Historical Record* Vol. xxx, No. 2, March 1977, pp. 51-7

Solomons, Bethel 'The History of Infant Welfare' *Journal of Paediatrics* September Vol. 53, No. 3, 1958, pp. 360-76

Spruill, Wanda and Charles Wootton 'The Struggle of Women in Accounting: The Case of Jennie Palen, Pioneer Accountant, Historian and Poet' in *Critical Perspectives on Accounting* Vol.6, 1995, pp. 371-89

Stopford-Price, Dorothy 'The Need for BCG Vaccination in Infants' in *Tubercule* Vol. xxx, No. 1, January 1949, pp. 11-13. Paper read at the conference of the British Tuberculosis Association on 1 July 1948

Townley, Christy 'UCG: A Short History - The Early Years' in *Cois Coiribe Journal of the U.C.G. Gtaduates' Association* 1993, p. 26

Travers, Pauric 'Emigration and Gender: the Case of Ireland 1922-60' in O'Dowd, Mary and Wichert (eds) *Chattel, Servant ot Citizen*, pp. 187-199

Tucker, Sara 'Opportunities for Women: The Development of Professional Women's Medicine at Canton, China, 1879-1901' in *Women's Studies International Forum* Vol. 13, No. 4, 1990, pp. 357-68

Valiulis Maryann 'Neither Feminist nor Flapper: The Ecclesiastical Construction of the Ideal Irish Woman' in O'Dowd, Mary and Wichert (eds) *Chattel, Servant or Citizen*, pp. 168-78

Valiulis, Maryann 'Toward "The Moral and Material Improvement of the Working Classes". The Founding of the Alexandra College Guild Tenement Company, Dublin, 1898' in *Journal of Urban History*, Vol. 23 No. 3, March 1997, pp. 295-315

Vinten, Gerard 'Requiem on Accountancy' in *Advances in Public Interest Accounting*, Vol. 6, 1995, pp. 373-4

W.W. (William Wynne) 'Kathleen Lynn' (Obituary) *The Irish Times* 1994 (no date)

Walsh, Bridget 'Nursing in the Charitable Infirmary' in O'Brien, Eoin (ed.) *Jervis Street*, pp. 135-54

Walshe, Katherine 'Iris Ashley Cummins: First Women Member of the Institute' in *The Engineers' Journal* September/October Vol.38, nos. 9 and 10, 1985 p. 57

Wangensteen, Owen 'Some Thoughts on Medical Education and the Training of Surgeons' in O'Brien, Eoin (ed.) *Essays in Honour of J.D.H. Widdess*, pp. 69-87

Theses

Bhreathnach, Eibhlin 'A History of the Movement for Women's Higher
    Education in Dublin, 1860-1912' (MA, UCD, 1981)

Calwell, H.G. 'The History of the Royal Belfast Hospital for Sick
    Children 1873-1948' (MA, QUB, 1972)

Chuinneagáin, Síle 'Women Teachers and INTO Policy 1905-1916'
    (MEd minor thesis, TCD, 1993)

Coolahan, John 'The Origins of the Payment by Results Policy
    in Education and the Experience of it in the National and
    Intermediate Schools of Ireland' (MEd minor thesis, TCD, 1975)

Cowman, Seamus 'Understanding Student Nursing Learning' (PhD,
    DCU, 1993)

Daly, Timothy 'The Training of a Teacher' (MA, UCC, 1914)

Donaldson, Margaret 'The Development of Nursing in Northern
    Ireland' (D.Phil., N.U.U., 1983)

Donovan, Hanna 'The History of Women's Higher Education During
    the Nineteenth-Century' (MA, UCC, 1919)

Eager, Clare 'Unequal Opportunity. Irishwomen in the Professions,
    1901-36' (MA minor thesis, UCD, 1988)

Finnegan, Belinda 'The Democratisation of Higher Education and the
    Participation of University women in the labour force, 1920-50'
    (MA, UCD, 1985)

Harkin, Patricia 'La Famille, Fruit du Passe, Germe de L'Avenir. Family
    Policy in Ireland and Vichy France' (MA minor, UCD, 1992)

Healy, James 'Teacher Education Policy in Ireland 1920-1975 with
    Comparative Reference to International Trends' (MEd, UCC,
    1981)

Higman-Robinson, Mary Beth 'The Woman Veterinarian: Origins,
    Education and Career' (PhD, Ohio State University, 1978)

Jones, Valerie 'Recruitment and Formation of Students Into the Church
    of Ireland Training College 1922-1961' (MLitt, TCD, 1989)

Kelly, Patricia 'From Workhouse to Hospital. The Role of the Irish
    Workhouse in Medical Relief to 1921' (MA, UCG, 1972)

Loze, Lara 'The Robertson Commission: Its Achievement in
    Contributing to the Admittance of Women to University Education
    in Ireland' (MA, minor thesis, UCD, 1994)

Magill, Isabel 'A Social History of T.B. in Belfast' (DPhil, University of
    Ulster at Jordanstown, 1992)

Maguire, Maria 'The Development of the Welfare State in Ireland in the
    Postwar Period' (PhD, European University Institute, 1985)

McIlhatton, Alexander 'Degress of Inequality. A Disaffected Teaching
    Profession in Ireland 1831/1922 and in Northern Ireland 1922/46'
    (MA, NUU, 1988)

Morrow, Alison 'Women and Work in Northern Ireland, 1920-1950'
    (DPhil, NUU at Coleraine, 1995)

Musson, John 'The Training of Teachers in Ireland, from 1811 to the
    Present Day' (PhD, QUB, 1955)

O'Brian, Diarmuid 'The Training of Primary Teachers in Ireland' (MA, minor thesis, UCD, 1963)

O'Callaghan, Margaret 'Language and Religion. The Quest for Identity in the Irish Free State 1922-32' (MA, UCD, 1981)

O'Connor, Anne 'Influences Affecting Girls' Secondary Education in Ireland, 1860-1910' (MA, UCD, 1981)

O'Donoghue, Thomas 'The Irish Secondary School. Curriculum and Curricular Policy in Ireland 1921-1962' (PhD, UCD, 1988)

O'Driscoll, Finin 'The Search for the Christian State - An Analysis of Irish Social Catholicism, 1913-39' (UCC, MA, 1994)

Orbach, Noreen 'The Evolution of a Profession. The Case of Women in Dentistry' (PhD, University of Illinois, 1977)

Paseta, Senia 'Education, Opportunity and Social Change: The Development of a Catholic University Elite in Ireland, 1879-1922' (PhD, Australian National University, 1994)

Rice, George 'The Royal University of Ireland 1879-1909' (MA, UCC, 1957)

Riordain, Patrick 'The Association of Secondary Teachers, Ireland, 1909-1968. Some Aspects of its Growth and Development' (MEd, minor thesis, UCC, 1975)

Summer, Pepi 'The Career Pattern of Women Graduates of the University of Buffalo Medical, Dental and Law Schools between 1895 and 1915' (PhD, State University of New York at Buffalo, 1980)

Tubridy, Rachel 'The Origin and Development of the Registration Council for Secondary Teachers in Ireland 1914-1960' (MEd, UCD, 1984)

Wyley, Roisin 'Changing Attitudes to Children: The State's Role in the Status and Welfare of Children 1952-87' (MA, minor thesis, UCD, 1990).

Index